Different?…You Have Always Been Different

by Isabella Clarence

This book is a work of non-fiction based on the life, experiences and recollections of the author. Some names have been changed in this book to protect the privacy of the individuals involved.

www.isabellaclarence.co.uk

ISBN-10: 1499298633
ISBN-13: 978-1499298635

DEDICATION

This book is dedicated to two very special souls, both of whom
saved me in so many ways. To my late Father, for his never-
ending love and support and to Nansi, without whose help I
can honestly say, I would not be here now.

You will both have my love, blessings and gratitude for all time

CONTENTS

ACKNOWLEDGMENTS

How many times have you skimmed over the acknowledgments page in a book you have read with a bemused look on your face, thinking to yourself, "I wonder why the author thanked Aunty Mary? What did Aunty Mary do? Did she proof-read the work, or did she perhaps keep the author supplied with copious cups of coffee?" With these thoughts in my mind I want to make sure that my acknowledgments page gives thanks, credit and love where it's due, to everyone that has helped me get my book to publication. If I have missed you out, please forgive me.

This is going to sound daft but I want to firstly thank a lady I haven't even met. That must be a first in anyone's book. I want to thank Lorna Byrne, so if you are reading this and you know her, please give her my gratitude and love. I had just finished writing my story and I had completely convinced myself that I couldn't possibly publish it, because I had gone way out on a limb and then some with what I had written, when a friend and patient gave me a copy of Lorna's first book, "Angels in my Hair" as a present. After I read it I knew beyond any shadow of doubt that I had to publish my manuscript. If Lorna had the courage to publish her story, then I had to find the courage to publish mine. Blessings to you, Lorna.

Now to everyone I do know.

Firstly to my husband for keeping me grounded for the past 40 years. Thank you, my love, for never getting cross with me during the writing of this book, when I forgot to make our evening meal and also when I slightly over-cooked (burnt) it because I was lost in my writing. Thank you for always being there for me. Without your love and support I couldn't have achieved half the things I have. The fact that you have walked this journey with me has to be a testimony to your patience and love.

Next to our beautiful daughter who helped me unscramble my mind, by helping me find the correct years for some of the events in my story. Also for sorting out what was a complete jumble of words in my book introduction. You unscrambled me amazingly well.

Next to three of my patients: Angela, Carole and Carole Gordon, who bravely read the first completed draft, complete with backward sentences, wrong words and goodness knows how many other errors. Thank you all for your time and patience, especially to Angela for her encouragement, helping me to realise that what I had written was worthwhile reading, and needed to be published. Also for editing my book, together with her friend Hilary. Thank you, girls. I almost agreed with everything you both did.

To Glenda for trying to help me find someone to proof-read my first draft.

To Liz for helping me put in the punctuation where we thought it was needed. We almost got it right, well almost!

Next I would like to thank Eileen Burrell for her expertise in proof-reading my book and also to Jeff Burrell for helping Eileen. I first met Eileen about twenty-one years ago when she was directed to my door by the very same lady this book is dedicated to, Nansi, and we have remained friends to this day.

It is now time to thank Nansi Morgan herself, and also Jean, Pat and Cath for allowing me to use their testimonials in my story.

I also need to thank Mary Lambton who, together with our daughter, came up with the subtitle for my book and I love it. Their words describe my story perfectly.

Now I would like to thank my dearest friend Carole Lowe. Time is a precious thing, but Carole found the time to write the foreword to my book. Thank you, my treasured friend, and now......

Last but very much not least, to our son for his patience with his mother. Thank you firstly for finding the title of my book from the book itself; I love it. You let my words talk to you and you heard them. Thank you for the final editing before

Eileen worked her magic, for all the work involved in getting my book to publication. Your genius with the computer and technology is amazing, including the book cover which I adore. And thank you for my Facebook and Twitter pages. I will always love you.

I will always love all of you.

You all have my love and blessings, always.

FOREWORD

I have known my dear friend Isabella for over twenty years now, and in that time have shared with her many life experiences, as well as 'out of this world' happenings too. I came to Isabella's door, for the first time, as a patient, not knowing what to expect. I was hoping for help and healing, as at that time I was suffering from the debilitating illness of M.E. It was the lowest ebb in my life and I had almost given up hope of ever becoming well again. (I had lived within the confines of the disease for seven years).

Little did I know how my life was to change in so many ways from that first meeting. This is not my story but suffice to say, through the many healing treatments I received and the journey to wellness that I had begun, I found that my strength returned and in time I made a full recovery. I am eternally grateful for the gift of healing that Isabella was able to impart, and the lasting impression this journey of trust has taught me.

Isabella is an extraordinary person in many ways, one of these being her seeming 'ordinariness.'

As a daughter, wife, mother and grandmother she is grounded in the everyday issues of family life. But she will tell you that it is here, within the framework of the family, that many of our lessons are learnt. She says she never stops learning herself, when it comes to the many ups and downs we all encounter as we go through life. She has been a woman in business, she has experienced loss and divorce. She has made her own mistakes along the way and has endured the pain and confusion of suffering herself, when at a young age she was diagnosed with a serious illness. A life less ordinary because of the gift she possesses, but a difficult life nonetheless. Throughout the roller-coaster ride she was to take, she held on to the belief and trust in the Universal energy, in God and in the spirit world (of which she had been actually aware since she was a child). She held on to that inner knowing through thick and thin and emerged a stronger person as the layers of her life peeled away and she was able to use all the lessons she had learnt. All the pain she had experienced, all the many obstacles she had overcome led her to be able to empathise with others of all ages, in a very unique way, to use the gifts she had been given to heal.

The countless numbers of people that Isabella has been able to help through her work as a healer have, I'm sure, all heard the same words upon coming to her door.

"How can I help you?" This is her mission. Even if she helps just one person through the healing energy she is able to channel, then that mission will be complete. Many of her patients have all asked the same question, after experiencing the healing energy for themselves.

How did you become a healer?"

They have probably all heard the same answer as she has always said, "One day I will write a book and tell you my story."

That day is here. The book is written. It contains the true story of Isabella's own journey and in writing it I'm sure many more people on reading it will be helped, as she gives a totally honest account of her own life. The loneliness she experienced as a result of being 'different' and the ensuing lessons of forgiveness she learnt along the way.

This is a story about trust and being true to oneself against the odds, following the inner voice that resides within us all. Isabella listened to that voice and followed it, even in her darkest hours. She may at first have been reluctant to take up the role of the Spiritual Healer in a sceptical world, but there are so many people out there who are so very glad that she did.

INTRODUCTION

Looking back over the past fifty years of my life I'd always thought that I was just an ordinary girl leading a fairly ordinary life, just like the rest of the human race. But I'm not, and it's about time I face up to the fact that my life is, and has been, anything but ordinary to date.

Am I of any importance? I've always felt that the simple answer is no. I'm not clever, I don't have any letters after my name and I'm not famous in any way. So that begs the question, why would I bother to take the time to write? Simply put, I have a tale to tell, and an extraordinary one at that. My daughter gave me some words of advice just as I was beginning to start to write this book.

"Mum," she said, "whatever it is you think you are going to write, trust me, it won't be."

I asked her what on earth she meant.

"You probably think you know exactly what you are going to be writing about but I promise you, you will end up with something completely different from what you originally thought."

Deep down inside, knowing that one day I would have to lead a different life from all my friends didn't exactly fill me with glee. But you will see as my story unfolds that the signs that kept appearing in my life, the guiding hand that I couldn't see but could always feel, and the 'voice' that was with me from being a child, had no intentions of letting me wander away from my own soul's journey. People say there is a book inside each and every one of us, but the problem I've been having recently is that there are at least six books inside of me, all jostling to be the first to the finishing post!

I have been asked many times by my close friends, people I have worked with and, most importantly, my patients, to write down all the healing stories I have accumulated over the past twenty years of my life as a spiritual healer. Almost all of them have told me that my storytelling has helped them to see their own problems in a completely different light, and it was these tales, analogies, examples and knowledge that I set out to write about.

As I started to write, I began to get a clear picture as to where my mind was taking me. How could I begin to tell you about the things I have seen, heard and experienced during my many years of healing work when I haven't explained to you how I came to be working as a Spiritual Healer in the first place? With that thought in my mind, I realised very quickly that I needed to tell you my own personal healing story first.

My story is the journey I was to take with an illness that the medical profession has no cure for, my own journey into wellness.

Thinking and remembering was what I had to try and do next.

As these thoughts rolled around in my head, I felt as if my mind was travelling backwards through a time tunnel, taking me back to my teenage years. Some of the pictures I found myself looking at were quite frightening to me at the time. Thank goodness those events happened many years ago and no longer hold any fear for me. I needed to give myself and my brain time to sort through all the old memory files that I had archived away in storages boxes. As I slowly dusted off the top of those boxes, taking one file out at a time, I had to stay single-minded when remembering how I felt.

All I want to do is share my experiences in the hope that something I may say will help someone. If I can help just one person, then I will have accomplished the task that I was given. If in the pages to come I don't mention lots of happy days please forgive me; we did have them. But it's not the good times that we learn from. If I forget to tell you what a wonderful husband I have and how much I love him, it's not because I'm not grateful for all the love and support he has given me over the years, or how much I respect him. If I forget to mention what wonderful babies both our children were in so many ways, so easy and happy and thank God healthy, again forgive me. The fact that both our children are now such wonderful caring adults, my husband and I must have done a far better job than I realised during their growing years.

This is my story and it's going to be very interesting for me to see how I feel when I finish writing it.

Had I really forgiven?

Had I really let go?

One thing I know for sure is that I most certainly had not forgotten. We are not meant to forget. Our memories are the building blocks of our lives. Every experience we have moulds us into who we are today. It's not necessarily the experiences that we encounter that can cause us harm. It's how we act, react and handle them. Sometimes we react to a situation with anger, sometimes with jealousy, or sometimes we hold a grudge for years. And sometimes, like me, we bury our hurts away in our minds and keep quiet about them for a very long time. If we all realised the harm we were causing ourselves by hanging onto these hurtful events we would soon change our ways.

People say we are what we eat. I like to say, "We are what we think" or "We are what we feel." Our feelings and emotions lead us up and down the road that we call life. If we could all change our way of thinking, what a different world this could be, what a different life we could all lead.

As we file these hurtful events away at the end of each day, each month, each year without forgiving ourselves and others, we find them resurfacing and haunting us in the years to come, causing us pain, both emotional and physical. That's where I like to think we get the word *disease* from.

Think about it.

Break it down into two words, dis-ease.

We become out of ease with ourselves, we become out of balance, we become ill.

Just like me.

CHAPTER ONE

Over the many years that I have been working as a Spiritual Healer, I can honestly say that I have lost count of the number of times that new patients have asked me, "How did you get into healing Isabella?" When I'm with someone during a healing session the time we spend together is for them, not for me. I have always kept my answer short. I just say that I was diagnosed with Multiple Sclerosis when I was thirty years old and, very soon after my diagnosis, I was directed to a wonderful lady who was a healer and the rest is history.

That is the very short version of a very long journey that I had to take to get me to where I am today. By telling you the whole of my story now, the question will be answered and I can move forward with lots of wonderful healing tales that we can all learn from.

I am actually feeling quite excited. I'm going on a journey down my time tunnel and I'm taking you along for the ride.

So let's get started.

I remember so very clearly the day, the time and place when a voice from 'somewhere' spoke to me in a very clear commanding tone and said to me, "Isabella, there is something very wrong with you." This was when I was fourteen years old.

Let me try and explain. I loved sport at school. I wasn't too sure about having to wear my grey knickers for P.E. and games, but that was the uniform at the time. My favourite sport at school was running and I was good. From the age of twelve years I was the fastest girl runner in our school. Not quite the achievement you might think when I tell you there were only about two hundred and fifty pupils in the whole school. Not like today's senior schools that have hundreds of pupils. Because I was fast, I was always picked to run the last leg of the relay race for my house team.

Sports Day, summer 1964. I remember the weather as always being lovely and warm during the summer term. This particular sports day was beautiful with a clear blue sky. I was in the hundred yards and won that, hurdles and won that, then the high jump and the long jump and then it was to be the relay race, which was always close to the end of the day's events. Our house team won the relay with me running the last leg as usual. But as I was halfway to the finishing line my legs began to feel very strange. I felt as if they had pins and needles running all the way down both of them and they both felt as if lead weights had been attached. I somehow managed to finish the race first, but only just. I fell onto the grass at the side of the track, exhausted. I was feeling so odd I stayed where I was sitting, trembling. I had such a very strong feeling not to try and get up.

Some of my friends and one of our teachers came across the track to see if I was alright. I was able to smile at them and say that I was just very tired as it was a hot day and, after all, I had been in quite a few events. They all said well done and then left me alone after I had reassured them.

But I was not alright and it was far more than just tiredness. My legs were trembling and tingling from top to toe. I felt very peculiar and frightened. I just sat there for ages, watching the last few events going on around me until I felt a bit calmer and a little bit better. I managed to get myself up and into the changing room. All I wanted to do was to get dressed and away from my school as quickly as possible and go home.

Normally I would walk home during the summer months but on this day I caught the bus. I knew there was no way I could have got myself home on my legs; there was something wrong with them and I didn't know what it was.

When I did eventually arrive home I said nothing. It may seem a bit odd to you, but I just knew not to say anything to my parents. This was something I had to sort out myself.

I may have only been fourteen years old but I had spent five years until the age of twelve suffering very badly from migraine headaches that ended when I had a very severe attack that lasted for three days, with me delirious for two of them because the pain was so bad. Fortunately for me, that was the last migraine attack I ever had. It seemed to me that the

16

previous five years of headaches had come to a head in one final episode. But because I had been carted back and forth to the hospital for head x-rays (no scanners in 1957-1962) and lots of horrible medicine that didn't help me, I was not going to tell my parents that I thought there was something the matter with me now.

My instincts were telling me not to say anything and, fortunately for me, I was listening.

I do remember that I spent a long time that night worrying alone in my bed, asking God to help me. From being a small child I have always talked to God and my guardian angels and trusted and believed that they would be there by my side to help me when I needed them, something I still believe to this day. I am not religious in an orthodox way, even though I was raised a Methodist, which is probably why I use the words God or Lord to refer to a supreme being. Of course I realise that my God may not be your God and my beliefs may not be yours, but that shouldn't matter. I gained a healthy insight into theology from a young age, but for many years have considered myself simply *spiritual* and independent of organised schools of thought.

The next day when I went to school I was still feeling very odd so when I got the chance in the afternoon I took myself off to the playing field where it was quiet and found a good spot on the grass to sit and think. There were so many questions running around in my head. "What was happening to me?" I didn't want to be ill again; I had had enough of that and lost far too much schooling with all my headaches and trips to the hospital. "Why were my legs still tingling? Should I tell someone?" These are just a few of the things I can remember, but I do clearly remember being frightened.

My instincts were always good. I had always had a way of knowing things from being a small child. I would finish grownups' sentences. I would answer a teacher's question and my friends' before the questions had been asked.

So from an early age my peers were very wary of me and I was labelled as being very cheeky by grown-ups. I never

17

meant to be; it just took me a long time to realise that I needed to keep quiet, in other words keep my mouth shut.

As I was sitting on the grass with my knees up to my chin, I adjusted my skirt and as I did I felt the frills. Frills? What the heck did I have on? To my horror, I still had my baby-doll pyjama bottoms on. Somehow, when I had got dressed that morning to go to school, I was so not with it. I had forgotten to take them off and put on my grey school knickers. Thank goodness I didn't have P.E. that day. I would have felt a complete idiot.

It was just after I adjusted my skirt and got over the shock of wearing my pyjama bottoms under my school skirt, that I heard the 'voice'.

"Isabella, there is something very wrong with you, but don't worry. One day you will be well."

I looked to my left and then to my right and behind me, to see if there was anyone near me but even as I was looking, I knew that I was sitting all alone.

I was not frightened by the 'voice' but I was frightened by what the 'voice' had said. It was confirming what I had been thinking. Something was very wrong. I just sat there by myself in the warm sunshine and cried.

Still snivelling, I got myself up to finish my school day and went slowly home. All the while I kept thinking to myself that the 'voice' said I would be okay so perhaps I should just try and forget what had happened to me for now and 'leave well alone'. My thoughts kept saying to me, "Trust the voice."

I can't remember anything much after that. I do know I only ran once more in a trial for the school and I had to stop before the finish line because my legs would not run for me. The trial was not at my own school so no one knew me and I wasn't questioned when I fell to my knees in the middle of the track (pretending I had hurt my ankle), as I watched all the other contestants running past me. I never ran for my school again.

It may seem odd to you that I wasn't frightened by the 'voice', nor did I question who it was or where it had come from. The reason for this was that I had been seeing things since I was a small child and also hearing voices, so I guess you could say I was used to this sort of thing. I only once told my parents that I saw things and heard voices, but they told me not to be so silly and not to talk about such things ever again. So I didn't.

But the 'voice' had never directed anything personally to me before.

CHAPTER TWO

I'm going to skip forward to 1974 (a very good year). I married for the second time and we had our beautiful baby girl. I was very tired through my pregnancy but I worked until four weeks before she was born and just thought being tired was a normal part of being pregnant. When our baby girl was ten months old I became pregnant again. My husband said we shouldn't wait to have another baby and I was quite happy with that. He knew far more than he was letting on at the time.

I knew the night I conceived each of our babies but I'm sure most people would say that I couldn't possibly have known that. I took no notice the first time because I thought I might be wrong. However, the second time I became pregnant, I felt a bit more confident in myself.

At the time my sister-in-law was working as a midwife and, as things worked out, she came to visit us on the Monday night, just after I had conceived on the Saturday night. As soon as she arrived I told her I was pregnant. She asked me how many weeks. I said, "No, not weeks, two days." Not surprisingly she laughed at me. But I did ask her to help me work out when the baby would be born. She did and my due date would be the 12th June (if indeed I was pregnant). My response was instant. I said, "The baby will be born on the 10th June." Please remember, I was only two days pregnant and, yes, he was born on the 10th June.

Things started to go wrong for me during my second pregnancy. I was so desperately tired. Being pregnant and having a little baby to look after was tiring, but this was more than that.

After our son was born I felt even worse. The only way I could manage to get through the day was to sleep when the babies slept, so every afternoon when they both had at least an hour's nap, I did too.

The tiredness I was feeling was very frightening. It came over me like a wave and I couldn't fight it, no matter how hard

I tried. But no one understood my explanation. When it happened all I could do was gather the two little ones up beside me on the settee or put the baby in his pram and I would sit quietly, as our daughter played beside me. As hard as I tried to explain to my family how I felt, I honestly think they thought I was just being lazy. Oh how I wished.

I was not managing very well but I had no choice. Somehow I needed to get through each day. Our two babies needed feeding and looking after, even though on some days I didn't feel I had the strength to look after myself. I just had to get on with it. When my husband came home from work each day he always took over from me.

There were days that I did manage and on those days I would be making the evening meal for us all when he arrived home, but some days I was so exhausted he would make our meal for us after he had bathed the babies. He did whatever he could to help me. But that was at the end of the day and some days were a nightmare for me.

All I kept thinking was, "Thank God both the little ones are so good." They both went to bed happily and, once the baby could smile, they both woke up smiling. We hardly ever heard either of them cry and I was very grateful that they were both healthy.

So when I took the baby for his six weeks check-up, I was quite upset when the doctor told me that there was something wrong with his feet. Both his big toes were turning inwards and almost touched his heels and we hadn't noticed. When our son was four months old our doctor made an appointment for us to see a foot specialist. Lots of photos were taken and, two visits later, the specialist decided he would like to operate. Our son would have to be in plaster up to his hips.

How was I going to manage to pick him up? I hardly had the strength to carry him as it was. He was now five months old and weighed twenty-six pounds, even though he was solely breastfed. Our doctor told me to cut down on his feeds and put him on solids because he was too heavy. (Just to let you know, he is now six feet three and wears a size twelve shoe. I don't think he was too big. He just needed his grub). I digress.

When the specialist saw how worried I was about carrying him and being able to lift him, he decided to postpone the operation until our son was walking. He said his feet might improve slightly once he was up and mobile, and that would make the operation a bit simpler. At least I had been given some breathing space. I was so relieved.

I did what came naturally to me. Each and every day when I was holding and cuddling him I would hold his feet in my hands, gently rubbing them and, of course, kissing them. I made a game out of it. By the time he was walking, at just under twelve months old, his feet were perfectly straight. He never did have the operation. He didn't need it.

We moved house when the children were about six months and just over two years old and I was twenty-six. This did help me a bit because we moved very near to a dear friend of mine. She is still my friend and I bless her for all the help she gave me.

Because we moved house we registered with a new G.P. The practice had two lady doctors and one male, so I chose one of the ladies because I felt a woman would be more in tune with me. Silly me!

Many times I went to the doctor asking for help. I was dropping things and I lost count of the number of cups and glasses that slipped from my grasp and broke. I was also having difficulty picking the children up and sometimes I would fall sideways for no reason. Trust me to be different. I used to fall upstairs and I don't mean on the next floor up. I mean I fell on the staircase forwards. At least I had something to catch my fall. I got bad headaches because I had to strain my eyes some days just to be able to see. It was as if a net curtain had been pulled across them and I had to really concentrate to be able to see through it.

One of the annoying symptoms that I had was that my speech would be affected. If I was very tired or upset, I would slur my words or stammer. Sometimes it almost sounded as if I was drunk. Another thing I found myself doing was, when I turned a corner into a room, I would knock myself on the wall and give myself a nasty bruise because I would misjudge the distance. The tiredness was getting worse as it came over me so quickly. One minute I would be alright and the next minute I would be almost falling onto the floor, as if I'd been unplugged.

Each time I went to the doctor's surgery asking for help I was told by her that there was nothing wrong with me. She kept telling me that it was all in my head.

I was getting desperate.

Then there was the day I took the children for their check-up with the health visitor. Our doctor was also present in the room. The health visitor checked the children over; they were both fine. Alexander was sitting on my knee and Marie was holding onto my right leg (the picture is still very clear in my mind) when the health visitor asked me how was I feeling. How were my headaches? I didn't have time to reply when our doctor spoke for me and said, "We take no notice of Mrs. Clarence's headaches. There's nothing the matter with her; it's all in her head."

I can't begin to tell you how I felt when I left the surgery that day. Was I going mad? I must be. I had all these symptoms and my own doctor was telling me that I was imagining everything.

Because I was being ignored by my doctor, my own family had very little patience with me. They believed what my doctor was telling me because, of course, 'She knew best'. How could she possibly be wrong? Consequently I got no help or support when I so desperately needed it. My husband did all he could, but even he seemed to be getting fed up with me. What probably made it worse was that my father-in-law was also a doctor of the 'old school'. If my doctor said there was nothing wrong, then there was nothing wrong.

Was I going mad? Was I really just imagining all of my symptoms? I must be because everyone was telling me I was.

Feeling desperate one day, I made another appointment to see my doctor. My appointment was for two o'clock in the afternoon. After leaving the children with my friend and, having given myself plenty of time to walk the distance to the surgery, I set off. I had only walked about fifty yards when my legs stopped working. It's hard for me to describe what happened but I'll try. I was still standing up but, as hard as I tried, I couldn't make my legs move forward. They felt very peculiar, not painful, just very odd. There was no way I was going any further. In fact, I wasn't going anywhere at all. I ended up having to sit down on the pavement, feeling frightened and very stupid in case someone, anyone, saw me sitting there. So I wriggled myself on my bottom a couple of feet to the low stone wall that ran along the side of the pavement and sat there, not knowing what to do next. I kept trying to get up, over and over again, but the same thing kept happening. I was telling my legs to move forward but they wouldn't. The only thing I could do was to sit back down. I was terrified in case someone saw me struggling. Somehow, I had to get up and walk so I sat there and said, "Please God help me."

That's what I kept saying to myself over and over. I had to get up and walk. I needed to get to the surgery. Just one more try and this time my legs did move, very slowly and wobbly at first, but at least they were moving and I could continue.

When I eventually arrived at the surgery the door was closed. I sat down on the step outside exhausted, not knowing what to do next. Plucking up courage, I rang the surgery door bell. After a few minutes the door opened. It was my doctor. She took one look at me and yelled, "If you think I'm going to see you now, young lady, you have another thing coming!" and slammed the door in my face. I sat back down on the surgery step and cried. Somehow I managed to get myself back home.

No help yet again. I was just going to have to try even harder.

It wasn't all bad days. There were good ones too. I would have a week or more when I felt almost normal. Then the wave would hit me again.

Our daughter was a very clever little girl. I not only needed eyes in the back of my head, I needed them everywhere.

She was so quick and so bright. I lost her for the first time when she was six months old.

Our first home was very small. I left her on the lounge floor, took about six steps into the kitchen to get her and myself a drink, which took about a minute and when I went back into the lounge she was gone and I mean gone. I was frantic. Had someone come into the house without me seeing them and taken her? I frantically looked in every nook and cranny, under the settee, in the cupboard under the stairs, but she wasn't there.

I was crying and desperate as I ran up the stairs and there, to my astonishment, I found her. She was in her bedroom playing with some toys. She was only six months old but she had managed to crawl up the staircase on her own. She walked at ten months. She was so small she could walk underneath our dining room table quite safely. From that day on, my life became twice as hard, as I tried to watch over her and keep her safe.

When we moved to a bigger house I had to be extra vigilant. One summer's afternoon when her brother was asleep in his pram in the garden and I was lying down in the playroom having a rest, her father was watching over her. She went out into the garden, pushed her brother's pram to the gate, climbed up onto the pram and untied the string on the gatepost that was supposed to keep the gate closed to tiny fingers. She then took herself down the street to my friend's house, climbed the stairs to their kitchen and down their back stairs to their garden to play on their slide. It wasn't just me that needed eyes in the back of my head. It was my husband too.

I kept away from the doctors for as long as I could. I was really beginning to believe I was going mad, that all of the symptoms I had really were in my head. I felt I had better keep quiet or I might be taken away from my husband and children. I tried very hard to cover up how I felt; I was confused and frightened. My doctor had to be right.

I remember quite clearly the days I let my daughter down. Not because I wanted to or meant to, but because I was ill. Late on a particularly difficult afternoon it was almost time for me to get the meal ready, in preparation for David coming home from work. But I just didn't have the energy or the will to even start. I needed to lie down before I fell down. Our son was not a problem; I could put him in his cot and he was safe. But our daughter was that bit older, very clever and very aware her mummy was not well. As little as she was, she tried to help me. I told her that her daddy would be in from work very soon. She was to play in the playroom until he came home. I told her I was taking Alexander and putting him in his cot and I was going to lie down because I was so tired.

I don't remember how long I had been in bed before my husband came into our bedroom to find me. He was obviously annoyed with me for leaving her alone downstairs and I don't blame him. Anybody with an ounce of sense would have known not to leave a two year old child in a room on her own but, when you're not well, common sense is non-existent. I do remember asking God to keep her safe that day. And He did.

I told myself I must try harder to stay awake, I must protect my two little ones. But when that wave came over me it was as if I was on another planet. I often felt as if I was out of my body, like a fly on the wall, watching what was going on around me, not being involved.

But I was involved, twenty-four hours a day.

CHAPTER THREE

You must be wondering if I had family other than my husband and our children. Yes I did. My parents lived about twenty miles from us and my parents-in-law about the same distance, in a different direction. My husband had an older brother and sister and I had a brother six years older than me and a sister six years younger. There was such a big age gap between my brother, myself and my sister that we all grew up as if we were only children. Consequently none of us were ever very close to one another.

But the one person that might have been able to support me, my own mother, had made it very clear to me years earlier that if I ever had any children they would be my responsibility and she would not be helping me to look after them in any way. That also meant she would not babysit for us. My father ran his own business so he had very little spare time. As the children grew older, my father would come and babysit, bless him, but my mother never did. Neither of our families ever came to our home to help me in any way. The children sometimes went to my husband's parents for a few days holiday, but that was later in our lives. They never did stay with my parents.

It never dawned on me that my family should have been helping me because I honestly believed that everything that was happening to me was in my head. It was all my own doing. That's what my doctor kept telling me.

Out of the blue, I was asked to do some book-keeping work. This gave me something else to think about, something to make me feel good about myself (and I needed that desperately) and, of course, the extra money would be a great help. Being self-employed meant I could work from home, just a few hours a week, and I could work my own hours. If I was not feeling very good or my sight was blurred, I didn't have to do the work that day.

This was a huge blessing because I was unemployable. It would have been impossible for me to work for anyone else. I was next to useless first thing in the morning, still am. Can you imagine trying to tell your boss, "I'm sorry I can't come in today. I'm too tired." Any boss would have lost patience with me in a very short space of time and I would have been sacked. So being self-employed was the answer for me. That was 1976 and I'm still self-employed. Some days were much better than others, but I was managing, just.

Then came the worst day of my life when my bubble burst!

I was so tired one morning I put Alexander back into his cot after I had given both the children their breakfast. Alexander would have been about ten months old at the time. I took Marie into our bedroom with me, thinking she would be safe beside me because I was desperate to lie down before I fell down. The next thing I remember was Marie by the side of my bed crying. That woke me up with a start.

She was standing with her hand wrapped in a tea towel. She was only about two and a half years old when this happened. When I saw blood on the towel I started to panic. I picked her up as best I could and sat her on my knee as I tried to see where the blood was coming from. Her hand was cut. She had gone down the stairs and climbed up onto the dining table to reach an apple. Then she had gone to the kitchen and climbed up to reach a knife from the bench. She had tried to cut the apple herself to eat it. She had cut her hand between her thumb and first finger quite badly.

I found this out as I followed the blood trail on the walls and floor of our home. My heart was in my mouth. I rang my husband at work and told him to come home immediately. I'd never done that before, so at least he realised I needed help and needed it fast.

For years after, I often thought about that day. As young as Marie was, she had had the presence of mind to close her hand and wrap it in a tea towel and, in doing that, she had managed to stop the bleeding herself.

When we arrived at A and E, David carried Marie into the room where they stitched her hand. I was in a waiting room not far from where she was and I could hear her shouting and crying for her mummy. We had to take Alexander with us to the hospital, as there was no one to leave him with at such short notice. I had him on my knee as I waited for my little girl to be seen.

My memory of that day is very hazy because I was in such a state. Marie had been given an injection before they stitched her hand and, from where I was sitting, I could hear her screaming because she was frightened and hurting. She had four or five stitches between her thumb and her finger and was bandaged up to her elbow.

It could have been so much worse and it was my fault.

If I had thought this was having a bad day, things were about to go from bad to worse for me. Big time!

My parents arrived not long after we got back home from the hospital. I am telling you this because I can still see my mother as if it was yesterday, standing in the doorway of the kitchen as I was making a pot of tea for everyone, when she said to me, "If you don't pull yourself together girl, they will take your children away from you. You are not fit to be their mother." My parents had a cup of tea after seeing Marie was going to be all right and left.

For the rest of that day I just wanted to run away, I wanted to curl up into a ball and disappear. I felt physically sick. Those words my mother said to me were carved into my heart. It would take me years before I could even think about that day without feeling tears well up inside me. My precious little girl could have been very seriously hurt and it was my fault.

That night when I went to bed my mother's words were ringing in my ears. I went over and over them, again and again. She might be right. Our children might be taken into care. I was going to have to try even harder to stay awake, but I honestly didn't know how I was going to do that. Please don't point out the obvious; they had a wonderful father. There was no need for them to be with anyone else. But common sense plays no part when you're not well.

As I lay in our bed that night I sent out a plea, "Please God, help me. Please tell me why my mother is so hard on me. She always has been and I don't know why. Someone please explain." Those were my thoughts as I fell asleep.

I don't know how long I had been asleep when I was woken by someone shouting my name. At first I thought I had been dreaming. But I was now lying fully awake and a bit unnerved when I heard the voice again. It was calling my name over and over. Then I recognised it. It was my grandmother. She had passed over when I was nineteen years old.

"I'm here, Gran."

Once she had got my attention and, oh boy, she'd done that, her voice went from outside of my head to her voice in my ear. She explained to me that she had been hard on my mother, just as her mother had been hard on her. My great-grandmother came from a family of fourteen brothers and sisters and my own grandmother was also from a large family, six girls and six boys. Several children from both generations died when they were very young. From what my grandmother was telling me, I was picking up the 'feeling' that the mothers down through the generations in our family had not been very close to their children, to stop themselves from feeling the pain of losing a child.

But of course I could have been wrong.

She said she was sorry she had been so hard on my mother and she was very sorry that my mother was being so hard on me now. She also said to me that it was for me to break the chain and make sure my little girl got all the love I could give her. At least now I understood. I had never heard my grandmother's voice before that night nor have I since. Just that once, but that's all I needed. I often send her my love. Bless you, Gran.

This was the first time that I recognised a voice, just like someone actually speaking to me. I had heard voices inside my ear from being a child, but I never knew who they were, that is, all except the voice I call 'my voice'. The 'one precious voice' that has been with me ever since I was very small.

Two years passed. There were good days when I felt almost well then all of the symptoms would reappear.

Our local playschool allowed Alexander to attend even though he was a bit young because his sister was also attending. They agreed he could stay three mornings a week which gave me a bit of a break.

Life went on. Some days and weeks I would be almost 'normal' and then the wave of tiredness would come from nowhere and I would be so tired that everything I tried to do turned into a monumental struggle. But somehow I managed.

Marie started school in September 1979 just before her fifth birthday. I managed most days to be able to walk with her the short distance to the school gates, with her helping me push Alexander in his buggy. But the memory of the odd days when I could not manage to walk with her is still very clear in my mind. I would stand at our garden gate and watch her, as she walked away on her own. First she had to cross over a side road. It was only about twenty yards from our garden gate but she still had to cross the road on her own, then she carried on to the top of our street and round the corner, out of my sight. It's as if it was yesterday the picture is so clear in my mind and I have to be honest and say writing this has brought tears to my eyes. It's not that I'm holding onto anything, or I'm cross or angry, it's just the thought of my little girl walking to school on her own still hurts me even now.

Fortunately, that wonderful friend of mine had taken the job of 'the lollipop lady' so, as Marie turned the corner and I lost sight of her, my dear friend, her Aunty Eileen, was there to take her hand and see her safely over the main road. Marie then had one more road to cross with another lollipop lady and then the school gates. It was very hard for me to stand there and watch her go. Alexander and I would keep waving to her and when she reached the top of the street, she would turn and we would all wave to each other and then she was gone. I would pray each time she had to do this that she would be kept safe and thank you God, she always was.

It has been many years since I have given much thought

31

to those days and it is an emotional recollection even now, but they are tears that are from 1979, not from now. Those tears are for the mother I so desperately wanted to be at the time. My legs not working very well, the net curtain coming across my vision, the waves of tiredness and everything else that MS could throw at me, all pale into insignificance compared to the hurt I felt not being able to walk my little girl to school.

At the beginning of 1980 I made a pact with myself that I was going to try and find out what the matter was. As my eyes were sometimes a major problem, an eye test seemed the first obvious thing. I was honestly beginning to think that I might have a brain tumour, not that I had a clue what the symptoms would be for this, but my head hurt, my eyes weren't working properly because of the net curtain and somewhere deep inside me I knew I was not imagining it all. But then, of course, I could be mentally ill. My mind was in a complete muddle. I was frightened and my doctor had no time for me. She just didn't hear the words that I said to her. If my own doctor was going to continually ignore my pleas for help, then I was going to help myself by trying to find somebody out there that could. I so desperately needed to know what was wrong. If someone could just say to me, Isabella you have green slime disease, I would have hugged and kissed them. At least I would have a name to my problem if one existed.

While the children were at school, I arranged an appointment with our local optician. But true to form, I was having a good day when I arrived for my appointment and I convinced myself that he would not be able to find anything wrong with me because I was feeling fine. I had no blurred vision and consequently no headache. The optician was such a kind, caring man and very gentle with me. After giving my eyes a thorough testing, he explained to me that my sight was fine, but there was a problem with my peripheral vision. He sat and wrote a short note that I was to take to my doctor, requesting her to make me an appointment in the eye department at the local hospital. He said he wanted someone else to check my eyes over because he felt that there was something not quite right. I agreed. At long last someone was trying to help me. He told me that I was not imagining my sight problem. Something was wrong but he wasn't sure what it was and then he reassured me again that it was not in my imagination.

I took the letter to my doctor who, in turn, made the appointment for me. It came through very quickly and in February 1980 off I went. After the specialist did his tests on my eyes, he said he wanted to do a field test, but it was getting very close to the time I was due to pick Alexander up from playschool so I couldn't stay for any more tests that day. I would have to leave and come back another time. The eye specialist said he would make me another appointment and I left to collect Alexander. But I waited and no appointment came and the year went on.

Alexander started school in September 1980. There was only one school year between him and Marie and she was always around for him during playtimes. I usually managed to pick them up at home time but again there were one or two days that they both had to walk to school on their own. That picture is also burnt into my memory banks. Marie holding her little brother's hand. She was the big girl at six years old and me standing at our garden gate watching my babies walking alone up our street, when I should have been walking beside them. That was a hurt I would carry for a long time. Thank God it only happened a few times. I had no choice. I had to completely trust that God would keep my babies safe because I couldn't. Thankfully they were.

Now that the children were both at school I had more time to organise myself during the day. I could rest if I needed to, or I could spend a few more hours a week working. The work came to me with no effort on my part and the extra money enabled me to buy myself a second- hand car. My very own little second-hand mini. It was great. I could drive the children to school and pick them up on the days that I was not walking very well. This made our lives so much easier.

Winter had arrived and I was having difficulty yet again with my sight, so I went back to my doctor and asked her to make me an appointment to have the field tests on my eyes as I had never received the appointment I had been promised. The letter for my new appointment came through very quickly although it was not going to be for another two months, but at least it was being done.

Never a day went by without me asking God for help. I would ask Him to keep me strong and well and keep the children safe.

You could say it's funny how things work out, or sometimes we say, "God works in mysterious ways."

But I have found over the years that there is always a right time, for everything.

CHAPTER FOUR

Christmas was fast approaching and I was waiting for my hospital appointment, but I was having difficulty again with my legs, my sight and the pain in my head was terrible. But it had only been about four weeks since I was last at the doctors and I was frightened to see her again so soon. I was having such a bad time with myself I felt I had no choice. I desperately needed some help. With great reluctance and a very heavy heart, I found myself ringing my doctor's surgery to make an appointment to see her. The receptionist told me that she was away on holiday. She said she could offer me an appointment to see the other lady doctor in the practice (who I'd never seen before), and I agreed.

I often wondered afterwards why I had never thought about seeing her before but, as I have said, there is always a right time for everything. Along I went at the appointed time. When I went into her room she introduced herself and a young student doctor who was sitting in on her surgery with her. She asked me what the problem was and my heart sank as I began to explain to her how I had been feeling.

After just a few minutes she stopped me and said, "Mrs. Clarence, do you have any numbness in your fingers? Do you have tingling sensations in your legs? Does the tiredness come over you like a wave and you can't fight it? Do you drop things?"

I just sat there with my mouth wide open listening to her telling me exactly how I felt. By this time the tears were streaming down my face. She was so kind. The complete opposite to her colleague. She said to me, "I think I know what's the matter with you." I couldn't believe my ears.

From my initial sinking heart I was beginning to feel elated. I told her how her colleague had said my problems were all in my imagination. She said, "No dear, it's not your imagination. There really is something wrong with you. I would like you to see my husband who is a Professor of Medicine.

Unfortunately, he is in the process of opening a new private clinic at the moment but we will get you an appointment as soon as it opens at the end of January."

I went home feeling very excited. She hadn't said what it was, but she had said it was not my imagination. There really was something wrong with me. It must sound daft to you that I was pleased there was something wrong but, having been told for the past four years that I was just lazy and I was imagining all the problems I had been having since before the children were born, I was so grateful.

That might not seem very long to some of you reading this but, trust me, if you are not well and you are feeling frightened, four years feels like forever. I know you must be thinking, you must have remembered the 'voice', but the memory of that day many years earlier had not surfaced, not yet.

When my husband got home from work that night, he didn't get through the front door before I was telling him what the doctor said. I kept saying to him, "The doctor knew all my symptoms." He was pleased for me but obviously worried because he had known for years there was something wrong with me. He told me that when we were first together at the beginning of 1973 he knew then, but he said nothing.

Bless him a thousand times over. He still wanted to be with me and still wanted to marry me. I think at this point we were both thinking that I might have a brain tumour, but we would have to wait and see.

A huge weight had been lifted from me because I now knew for definite that I wasn't imagining things. If I just knew exactly what the problem was, then perhaps I could fight it. But I had been trying to fight an unseen, unknown enemy for years, that everyone told me didn't exist.

Wouldn't you think the family would have been pleased with the news? Both our parents reacted very strangely. Well, I thought they did.

We had a visit from my husband's parents within days of me being told I would be seeing Professor Branson. They were both very cross with me and I couldn't understand why. My mother-in-law asked me, "Why did you ask to see Professor Branson?" I told her I hadn't asked. The doctor said she wanted me to see him. Then she said, "What do you think he will find?" I tried to explain to her I had no idea who this man was and I certainly didn't have any idea what he would find. This was a very odd conversation and quite upsetting. They were both making me feel as if I had done something, or said something, wrong. I found out later that my father-in-law had trained with Professor Branson many years earlier and they both knew he specialised in Multiple Sclerosis. He had carried out research work at our local hospital and had only recently left. They knew who he was but my husband and I didn't. The Professor was opening his new private clinic so that he could continue his research. But I didn't know who he was, or what he specialised in, not for a few days anyway.

When I told my father what had been said to me, he avoided me the best way he could for the next six months and hardly spoke to me, again as if I'd done something wrong. Oh boy, family dynamics can drive you crackers.

I found out much later that he felt if there was something very wrong, I would not be able to cope and he would not be able to help me. He was certainly having difficulty with the fact that there was something wrong with his daughter. This was how he reacted when I was a small child. If I had a migraine attack he kept away from me, I didn't understand at the time why he seemed cross with me, but I do now. He didn't like me being ill; it hurt him because he could do nothing to help me.

It only took me a few days to find out about this Professor and what his speciality was. I don't think I had heard the term MS before and I certainly didn't know what it was, so I went to our local library and found some literature on MS and read up about it. This is going to sound daft to you, I didn't feel as frightened by the disease as you might expect. I should have been, but I wasn't. I think perhaps I had spent too long trying to fight something I didn't have a name for and the whole family didn't think existed anyway.

At the beginning of December I received a phone call from Doctor Branson. She said an appointment had been made for me to see her husband, Professor Branson, at the end of January 1981 on the first day his new private clinic was to be opened. At long last I was getting somewhere with a doctor I trusted.

Christmas passed and I could hardly wait for my appointment with the Professor. But my appointment in the eye department at the hospital was also in January, two weeks before my appointment with the Professor.

Off I went on my own. It was a cold wet miserable Friday morning, one of those typical dark damp winter days. After the series of eye tests were complete I had a talk with the doctor, who asked me lots of questions about how I felt and all my symptoms. That's when, dare I say it, 'all hell broke loose.' This specialist said to me, "I want you in here first thing Monday morning. I am going to do more tests on you. You will be in hospital for at least four days, possibly longer, so you better make sure you come in prepared to stay." Please remember I was still just thirty years old. I stood there and I said, "No." He looked at me in sheer disbelief.

The conversation that followed went like this. (Trust me, I can remember this as if it was yesterday).

"You will do as I say - I want you in here on Monday morning at eight o'clock."

"No." said I.

At this point he started to turn very red in the face.

"You will do what I tell you."

"No I won't." (Me again)

"You will. You have to!" He was yelling at me by now.

At this point, the two nurses who were in the room with him started to back away from him.

"How dare you. You will do what I say."

"No I won't. I don't have to do what you say, I'm not coming into hospital. You're not touching me," and with that I turned to leave the room, with him screaming behind me, "You'll be back. You'll be back!"

"No I won't," I replied as I left his room and walked out of the hospital.

Where the strength came from, where the words came from, only God knows, of course He does. It was not me speaking. My mouth might have opened but the words that came pouring out were not mine. Someone was protecting me big time and this would all become clear to me as the following months and years went by. My legs were trembling, my stomach was in my boots and I may have been shaking all over, but I had followed my instincts. In fact I had done more than that. I had lived my instincts. Every fibre of my being told me to get out of that hospital and don't look back. It was a knowing from deep down inside of me that I could not have explained for the life of me. I didn't stop to think about the consequences.

That was one appointment that I would never forget and I was about to have another one.

My big day had arrived. I was the Professor's second patient in his new clinic on that Monday morning in January 1981. He sat me down and started to ask me a long list of questions. Could I remember anyone in the family who had been ill with what was, or might have been, MS? But, as far as I knew, no one had. He asked me to go back two generations because he told me that he had found that MS often misses a generation. As my grandparents on both sides of the family had come from very large families and most of them had died before I was even old enough to remember their names, let alone know them, I'm afraid I wasn't much help to him.

He then examined me by testing my reflexes first. Then he tested the strength of my grip in both hands and also measured them. Apparently my right hand is slightly smaller than my left hand and doesn't have the same spread. Then he took a blood sample. Professor Branson had spent many years researching and developing a special blood test that apparently could detect MS. My blood would show him if I had MS or not.

I was later to find out, almost ten years later, that the rest of the medical community did not agree with his findings. But that's another story.

There were no brain scans available in 1981 to diagnose MS, only lumbar punctures. The Professor told me never to allow anyone to perform a lumbar puncture on me. He told me that the damage they could cause far outweighed any benefit that might be derived from having one. The testing was over and I would now have to wait a week for my results.

Professor Branson did explain to me, that if my blood test came back positive, he would get his wife to ring me and make another appointment for me to see him. He would also need to see both our children to test their blood, to see if either of them were positive for MS. He said because MS is usually found within family groups, he would also need to see my parents and some other family members.

David and I had a week to think about the outcome of my test. It would be fair to say that we were both now beginning to realise how serious MS was and we were both worried, but I was still grateful that someone was taking me seriously.

We were not expecting to hear from the Professor until the following Monday, so when our telephone rang Friday lunchtime I didn't think anything of it. I picked the phone up and immediately recognised the Professor's voice. Without hesitating he said, "Isabella, I would like you and your husband to bring the children to see me next week, so that I can test both of them. We will also organise for your father and mother to come in to see me, as soon as possible." Then he said, "You also need to ring my wife and make an appointment with her so she can explain things to you."

"Professor Branson, do I have Multiple Sclerosis?"

"Yes. Your test has come back positive. I'll see you next week," and he rang off.

Our phone was on the hall floor and as I was speaking to the Professor I had been kneeling on the carpet. I was still kneeling in a bit of a daze. It took a few moments for his words to sink in and I started to cry.

But I'll never forget the next thing that I did. It's still as clear as if it were yesterday. I said in a very loud voice, "Lord I can't take this, but you can. I can't cope with this, so please take it away from me and make me well." And that's when I remembered the 'voice' from when I was fourteen years old. My higher self knew I was going to be alright, I was going to get well. I can't really explain the knowing. It was as if someone had switched a light on inside of me. I had no idea how I was going to get better, or when. I just knew that I would.

Please don't think for one minute that I wasn't frightened. I was. But somehow, one day, I would be well.

After I blew my nose and dried my eyes I rang my husband at work to tell him the news. He said, "I'm sorry." I guess there was not much more he could say. But when he came home from work at teatime that day he had bought me a bunch of flowers, freesia if my memory is correct. This was his way of saying, "I love you." In all the years we had been married, flowers had been a rare event, so this was major for him. He's a wonderful man but he hasn't got a romantic bone in his body.

After I had spoken to David I rang the surgery and made an appointment to see the Professor's wife that afternoon. She explained as much as she could about MS, more or less everything that I'd learned from the books that I'd read. But she was also able to tell me what foods to avoid and what vitamins to take and how to look after myself. When I left her surgery I was feeling a bit down because she said there was no cure.

That appointment was in 1981 and there is still no cure. You would think if they can put a man on the moon, they could have got somewhere by now with all the research that has been done. But I don't think they are any further forward. They don't know what causes it and they don't know how to cure it.

Me, I have my own theories which we will come to somewhere in my stories.

David and I took the children to see the Professor the

following week for him to test their blood. Marie managed alright with her blood being taken but little Alexander almost passed out. He doesn't like needles to this day and I don't blame him. Fortunately, both their results came back clear.

The only slight concern, the Professor had said it usually misses a generation, so we would need to keep a watchful eye on our grandchildren when they started arriving. But I'm not worried. Their grandmother is a healer with a lot of experience, especially with MS.

The only tears David and I shed the week we were told that I had MS were over the fact that Professor Branson advised us not to have any more children. We had both always wanted four, but I guess we were very fortunate to have two children and one of each at that. In truth, I was not well enough to cope with a new baby, not at that time anyway.

When we gave David's parents the news their response was very negative. They were obviously sorry and concerned about the consequences on our family. My father-in-law said to me that I would be in a wheelchair within a year. You can't get much more negative than that. I said to him, "I won't. I'm going to get well." He just looked at me and shook his head.

My father told me I would have to stop working, even though I was only doing a few hours a week after the children had gone to bed. But again I said, "No. I'm not going to stop. I'm going to keep on working and perhaps even do a little bit more."

I now knew what I was fighting. It had been given a name and that's all I ever wanted. I knew my tiredness was because of the MS and I wasn't just being lazy. I didn't have a brain tumour and I wasn't going mad. There was a reason why I had been so unwell.

I was to see that other lady doctor once more just before she retired. When I walked into her consulting room, her words to me were priceless. She said, "Well, I hear you have MS. Of the three major neurological diseases, motor neurone disease, muscular dystrophy and MS, MS is the best one to get." That's what she said to me, word for word. It's thirty years on now and all I can do is sit and shake my head in disbelief, as I did all those years ago.

You may be thinking, thank God that's all over, but of course this is just the end of the beginning of my story.

It's time for me to have an inquest on myself. How do I feel now after writing all of this? Have I really forgiven and let go? Yes I have. I feel fine.

It was almost as if I had been writing about someone else and not me, but it was part of my life and definitely one of the hardest. This has been the first time in many years that I have thought about such a lot of the things I've been writing about. I must have done a good job of keeping my storage boxes safe and, after taking a thick layer of dust from the top, my memory files inside are all still crystal clear. Those memories may still be very clear but I don't feel particularly connected to any of them anymore. I don't feel angry, I don't feel any of the hurts and I certainly don't have any of the fears.

But I have to be honest and say I do feel a bit sad. I'm sad that my mother never understood me during her lifetime and I'm sad that I let my daughter down so badly when she was such a little girl. And I'm also sad that I didn't have a lot of energy when the children were small, the energy to be able to play with them and really enjoy them both when they were young. And last but not least, I'm sad that I put my husband through so much worry, that he very rarely showed.

As for the doctors that were so unprofessional with me, what can I say? Not much. The word 'ignorant' comes to mind.

If I had one pound over the years for every time I have heard my patients say to me, "My own doctor doesn't listen to me," I would be a very rich lady. I wonder how many times over the years doctors have sat and listened to their patients and taken absolutely no notice of what their patient was trying to tell them. They completely ignore their patient's own words and instincts, always assuming that they, the doctors, know best.

We all need to listen more carefully. I do. That's one very big lesson I learned the hard way.

CHAPTER FIVE

Every day, without fail, I would ask to be guided in everything that I did, from everyday chores to the paperwork I was doing; asking for help was second nature to me. But the most important and constant thought in my head was, somehow God please show me how to be healed. I know I will be, but I have no idea when and I have no idea how.

I must have driven the Universal energy crackers with my pleas for help. But I had the sense to realise that I had to live each day and somehow make each day count, until the right day and the right time.

I really did and do believe those words. There is always a right time for everything.

My new doctor suggested to me that I should join the MS society where we lived. She thought it would be good for me to meet other people with MS. It seemed like a good idea at the time, so I arranged to go to one of their meetings. They were a lovely group of people, but they were all 'well into' their medications. That was the primary topic of conversation every time I met them. Who was taking what and for how long and what were the side effects. Not once did I hear any one of them say how the drugs were helping them.

After a few weeks the committee, which included two people who had MS themselves, asked me to be, for want of a better word, an MS support worker for people who were newly diagnosed. They all felt because I had MS myself, I was the perfect candidate for this new voluntary post.

I was happy to help where I could and, of course, if I could. But it didn't take me very long to realise that my way of thinking was so different from theirs. It was hard for me to be able to talk with them. They were all happily taking lots of drugs, thinking that the drugs would help them get better, or at least improve their condition, and they just couldn't understand why I was not taking any of the drugs myself. If I tried to explain my reasons for not taking any medication it fell on deaf ears. If I tried to talk about my trust in the Universal energy I was met with a blank stare.

We all have choices in this life. Their choice was to follow the medical path of medication, while mine was to trust that, one day, the Universal energy that I knew and trusted would somehow heal me. It was just an inner knowing and very difficult to put into words. It was hard enough to explain my thinking to my closest friends and family, let alone a complete stranger. Anyway, none of the people I met were in the least bit interested in my opinion and that was fine by me. Whatever they thought was best for them was right for them.

But I really did wonder if any of them had stopped to think for a moment that by following their doctor's advice, or their family's advice, or anyone else's advice for that matter, was this really the best thing for them? Why is it that some people don't want to stop and think for themselves, or more importantly use their own instincts and follow what they themselves think they should do? If they did but realise it, their own instincts would keep them safe. If I had listened to the doctor from the hospital and done exactly what he wanted me to do and I had taken the road into the hospital in January, I would also now be taking lots of drugs.

Thank you, Lord, a thousand times over for protecting me. Thank you for giving me such strong instincts and the strength and sense to use them.

It didn't take me long to realise that, unfortunately, this voluntary post was not for me. I decided to tell the group that I was going to stop going out to see people who had just been newly diagnosed because I didn't think I was the right person for the job. I did keep in touch with one or two of them over the next few years. But sadly, one by one, they passed over into the next life. God bless them all. In fact within ten years of my diagnosis, everyone I knew that had been diagnosed both before and around the same time as me had all left this life.

Through visiting the group on a regular basis I had got to know quite a few of the people really well and I feel confident in saying it wasn't the MS that killed them, it was the drugs they were all taking. Their immune systems became non-existent over a period of time because of the high levels of drugs in them. One or two of them were so huge in bodyweight because of the dose of steroids they were on, it didn't take a genius to see how their bodies just couldn't cope.

One of the members in the group was a lovely lady who I grew quite fond of. I liked to spend time with her, listening to all of her stories. She also said to me how lucky I was that I had never taken any of the drugs that she had been given. She personally felt that the drugs had put her into her wheelchair and it would be the drugs that would eventually kill her. That's what she had told me then; those were her words not mine. I believed her then and I feel the same way now.

I had had a 'knowing' not to follow the hospital doctor's advice and, after meeting the people in the society, I realised that my 'knowing' had been keeping me safe. It seemed to me that my friend and all the other people that I met with MS were being treated like guinea pigs by their doctors for the drug companies. The doctors knew the drugs would not help or cure them, but they were given them anyway. That lovely lady friend I had known told me that she was under nine stone when she was first diagnosed with MS and when she died she weighed well over sixteen stone and this was not through overeating.

That was 1981. I would like to think things have changed by now, but I'm not sure.

Makes you think doesn't it?

Since 1981, when I finally got my diagnosis, I have never taken any pharmaceutical medication of any sort for MS because for me there are always other ways. I have always believed that somewhere in the natural world around us and in the unseen forces surrounding us, that there will be a cure for each and every illness that we as humans suffer from, be it healing energy or healing plants, all natural safe and harmless.

Professor Branson had advised me to start taking 'Naudicelle', pure evening primrose oil, in capsule form. This was a natural medicine that could do me no harm. So I started to take it as soon as he suggested it to me and I kept on taking it for years. 'Naudicelle' helps make myelin in our system. MS is the breakdown of the myelin sheath, which is the covering that protects our central nervous system. When my legs would not work there was nothing wrong with my legs. It's just that the messages from my brain to my legs didn't get through because the protective covering on my nerves was damaged. Just like a wiring system in our homes. When you put the lights on by pressing a switch the message travels along the wires and the bulb comes on. That is providing the wires are covered in a protective plastic covering. But because the covering (the myelin sheath) in my central nervous system had broken down, the messages my brain was trying to send just didn't reach my legs, or anywhere else very well for that matter. 'Naudicelle' helps repair damaged myelin. It might not be able to completely restore or replace it, but it can and does help to stop any further deterioration and that's got to be good.

I mentioned before that both our children were tested by the Professor and that their test results come back clear, but should one of our grandchildren show any signs of MS one of the first things I would be suggesting to my family would be to start taking 'Naudicelle' to help protect them.

Because I was very much in tune with alternative medicine I began to use homeopathic medicine for myself, mainly to help me keep calm when I was having an MS attack. And I also used it on both our children whenever I felt they needed it. Homoeopathy was always there to help and we all still use it.

Once the family found out that I actually had a real problem, both our parents offered to help me but you know how it is, people sometimes make promises that they just don't keep and nothing changed. I remember being told they would come and help me with the washing and ironing. The ironing was particularly tiring for me but no help came. Somehow I managed with David helping me when he was at home. At least now he knew why I needed it (having known himself for years that something was wrong with me).

In September 1981 both the children were due back to

47

school. I was still having the usual good days and bad days, but because we all knew now what the problem was it wasn't such a big deal. But I desperately wanted to be well. Apart from having trouble walking on some days, I had also found that when I was in some of the big shops in our local town I would begin to feel ill very quickly and I couldn't understand why. I would have only been in the shop a few minutes when I would begin to feel panicky and very odd. It turned out that a few of my new friends, who also had MS, had experienced the same thing. They had managed to find out that it was due to the lighting systems in some of our larger stores. If you look closely even today some of the lights flicker ever so slightly. This can spark an MS attack, so I started to wear sun-glasses inside the stores and this stopped the symptoms.

My dear friend Eileen had helped me such a lot at the beginning of the previous summer when I was going through a bad patch. There is a saying, a friend in need is a friend indeed. I think that's how it goes. This friend was more precious than gold. One summer's afternoon when I was sitting outside in the garden with the children, my dear friend Eileen called in to see us. She just lived four houses away. I asked her if she would please do me a huge favour because I was going through a bad spell. Would she please go shopping for me and buy the children some new summer clothes? She said of course she would. I gave her the money and a list of things the children needed. New summer dresses for Marie and little shorts and tee shirts for Alexander, underwear and socks for both of them. She came back with all of their outfits and they were just what I would have chosen myself. I can't thank her enough for all the support she gave me. Thankfully it was a two-shop trip as the local Mothercare store and, of course, Marks and Spencer had everything we needed. I just could not have done this myself at the time. That to me was real friendship, lifting the load from me. My prayer on that day was that one day I would be able to lift someone else's cares away for them, the way she had done for me. It was no good asking David to go shopping for clothes for the children because he had no idea about their sizes, or what suited them. If I had sent him to buy new outfits goodness knows what he would have come home with. We may have had a good laugh but everything would have had to be returned.

But this year I was feeling stronger; I knew to wear sunglasses inside the shops. At the end of August, just before Marie and Alexander were due to start school, I was able to go shopping with David and the children. I was going to buy some new clothes for both of them and I was going to choose them myself. What a treat that was for me, just a very ordinary everyday thing to do, but for me it was great. It was such a pleasure being able to choose warm cardigans, jumpers and lovely warm tights for Marie and warm jumpers and trousers for Alexander for the winter months. I did enjoy myself but I paid the price; for two weeks afterwards I was so tired.

I was trying to stay as positive as I could. Just knowing what the problem was had made a huge difference to me. Green slime disease or MS, it didn't matter. I had a name and it was not my imagination.

After the initial consultation with Dr. Branson when I'd been given the explanation from her as to what MS was and how best to cope with it, I made a decision. I decided I was not going to go to the doctors ever again with what I now knew to be MS symptoms and there was a long list. I had no intention of taking any drugs and I was certainly not going to allow anybody to treat me like a guinea pig and experiment on me in hospital, trying out different medications. If I felt there was something else wrong with me, other than the MS, then maybe, just maybe, I might go to the doctors, but only maybe. Most of the medical profession I had come into contact with had let me down so badly and treated me abominably.

I wanted to take control of my own life. I wanted to take responsibility for myself. If someone was going to let me down it would be me. But of course, as always, I was going to put my trust in God. Not faith, not hope, but trust. I had trusted Him or what I also call the Universal energy from being a child. That precious 'voice' that I heard, that never let me down. The only

49

time I ever got into trouble was when I didn't listen to what my 'voice' said. If I followed my 'voice' I was safe.

I was working part-time from home and I was enjoying the work. It made me think and it made me feel good about myself. I had also been doing some voluntary work for the Samaritans. This suited me fine because I wanted to help other people and this was one way that I could. The job entailed sitting at a telephone, answering calls from people who needed help. This was something I could do, sitting and listening.

The training programme they gave all the volunteers before we were allowed to answer the telephones was excellent. We were all taught to turn a caller's conversation around, in other words throw the ball back in their court. We were taught never to tell anyone what to do and why. It was common sense put into practice. It was so well done that by the time we (new recruits) were ready to answer the telephones we all felt we had been given the skills to be able to handle whatever calls may come in. We all did. I did it for about three years.

When I'm now asked, "What should I do, Isabella?" I gently turn the question around by saying, "What do you think you should do?" Then I will try and get the person to see their problem from lots of different angles. In other words they will answer their own question. Although I sometimes make suggestions, I would never tell anyone what to do. Being a Samaritan was a very valuable experience for me. I would use what I had learnt in the years to come.

When I saw Professor Branson in January 1981 he told me to avoid anyone with the flu, not to get stressed and keep out of the sun. These were the three things he felt could trigger an attack of MS. He explained that sunshine or rather hot weather did not suit people with MS. But I loved sunshine and hot weather. I could understand the flu and stress bit, but I liked to look well, not white and pasty, and because of this I used to have sun beds in the winter. (How daft was that?) I only had a few, but I had them.

Autumn 1981 when the children were at school, off I went to have some more. After only two sessions my net curtain started to come back and I was having difficulty seeing again. That's when it dawned on me, that the flickering lights on the sun bed had triggered my attack, so I stopped immediately. I had managed to give myself this attack and probably at least one other. At least now I was recognising what was causing some of my problems. I only started the sun beds two years earlier, so not all of my attacks could be put down to them. But I vowed never to have any more. I had managed to set off another attack. How clever was that?

It was difficult for me to see anything close up, which meant I could not do my work very easily. I was straining my eyes so much to be able to see that I ended up having to ask my father for his help. By coming to our home a few times he was able to prepare the wages for two small businesses for me. This had to be done every week regardless of how I felt.

Fortunately for me, my father had had his own business for many years and if necessary he could do his own company wages. His company secretary had taught us both how to do book- keeping and how to prepare wages, many years earlier. So he was able to step in for me at short notice and help me, thank goodness. But this was not a good situation and it really couldn't go on.

I knew I must get well soon, but how?

I managed to keep myself positive most days. Trust me, it wasn't easy. Obviously when I was going through a good spell I could stay positive, but when that wave came over me and I knew I was in for a few bad days or, worse still, a few weeks I would begin to get frightened. Would I ever find out how I was going to get well?

We all know how rotten and miserable we feel when we get a bad cold. We start sneezing and our nose starts dripping like a tap and we generally feel rotten. Well, I guess my symptoms just made me feel so down and negative that fear crept into every thought I had.

People died of MS. Would I see my children grow up, would I be there for them when they needed me, would I see them get married? On and on my thoughts would race away on a very negative track. Then I would pull myself up and remember the 'voice'. But it was getting harder and harder for me to keep smiling.

My trust in God was never failing, but my trust in myself was melting away fast.

This was a bad attack and the first time that I had been unable to do my work, the first time that my father had come to help me.

CHAPTER SIX

It was during my next evening shift at the Samaritans a week later that I explained to one of the other volunteers how I was feeling. She hesitated for a few moments and then said to me that she might know of someone who could help me. I asked her to please explain. She said she knew a lady who worked as a healer. She asked me how I felt about healing, I told her that I had no idea what it was all about but I would love to find out; it sounded so right. It not only sounded right, it also felt right because I realised that I had a shiver running down my spine and the hairs on my arms were standing up. This always happens to me even to this day when I'm on the right track, when I'm plugged into the Universal energy and this was one of those times. Then she explained to me that this lady didn't see very many people, only those she chose. She said I may ring the lady's door bell and when she answers the door she may say, "I'm sorry I can't help you," and close the door in your face. "How do you feel about that?"

"Well, obviously I would be worried in case she turned me away, but I'll pray that the lady will take me on as a patient."

"Ok, I'll speak to her for you and find out if you are allowed to get in touch. I can't give you her phone number and address without her permission."

I remember feeling excited inside, but very nervous and frightened all at the same time. I could hardly wait until my next shift.

The following week when I went into the office to do my shift on the telephones, my colleague handed me a piece of paper with the lady's name and address on it. It turned out that the lady I was to go to see only lived three streets away from our home. I felt that this was incredible. She could have been a hundred miles away from where I lived. I was told that I didn't need to telephone. I was just to go and ring her door bell. My colleague said to me, "Remember, you must be prepared to be turned away. She may not want to take you on as a patient."

Was this what I had been waiting for, for so long? Please let it be.

It took me a few days to pluck up the courage to go to the lady's house and I must be honest and tell you that I walked backwards and forwards past her front door at least four times, before I plucked up the courage to ring her doorbell. I was so frightened that I would be turned away. I was shaking from head to foot and it wasn't the MS. I was so worried she wouldn't want to help me; she might turn me away and close the door.

Oh boy, talk about being nervous, but something was telling me this was a very important step in my life. It felt as if my life depended on it and I guess that was exactly right. Taking a deep breath and saying a prayer, I rang her doorbell and waited.

She opened the door, looked at me and smiled, saying, "Where have you been? Come on in. I've been waiting for you." I was so relieved she hadn't turned me away I don't even think I said hello to her. I just followed her into her home and into the room she worked in. She invited me to sit down; we were going to have a chat.

When she asked me what was wrong, the flood gates opened. All the negative thoughts I was having, all the hurts that I felt, all the upset caused because of the way a certain doctor had treated me all came flooding out. I remember finishing off by saying I was dying.

She laughed at me, yes laughed.

"No, you're not going to die. You're going to spend the rest of your life healing other people and you're going to be fine."

I honestly thought she was crackers at the time. I couldn't see properly, I was having difficulty walking and she was sitting there telling me I was going to heal other people. I couldn't even heal myself, so how the heck was I going to heal other people? But somewhere deep down inside me, I knew that what she was saying was right.

Then she started to tell me things about myself as if she'd known me all my life, especially when I was younger.

"You know you can heal. You did it as a child without ever thinking about it. You healed injured birds and small animals. You have been healing your children with no conscious thought because it comes naturally to you. You've been seeing things for as long as you can remember, hearing voices from another world and you've given it no thought because you have been like this from the day you were born. Different, you have always been different. You drive your car along a country road and for no reason whatsoever you slow down to almost a stop, just before an animal crosses the road in front of you. But because you slowed down both you and the animal are safe. You have seen things of other worlds. But the most important of all is your trust in what you call God, the Universal energy, because this trust you have cannot be taught. It's priceless."

I just sat there listening to her telling me all about me. I told her just how useless I felt I was. What was the point in unconsciously knowing these things if I had no idea how to help myself by using them?

"That's why you have found the path to my door and not before time," was her reply.

Then she explained to me that she would help me get better, but she was also going to teach me how to heal myself. She was going to teach me how to use the wonderful healing energy that she used, so that I would be aware of the energy that I had been tapping into without realising what I had been doing for years. It was not going to be an easy ride. She wanted me to learn how to heal myself alongside her healing me. For a long time afterwards I thought that she had been very hard on me. But, of course, she was right. I had to take responsibility for my own healing. I had to learn everything there was to learn from her. This was the only way for me to become the healer she knew that I would become in the future.

So my journey was about to start. She made an appointment for me for a couple of day's time for our work together to begin.

Do you remember the words I used when I first started writing this?

Question: "How did you get into healing, Isabella?"

Answer: "I was diagnosed with MS, then I was directed to a healer and the rest is history." That was the short version I have used for many years now. Well now you know why I kept my answer short.

I was a bit apprehensive when I went along for my first appointment with Nansi because I had no idea what was going to happen, what she would do, or how I was supposed to react. But this was all part of the learning process. When someone comes to see me now as a patient for the first time, I know exactly how they are feeling because I've been there. Nansi first explained to me that my healing was not going to be a quick cure. There were three very important words that I was to learn by heart and never forget. And thirty years on I still use them.

Patience, perseverance and persistence. I call them the three 'P's.

I was going to have to be patient. I wasn't going to heal overnight. She explained it had taken years for me to become so unbalanced and it was going to take a while for me to correct this and heal. I would need to persevere. I must never think about giving up no matter how ill I felt. I must be very persistent and constantly practice all that she was going to teach me no matter what. Nansi then explained to me that the Universal energy that I called God was connected to everything. We were all connected, nothing was separate. No one was. We are all connected to God, I was connected to God. Amazing.

"We all are."

I'd never thought about it like that before. I had felt it but never thought about it.

When my friends say to me now, "It's alright for you, Isabella. You have a direct line to God," my answer is and has been for a long time, "We all have. It's just that I know I have, but you've yet to realise it."

Nansi then explained about the energy that surrounds every living thing. Another word that healers use for this energy is the aura. Every living thing has an energy field or aura, even this beautiful planet we live on. Plants, animals, flowers and, from inside the Earth itself, crystals all have an energy field. People still look at me sideways sometimes when I say this (but not nearly as often as they used to); crystal healing was not around in the early 1980s. Ask yourself what was in the first radio ever invented and what is in a computer today? A crystal. This energy/aura is all around the human body and also inside us sitting beautifully in our chakra centres. It's actually the real us. I often explain to people that our bodies are just our spacesuit. If we lived on another planet our spacesuit would look completely different. The real us is our beautiful aura which can travel anywhere and often does.

Here's a very good example to help explain. A friend took me for a day out a little while ago and one of the things we did was to visit a friend of hers, an elderly gentleman who my friend has been helping for years. It was to be his eightieth birthday the following day. He had had to have his left leg amputated just above the knee last year. This precious friend of mine came to me as a patient some eight years ago. When she first started to come to my home for healing she used to bring this old gentleman with her in the car to get him out and about. He would patiently wait in the car while she had her appointment. I would always pop out and say hello to him and invite him into the house but he preferred to sit in the car and listen to the radio.

On this particular afternoon I suggested we went to see him for a short visit, as I hadn't seen him since his leg had been taken off the previous year. He told me that he still sometimes feels his foot, even though it's not there anymore. I was able to explain to him that actually it was still there. Just because he'd had his leg amputated the energy of his leg was still whole, his foot was still there in his aura. When it was time for him to pass over into the next world he would go over complete, left leg, foot and all. He would be able to run just like he did years ago.

I then explained to him that quite a few years ago a camera was developed that can photograph the aura. It's called a Kirlian camera. If you take a photograph of a whole leaf on a live healthy plant with a Kirlian camera you will see the beautiful energy all around the leaf. If you were then to cut one of the leaves of the plant in half and were to photograph the leaf again, you would see the energy of the leaf will still be complete, providing it is still attached to the live plant. The aura is not injured in any way because the energy or life-force of the whole live plant is still intact. The same thing applies to everyone when a limb is amputated. We are still whole and our auras are still complete, just like the leaf on the plant. This, as you can imagine, made him very happy.

Nansi then explained to me that when we become ill, it's because we have knocked the balance out in our energy/aura and that in turn affects the human body. I had caused my MS myself because my aura was so out of balance. Patients often say to me, "I think I get how my aura has gone out of balance, but how come this affects me physically?"

My simple answer:

You know when the wheel on your car is a bit out of balance because you can feel something is wrong through the steering wheel? The car does not drive right and it feels heavy even at low speed. Then if you try and drive your car a bit faster you will experience a wobble through your steering wheel. The faster you go the worse the wobble will become and this is not a good thing to be happening to your car. So if your wheel was out of balance you would get it fixed as soon as you could. I'm not very good with cars but I think what happens is that when the wheel is out of balance it then affects the drive shaft which, in turn, affects the crank-shaft and so on. So if that wheel is left out of balance you would end up with a very poorly motor car, which could also cause an accident. Well, if our aura is out of balance and it's not corrected it then begins to affect other parts of us, our physical body. Just like the wheel on the car. Remember, everything is connected.

So what made my aura go out of balance? That was for

my next session.

As Nansi explained to me, my healing was going to be a journey, taking one step at a time. I needed to learn and understand each step as we went along. All the time she was explaining things to me she would be working on my body with her hands. As I lay on her healing bed Nansi would start at the top of my head with her hands. She told me to imagine the top of my head as a lotus flower and as she was drawing down energy from the Universe (or God's loving, healing energy) the lotus petals would open to allow the healing energy to flow into me, in through the top of my head and then down through my body and through my chakra centres. She also explained to me all about the chakra centres in the human body, how each one was an energy wheel, and because I was so out of balance with myself, most of these unseen energy centres were almost closed down.

Boy, I was in a mess.

Along with me imagining the lotus flower, I needed to learn to breathe properly as she was working with me. I learned to breathe in through my nose deeply and then out through an open mouth, slowly. As my mind saw the petals opening on top of my head, I would breathe in the energy through the top of my head and slowly down through each part of me. I was to visualise or imagine it passing through me, through each energy centre in turn and also down my arms and legs as I was breathing.

This sounds easy, but it took me about three months before I was able to do this with ease. But once I had mastered the technique I would be buzzing all over with healing energy after each healing session. This would be the basis for all the work we did together. I was to see Nansi once a week for my treatment but I had my homework to do each day. I was to practise the breathing every day and at night when I was in bed. I was to practise drawing down energy through the top of my head. She also gave me an affirmation that I had to say every morning before I got out of bed and I had to say it ten times out loud.

Every day, in every way, I am stronger and stronger. Not was, or may be, or could be, or even I would like to be.......I am. Nansi used to say to me, "I don't care if your leg drops off, you will say: Every day, in every way, I am stronger and stronger." I didn't understand the reasoning behind this at first. It would take me a long time before I could honestly say I owned those words.

Because I was still having difficulty with my net curtain, she taught me to imagine the healing energy passing through my brain into each eye, before it travelled through the rest of me. I was learning how to heal myself with her wonderful help.

Action follows thought. This was very powerful thought, along with wonderful healing energy. Patience, Persistence, Perseverance.

CHAPTER SEVEN

My next healing session with Nansi was going to be very important for me because she was going to help me find the cause of the huge imbalance in my aura and I was feeling a little bit apprehensive, to say the least, as to what we might find. I realised that I had so much to learn and, thank God, I had been directed to such a wonderful lady. She was to be my healer and my teacher for the next few years of my life.

Nansi explained to me that because every part of us is connected, our physical body is connected to our aura and our aura is connected to our chakra centres. Our emotions and thoughts are the fuel that fires all of these, allowing and enabling us all to cause ourselves great health problems without ever realising what we are doing. And, of course, our auras are connected to the Universal energy, if we did but realise it. But all of these connections can also allow us, when we know how, to create a wonderful balance in our aura and then in ourselves. It was quite something for me to realise that whatever the disease or problem was that I had, I had caused it all by myself. So there was no point in looking for someone else to blame, (not that I ever had). It squarely put the onus on to me and no one else.

Once we all know and understand this we can make such a difference in a good way to begin to help ourselves. I am aware that this will raise many other questions and comments such as, "That can't be right." Babies are sometimes born with serious health problems. Some babies die before they are born, young children become ill and die and so many other instances that we all could mention. Children and babies couldn't possibly have caused their situations so what I'm saying must be wrong. Because the answers to these questions are so very hard to understand if you have no knowledge or understanding of the laws of the Universe, I would like to leave these sad situations for another time. I will come back to these questions at a later stage, or perhaps even in another book.

But I could only learn one step at a time. There was much for me to take in and think about, or as my father would have said, 'to ponder on'. My own situation was the first disease that I had to understand before I could move forward.

So please bear with me and allow me to explain all these things in the order that they were explained to me. Each healing session was as much about me learning and remembering as they were about the treatment I was having. It was explained to me that each of us has the possibility for any illness to occur. In other words, I could have triggered any illness known to man. It just so happened that I triggered MS. Depending on what the trigger is to cause the imbalance, this will then have its own relevant outcome. To help me understand this she used a simple example. Picture a beautiful tree on a windy summer's day. The branches are swaying gently in the breeze and as the breeze blows stronger and turns into a strong wind or gale, the branches and the trunk move more quickly, bending and swaying in harmony with nature. Now try and imagine what would happen if the same tree refused to bend in the wind. It would be relatively safe in a light breeze but if a gale force wind was to blow, the tree would break. Firstly branches would be broken off and then the trunk itself would snap and the tree would fall. The tree would eventually die, all because it wouldn't bend. Then she said think about the tree as a person. If a person is happy and content within themselves, easy-going and willing to compromise with family and friends, their nature is to bend and go with the flow. A person like this will very rarely have a back problem because simply put, they bend with the winds of life.

Over the many years that I have been working with people, I have occasionally found very easy-going people with back problems because they have either had, or they have been involved in, an accident of some sort. My experience has shown me that at the time of their accident the person's energy was 'all over the place'; they were in a jack-in-the-box state of mind, where one minute their thoughts were 'here' and the next minute their thoughts were 'there' and that in turn affected their energy/ aura around them. Because their energy/aura was so out of balance, it created chaos.

Unfortunately that sort of energy doesn't just create chaos around a person. It also attracts chaos and makes them very accident prone. Think about this. Whatever the energy/aura is around us all, then that's what we are attracting towards us because like attracts like. So if our energy is angry, we will attract anger towards us, but if our energy is full of love then we will attract love to us. We all need to remember this. Balance in ourselves and the energy around us will keep us safe and well.

Now let's look at the person who is not willing to compromise. They think they are always right no matter what and refuse to compromise with family and friends. This person has a completely different personality from the first example and is often very stubborn. This personality will complain of back pain and sometimes suffer very badly. If a person like this could learn to give a little, in other words bend and give in their relationships, they would find their back problems would begin to ease and the more they can give and take, the better their backs would be. It made a lot of sense to me then and even more sense to me now.

So what about me?

After Nansi had explained to me that every 'dis-ease' has its own trigger, it was now time for me to find mine. I needed to find the root cause of my problem to be able to clear any emotions that the cause had left me with. I needed to be able to let go of any hurts that I was carrying to allow my life to move forward and heal.

This was how she explained it to me:

Firstly we have our skin, then below that we have muscles and veins, then bone then, very deep inside us and well protected, we have our central nervous system. It's our central nervous system that sends the messages from our brains all over our bodies. The important words for me were 'very deep inside'.

The trigger that had caused my aura to go out of balance

had to have been something quite traumatic. An event that happened to me that had not just frightened me but had terrified me. An event so horrible for me that the hurt had gone very deep and in turn the dis-ease that I had triggered had gone deep. Even a shock of some sort or a minor accident would not have been a powerful enough trigger.

Then Nansi told me a story she had read a few years earlier. Unfortunately, she couldn't remember if she had seen it in a book or if it had been an article in a magazine. The story was about American fighter pilots during the First World War. There can't have been very many of them, as there were not that many fighter planes in the skies all those years ago. The story was all about the American pilots who survived and went home after the war. It was reported and investigated that over eighty percent of them developed MS within two to three years of returning home. Why did this happen to them? What was the common factor? The researchers, at the time of writing the book, thought there must have been one. I don't know how the story ended, or what the researcher's conclusions were, but Nansi certainly had her own conclusions. Whether Nansi's had come from the story or not, I'm not sure. Those American pilots all flew during the First World War without parachutes; they had not been invented at the start of World War One. So every time they took to the air in combat they knew that if their plane was hit and damaged in any way that would be the end of them. They would go down with their plane; no way out. I can't begin to imagine how frightening this must have been for them. Every day they had to fly they must have been terrified. Would today be the day that they would die horribly, burning along with their aeroplane as it fell out of the sky? Each and every day they flew. It's no wonder they developed MS.

Now it was my turn.

After Nansi had told me the story about the American pilots, I knew what the cause of my imbalance had been. It had come to me in a flash as Nansi had been telling me the story. An event I had not thought about for many years. In fact, I could honestly say that until five minutes earlier I had completely forgotten the whole thing ever happened.

I sat with Nansi and cried. She just sat patiently beside me and waited for me to start talking when I was ready.

Summer 1962. It was the school holidays.

It's important to remember that the mobile phone had not been invented in 1962 or the internet. The only way young people could keep in touch was by walking around to each other's homes to find out who was in and what was going on. We did have a telephone at home but I wasn't allowed to use it and that was also quite normal. Only on rare occasions did young people get to telephone their friends. All my friends, and there was quite a group of us, lived on the same housing estate but at least half a mile away from each other, so getting together involved quite a lot of walking or cycling. This particular warm summer's afternoon was turning into a bore for me. I didn't know where any of my friends were, so I decided to try and find one or two of them.

Because the day was so lovely and warm, I thought that some of them may have gone for a walk down to the river. It was a favourite place where we all went when it was hot and sunny, to go for a swim. So off I went in search of at least one or two of them for someone my own age to talk to. The river was about a two mile walk away from where I lived. As I had to pass both of my friend's homes on the way I decided that I could call to see if they were in, before heading off on the long walk by myself to the river. Unfortunately, no one was at home so I continued on my way.

The river was at the end of an old disused railway line. It was a beautiful walk, but it did take a while. Having passed through the housing estate, I left all the houses behind me as I began to walk along the old railway track. All I wanted to do was to find some of my friends; they had to be somewhere near.

It must have taken me well over an hour to reach the river from my home. As I approached the river bank I could see in the distance what I thought were some of my friends. I could see a group of eight young people and, as I walked closer towards them, I could see that there were two girls and six boys. As I was nearing the group I could now see who they were and, unfortunately for me, they were not my close friends. The two girls in the group were at my school but were not my close friends. Two of the boys were also at the same school as me but the other boys were not from my school and they were much older and I didn't really know them. I was only twelve and a half years old and I knew that some of the boys in the group were over fifteen and to me they were all grown up and I wasn't.

A feeling of unease swept over me as I approached them. I can remember asking them if they knew where my friends were. They all just shrugged their shoulders and said, "No."

So I said, "That's fine. I'll go back home and I'll call again at their homes on my way."

As I turned away from them all and started to walk back along the old railway track, I heard one of the older boys shout, "Let's get her!" and, to my horror, I heard the two girls join in and say, "Yes, let's get her," then the rest of the bunch also joined in. Something in me took over and my legs started running without me even thinking about it and, at the same time, a very loud voice in my ear shouted, "Run!"

And run I did, like the wind.

As I started running I could hear the boys' voices behind me, all six of them shouting at each other, "Get her!"

"You get her."

"I'll get her."

"Come on, we can catch her."

I could also hear the girls' voices joining in, saying, "Come on, you can get her." It was horrible. I was terrified but I kept on running. I don't think my feet touched the ground. In fact, I know they didn't. I can honestly say I can still remember thinking that I was running on air.

"You mustn't look back," said the 'voice' in my ear. "Don't look back." I seemed to know that I would have fallen if I'd tried to. I was running so fast and the ground was so uneven, but on and on I went.

The old railway line was about one mile from the nearest house. Those boys were so much taller than me and I was sure they would catch up with me at any moment. All I could hear from behind me were all eight voices shouting, "Get her!"

I knew I had to run faster than I'd ever run in my life as they were right on my heels. I could hear and feel their puffing breath on the back of my neck right behind me; they were so close but they still hadn't caught me. All the time I was running I was listening to all their voices.

"Grab her."

"Stop her."

Then I heard one of them say, "I can't keep up with her."

My 'voice' was telling me to keep running and as terrified as I was I just knew I had to keep going no matter what. But gradually, one by one, the boys were giving up. The last two voices that I heard were saying, "I can't catch her," and then the last one, "I just can't. She's too fast." The sound of their voices was fading into the distance, but I kept running like the wind until I reached the bottom of the gardens of the houses on the estate.

As I ran towards them I saw a gentleman leaning on his garden fence watching me. When I eventually reached the bottom of his garden he told me that he had been watching me running from the boys for quite a few minutes and then he asked me if I was feeling alright and was there anything that he could do for me. I couldn't speak to him at first because I was so out of breath. I just stood beside his fence and nodded my head to indicate to him I was okay.

He said, "Are you sure?"

I somehow managed to say, "Yes."

I still hadn't turned around to see where the boys were, the only thing I wanted to do was go home, where I would be safe. There was still about a mile to walk. I was trembling, my legs felt very weak and I felt sick. But at least now I was amongst the houses and I couldn't hear their voices any more. I honestly think I'd have won the gold medal that day if it had been an organised race. In fact, I know I would.

Six boys, some older and all taller than me, had not managed to catch me, thank God.

When I eventually reached home I went straight into our kitchen and collapsed onto the kitchen chair. My mother was in the kitchen and asked me if I was alright. Then she asked me what the matter was. "I'm okay, Mum. I'm just tired and I don't feel very well." I took myself off to my bedroom and sat shaking for about an hour.

I felt physically sick. I asked Mum if it would be alright if I went to bed to have a lie down for a little while. Looking at me strangely, she said, "Yes, if you think that will help."

She never did question me further and I never did tell her.

I never spoke to the two girls and the two boys from my school ever again. The older boys were not in my circle of friends, so I didn't need to have anything to do with them.

I didn't understand it at the time but I must have been in shock for quite a few days. I was very upset when the reality of what happened sank in. I didn't go out on my own for the rest of the summer holidays and I didn't want to go back to the river. Yet my parents never noticed that anything was wrong. I didn't tell them because I felt they would have blamed me, that somehow it must have been my fault.

"Was this the trigger, Nansi?"

"I should say so. Why did you think your parents would not have supported you?"

"Because as I was struggling to walk home that day I went back over in my mind the number of times my 'voice' had told me not to go. It had told me to stay at home, but I was bored and I wanted to see my friends. After I left the first of my friend's houses, when no one was in, my 'voice' told me again to go back home, but I ignored it."

How many twelve year olds in 1962 do you know would have heard a voice, let alone listen to what the voice said and then take any notice? My 'voice' had tried to keep me safe, but I wasn't listening. If I'd followed what my 'voice' had said to me on that day, this would not have happened to me, so in a way it was my fault.

This was a lesson I needed to remember for the rest of my life. If I hear my 'voice' telling me something, I would listen to whatever it said and follow its advice.

"How do you feel about this now?"

"It's been so long since I have even thought about that day and, to be honest, I'm amazed I can still recall it all so clearly, just as if it were yesterday."

"Why do you think that is?"

"I guess it's because it was such a very frightening thing to have happened to me. I'm never going to forget it now."

Nansi explained to me I wasn't meant to forget. All of our life's experiences are helping to mould us into who we are today. She then explained to me that there are no mistakes in this life, only lessons and the bigger the 'mistake', or nasty experience we have, the bigger the lesson there is to learn.

If we can learn the lesson, then the lesson is complete.

My simple explanation for this is that it's a bit like when we were all at school and we learnt our times tables. Once we knew them we didn't have to keep repeating the lesson. This had been a very hard lesson for me. I had found my trigger and now I needed the time to think about that day all those years ago. The terror I had felt while I was running that mile had left its mark on me 'big time.' But I needed to learn to forgive what had happened, let go and then I could move forward.

It also became clear to me I needed to forgive my parents, especially my mother. If I had been able to approach her that day, if she had been more loving towards me, then perhaps I would have been able to tell her what had happened to me and I wouldn't have had to keep the whole episode buried away for all of these years. I would have had someone to talk to. But, unfortunately for me, my mother had been distant from me for as long as I could remember.

Then the penny dropped - I needed to forgive myself.

It was time for me to think.

CHAPTER EIGHT

I had had no one to talk to, no one that I could confide in and share my problems with and no one to explain to me who or what the voices were that I heard, and I heard them and my 'special voice' a lot.

When I had mentioned to my parents years earlier that I heard voices and saw 'things', I was told not to be so silly and not to talk about 'such things ever again' so I never did; I kept quiet. And I'm sure because of this I had been very much on my own, keeping my thoughts and my voices to myself all of my childhood and young teenage years.

This was the very first time that I had told anyone about that day. In fact I've never told anybody since, not even my husband. It's not that I'm keeping it a secret; that memory has not had a hold on me for many years now. It's just that none of my family have ever asked me if I knew what had caused my MS, so I have never had a reason to talk about it.

Nansi said I now had someone to talk to. She would try and explain anything to me that I didn't understand. At long last, I didn't feel strange or odd any more or, as a friend of mine has often said, I didn't feel as if I'd got off at the wrong bus stop. I often used to think I had got off on the wrong planet.

As I was sitting talking with Nansi, it dawned on me that the first time I knew something was wrong with me all those years ago was when I was fourteen years old, during that race at school. Then the next day my 'voice' told me something was very wrong with me, which was about two years after my horrible experience. It had taken two years to transfer the terror from my aura to my physical body and show itself, just like the American pilots.

How I wish I had had someone like Nansi in my life to talk to when I was a child. But there is always a right time for everything and the right time for me was now.

Over the years I have had the privilege of seeing quite a

few pregnant women as patients and at some point I would love to tell you some of their stories, perhaps even in the coming pages. But there is one important thing I have said to all of them. Please make sure when your baby starts to talk to you, find the time to listen to the words they may say, really listen to what your little one is telling you. If they have an imaginary friend, if they say they describe a loved one who you know has passed over, if they say they can hear people that you can't and much more, please be gentle with them and don't discount what your children might see and hear. Please be there for them. They may be far more aware of the other worlds around them than you are. Just like me as a child.

What did I learn? What can we all take away from my experiences?

If I had listened to my 'voice' in 1962, I wouldn't have been in trouble on that day, many years ago. So I learned that I must always listen and follow my voices, especially the voice I call 'my voice'.

Everyone has a sixth sense; everyone has that inner voice that tries to keep us all safe.

Okay, I know not everyone hears an actual voice the way I do but if people would just learn to listen to their inner voice and follow it everyone would be much safer. The more you follow the voice on your shoulder the more it will be there for you and the stronger your sixth sense will become. You are going to ask, "How can I do this?" Here are a couple of simple examples.

When I go food shopping I take a list with me of everything I need to buy so I don't have to spend ages wandering around the shop looking at all the shelves, wondering what to get. I take my list and stick to it. That way I don't waste time and money on things we don't need. But I have learnt over the years that if my hand goes out without me thinking about it for, let's say, a lemon I now know to keep it in my basket. It wasn't on my shopping list but I can guarantee that when I get home, within a few hours, the one thing I will need above everything else will be the lemon. Doing things without thinking. I wasn't thinking of a lemon; my hand just went out for it. That's your higher self, your intuition working for you and the more you follow it the more it will be there for you.

If you should find yourself thinking of a friend for no reason, ring that person; get in touch. I can almost guarantee your friend will be thinking of you. I have a few very close friends and when I ring them they will often answer the phone and say, "I was just about to ring you," and vice versa. We all follow our instincts; trust me, you can do it too.

If you are ever out with friends or family and something feels wrong, you feel uneasy or you are somewhere away from home on your own and you feel uneasy and don't know why, please follow your instincts, your sixth sense and get away, or out, from wherever you are. This is how the Universal energy works, trying to warn and protect you. Again, the more you follow it the better your sixth sense will become. It's like everything else in this life, practice makes perfect.

I had learnt that my awful experience was the cause of the huge imbalance in my aura which in turned triggered the MS. I hadn't meant to make myself ill or give myself a dis-ease but I had. So there was no one to blame. I understood it now. In fact I was seeing and understanding an awful lot more than I realised. It was as if my eyes had just been opened for the first time. You might be thinking that's a big one to take in. I'm still not sure that I fully understand. So I'd like to go over the lessons I had learnt to date once more in the hope that, like me, you can say yes, I understand now.

Let's start with our aura or energy.

A scientist would call it the human energy field but because I work as a healer I always use the word aura. So from now on throughout my tale that's the word I'm going to use. How I wish you could all see your own aura the way I often do. Everyone on the planet has an aura and, just like our fingerprint, your aura is unique to you. Someone else may have an aura similar to yours, but never exactly the same. Our auras are made up of all the colours of the rainbow and then some.

Colours that we, here on Earth, haven't even got names for. Think of the colour blue, then try and imagine hundreds of different blues. We can't. So if anyone ever tells you your aura has lots of blues, greens and pinks in it, just these three colours will have a thousand different combinations, a myriad of different shades. When we are happy our aura shines brightly. The colours are clear and true. But when we're not well or we are feeling down, our aura reflects this in its colours and in its shape.

Over the past few years I've often been asked by patients, "What's my aura looking like today?" My answer has sometimes been, "When I was a little girl my mother had two brass kettles that I loved to touch and look at. She would polish them every week and when they had just been polished I could see my face in both of them, they shone so brightly. But when they needed cleaning they were dull and lifeless. Your aura needs a good polish today, just like my mother's brass kettles, so you can shine again."

Our aura goes out on average about twelve feet around our bodies.

There have been many books written on this subject so I'm not going to spend ages explaining all the different layers. I'm just going to explain it in my own simple way for you. Your aura is all around you, surrounding you just like the shell of an egg, with your body inside it. But please remember this aura is the real you. It is also inside of you in your chakra centres, those energy wheels and, of course, both your aura outside your body and your aura inside of you are both connected. Our bodies are the vehicle that we need to be able to live on this planet, just like a spacesuit. If you could see your aura or if you saw a photo of it, you would describe it as a multi-coloured sphere stretching out all around us, above, to the sides and below. Our twelve foot egg shell.

Have you ever gone out to meet some friends for a drink in a pub, or a meal in a restaurant, and as you approached your friends, with them was a stranger and the thought went through your mind, "He or she seems nice," yet you were still about twenty feet away from them. Or you might have thought, "I don't like him or her." Yet you still haven't been introduced. I'm sure most of you will have experienced this at some time in your life. Well, think about it. Your aura goes out about twelve feet and so does the stranger's. As your aura walks into the stranger's aura you can actually 'feel' the real person. You could be twenty feet away from the stranger but you are in each other's aura.

This is another lesson for us all to remember.

If your first impression, your first thought, was that you didn't like the person, no matter how charming the stranger might be to you, please remember your first feeling. Let your instincts be your guide and trust your sixth sense. You felt the real person. This is the way you will spot the wolf in sheep's clothing. Always go with your first impression. I know I have said that I never give advice, but that's not quite true. This is what I tell my family and friends and my patients and I promise I practise what I preach.

So here are a few words that may help you. 'Let your instincts be your guide.' Always and I do mean always, follow your own instincts. Not mine, not your partner's or your friends or anybody else's...... just yours.

If you're not sure which way to go, if you are hesitant about doing something and you doubt your own instincts, then here's my next bit of guidance. 'When in doubt, do nowt.' In other words don't do anything until you are sure.

And last but not least: 'Unto thine own self be true.' It really is alright to be you.

Perhaps now you can see why I say I never give advice, well not really.

74

CHAPTER NINE

Now let's look at what can happen to put the balance out in our aura. It doesn't have to be a major trauma, or a situation of fear beyond words, to knock the balance out. It can often be something quite simple.

This is a special little story I would like to share with you, which is very close to my heart because it is such a good example of a very simple everyday occurrence which caused a major health problem. Many years ago my mother-in-law's sister came over from Australia for a holiday. She had emigrated in the 1950s along with her husband and four children. Her children were now all grown and married and had children of their own. We spent a few afternoons together getting to know each other and, in a very short time, we became great friends, even though she was forty years older than me. She was a lovely lady.

When she went back home to Australia she told her granddaughter Diane that she had met David's new wife. She told her that she loved me. Diane promised her Grandmother that if, in the years to come, she ever had a baby girl of her own, she would call her Isabella, after me. Apparently her grandmother was very pleased with this.

Years passed and then Diane came to England for a holiday with her new husband. They both stayed with us for two nights before moving on through Europe. It was during that visit she told me the above story and I sat and cried. They had their first baby boy about two years after their visit to us. Then three years after that we received the phone call from Australia to say their little Isabella had been born.

Now the reason I am telling you about this is because five years ago Diane and her husband Gary and their two children came to stay with us in England for a week's holiday just before Christmas. They were spending two months travelling through Europe and our home was one of the places they wanted to come to stay. I was going to get to meet my namesake. Their little Isabella was now two and a half years old. They duly arrived. The children were both wonderfully behaved but little Isabella had a very bad stammer. Diane told me that it was trying both her and Gary's patience to the limit and she felt the stammer was getting worse. I have to be honest, her stammer was bad, poor little mite; she would take ages just to get one word out so we all needed a lot of patience when Isabella was speaking, to allow her to say what she wanted to. I could see it was causing problems for the rest of their family.

They had been staying with us for about four days when I asked Diane if she knew what had caused the stammer. Did she know what the trigger had been? She said she felt it had been her fault. About six months earlier when Isabella had just turned two, she shouted at her because the little one was being stubborn. She said to me, "I really shouted and I realised straight away that I had reacted too harshly. After all, she was still just a baby." Anyone who has children will understand that little ones can be very trying; we have all heard of 'the terrible twos'. Diane told me that she was having a particularly bad day herself that day; she was tired and yes, she knew she shouldn't have shouted at the little one, but she had. Isabella had started to stammer very soon after. That was six months ago and it was getting worse, not better.

It just so happened that the two children were sleeping in a bedroom right opposite my husband and me so when Isabella woke up whimpering that night I went into the bedroom to comfort her. I sat on the floor beside her and gently stroked her head, just like I used to do with my own children and after a few minutes Isabella went back to sleep.

The following morning I noticed that her stammer was not quite as bad as yesterday. Diane asked me if I would give her (Diane) a treatment because she was having a problem with her hip. I said of course I would and I suggested that I could also give little Isabella a small treatment. If Diane agreed, the little one could come into the room while I worked on her mummy and then she could have a turn on my electric healing bed herself. Diane thought that this was a very good idea if we could get Isabella to agree.

My healing room is a joy for me to work in and a little girl's dream, partly because it's decorated in pale pink with a pink carpet but also because I have lots of lovely crystals, angels, fairies and butterflies all over the place. So I didn't think we would have a problem getting Isabella to come into my room with us and I was right. We told her it was a magical room full of lovely things and actually it is.

As I was working on Diane little Isabella was happily playing on the floor with my crystals. When I had finished treating Diane, I asked Isabella if she would like to get onto the magic bed. I didn't have to ask twice. She climbed up onto my bed before I had a chance to help her. I gave her the remote control to operate the height of the bed.

Up and down she went for about ten minutes and while she was doing this, I was doing my healing work. I didn't need to touch her, just her aura around her. So as she was going up and down, so was I. She had a great time and when she decided she had played enough the session was finished. My prayer was that this short treatment would be enough to clear what I can only describe as a shock wave in her aura.

The following morning there was a marked improvement in her stammer and Mummy's hip was feeling much better. It had been a joy to have them all to stay with us and there were quite a few tears when they left. But this was not quite the end of the story.

After they left us they were travelling to London for Christmas. We received a Christmas card from Diane. Needless to say I have kept it. It's one of my many treasures. The card was to wish us all a wonderful Christmas, with many thanks for their stay. But most important of all Diane wrote, "Little Isabella left her stammer in your magical pink room."

Our daughter travelled to Australia three years ago and stayed with Diane, Gary and the children. She reported back to us that Isabella is a lovely seven year old girl, very clever and very aware. Her stammer went completely, three days after they left our home in England, never to return.

A young mother shouting at her young daughter would seem like a very ordinary everyday occurrence. But this had caused her little girl's aura to be shocked which, in turn, transferred into a physical problem for her, a stammer. If we as mothers are honest, I'm sure most of us at some time or another have done exactly the same thing, shouted at our children. Hopefully we didn't cause them any damage but the problem is that sometimes we don't know what damage we might have caused.

This should be a lesson for all mothers everywhere; take care when handling our children, take great care.

I felt after they left that the Universal energy had brought them to us, to enable me to work with little Isabella, allowing the wonderful healing energy that flows through me to heal her. This was one of the many times over the years that I have recalled receiving help when I needed it.

My prayer on that day was, one day I will be able to lift someone's cares away for them as someone had lifted mine.

CHAPTER TEN

Having found my archive filing boxes I was able to access all my files, exposing so many more memories.

It was about nine months after I first started my treatments with Nansi that I began to notice a real difference in the way I was feeling. I had more energy; those waves of tiredness had stopped and I was beginning to feel much stronger. In other words, I was feeling so much better. But it would be another two years before I could honestly say, hand on heart, I was wonderfully well.

The first few months of me having my treatments must have been very difficult for my husband. He knew I was putting my trust in Nansi and what I was calling the healing energy and he had no idea or any comprehension of what this was, or what my treatments were all about. All he could see in the first few months was that I was still suffering from my blurred vision and the waves of tiredness. There had been times during those first few months when he said to me that he didn't think my treatments were doing me much good but I was insistent that I was going to get better. It was just that it was going to take a while and he needed to be patient with me, just as I needed to be patient with my own progress. It must have been very hard for him to understand my reasoning, as he was on the outside looking in and all he could see was that his wife was still ill.

Let's be honest here, it wasn't easy for me to keep positive when everyone around me was questioning what I was doing but the strength and determination came from somewhere and I knew where that somewhere was.

It was after the first six months that I began to understand more clearly those three words that Nansi had given me when my journey into healing first began because I was living them now.

Patience, Persistence and Perseverance.

In fact it would be safe to say I was beginning to own

those words. I had learned so much but Nansi had helped me to remember so much more.

Can you remember how Nansi had explained to me when I first met her how everything in the Universe is connected, nothing is separate and I mean nothing? All the knowledge that we could ever want and need is there to access. All the understanding of the things that our conscious minds can't comprehend is there for us to access. Other worlds, other times and other dimensions of existence - it's all there for us to tap into if we only knew how. That's what Nansi had shown me was possible. That's what she helped me to remember because I had understood and had known all this before I came into this life and it was mind-blowing.

I was reconnecting myself to all the wonders of things not of this world but I also understood that this connection applied to everything, right down to the smallest of things and the smallest things I could picture in my mind were the cells in our bodies. When someone says to me now that they have this or that condition, one of the things I always try and explain to them is that all the cells in our body are all connected. They are connected through our thoughts. I actually believe that all our cells 'talk' to each other. Just because some cells are not well today doesn't mean that next month they still have to be poorly. The cells in our bodies are constantly being replaced. A simple example of this: We lose skin cells every day but new ones replace them without any conscious thought on our part.

But what if our thoughts are constantly negative?

If you are constantly telling yourself, your loved ones and friends how unhappy and unwell you feel or you're keeping all your hurts to yourself like I did, then that's the message that you are passing to every cell in your body, every day of your life and that message is going from cell to cell. Just stop and think for a moment of the damage you could be causing yourself. You need to change your thoughts.

Trust me, I know it's not easy. I spent months and months repeating the words that Nansi gave me. Remember, 'Every day in every way I AM stronger and stronger.' Positive thoughts. This is just another way of showing us how everything comes together, everything is connected. That's what I'd been learning, remembering and practising for the past few years. I had also been learning how to remember.

Once I had mastered going within in my deep meditations I was able to reconnect myself. The whole of the Universe was there for me to explore when I was ready. To be honest my feet were not quite on the ground. My mind was so full of Heavenly things I was 'no Earthly good'.

That's exactly what my father said to me and he was right.

Dad and I were sitting out in his garden on a beautiful summer's afternoon having a good old chat together, as we did whenever we could. I had brought the children for the afternoon to their grandparents. They were happily busy doing something and Dad and I were 'putting the world to rights'. I had been trying to explain to him how I felt when he came out with, "It's no use being full of Heavenly thoughts, if you're of no Earthly good." He was smiling at me at the time, but he was right. I needed to find the balance in my life.

Me finding myself and exploring the spiritual side of my life was all well and good, but I needed to learn to be in the world and to find the balance between this world and all the others. That afternoon while I was talking to my father, I realised that it was time for me to stand back and be still for a little while. It was time for me to assimilate all the information, all the knowledge that I had taken in and remembered over the past few years. Time to think about all the wonderful journeys I had taken when in a deep meditative state with my teacher's help. Time to ground myself. Otherwise, as my father said, "I was going to float away". It was time for me to find my own balance.

Fortunately my work was a good grounder, as were my family of course. Any parent with two children will tell you they keep your feet on the ground and our two certainly did a good job in helping me, but probably the best grounder of all was my husband. It may seem daft to you but all I wanted was to lead a normal life, whatever that was. Ordinary things like working, cooking and cleaning and looking after the family, things that I hadn't been able to do very well for years. In fact, since before the children were born I had not been 'normal'. Going out and having fun. It wasn't that I was getting my life back – I was actually finding my life for the first time. I was finding out who I really was. Not the ill person I had been for so long. This was a new experience for me and I liked it.

I was still seeing Nansi every few weeks for my treatments and growing stronger in so many ways all the time. During one treatment Nansi said to me, "There is one thing I would like you to be aware of and remember. What do you think your ego is like?"

"I'm not sure what you mean, Nansi."

"When you begin your healing work, when you think it's the right time to start, I want to make sure you will not be working from the 'I' in you. I don't think you will be but I'd like to make sure. How do you think you will feel when you heal, let's say, someone's bad back. Will you feel proud of yourself? Will you say, look how clever I am?"

"Now I see what you mean. How could I be proud Nansi, when I know it's not me that will have done the healing? It will be the healing energy flowing through me, but never me. I think if I ever had an ego it got flattened years ago." My words made her laugh. "Having been able to experience all the wonderful energy that I have felt running through my body over the past few years, when you have been working with me, all the beautiful colours of the healing energy that I have seen surrounding me and healing me, I have always been in complete awe. I honestly don't think I will ever lose that feeling. I know I never want to." (And I never have.)

If you should ever come to me for a healing treatment and I was to say to you, "I can't make any promises but I think 'I' can help you," please forgive me. Because I should have said 'we' can help you. That's me as the instrument and the Universal healing energy flowing through me, 'us'.

I explained to Nansi that I just wanted to lead a normal

life for a while. It didn't feel right for me to start healing other people, not yet anyway.

To be honest I was feeling a bit reluctant about starting to heal because I didn't want to be different again. If I were to start healing other people I would surely be thought of as odd. I had been 'different' when I was at school, as I have said before. My friends were very wary of me at school and I didn't want that to happen again. I just wanted to be able to lead a normal life, doing normal things. Nansi said I would know when the time was right. I just trusted that I would. It was time for me to enjoy my life, enjoy my family.

Find myself and find my balance.

CHAPTER ELEVEN

Having told Nansi I just wanted to lead a normal life for a few years, the spirit world obviously had other ideas for me.

This is a tale I really must share with you.

We moved house in 1984, a few months before our son's eighth birthday and at the same time he started a new school. Without going into great detail I will just say that in the small class of seven year old boys was a little boy called Daryl. Alexander didn't meet Daryl until nearly the end of his first term because Daryl was in hospital receiving treatment. When Daryl did return to school it was for a few hours only each day, as he was very weak.

I always find it wonderful the way children seem to be blind, not only to different skin colour but also to their friend's infirmities. Daryl had no hair when he came back to school due to the 'treatment' he was receiving, but Alexander and the other boys in their class just didn't seem to notice; he was just another of their little friends. The only time Alexander talked about Daryl was the day he came home from school and told me that Daryl had been punched in his stomach by another boy and Alexander proudly announced that he had thumped the offender. This, to the best of my knowledge, is the only time in our son's school years that he resorted to any sort of violence.

Parents' evening towards the end of the spring term in 1984. The form mistress was very fond of all her boys. She told me she had given them an essay to write entitled, 'My greatest wish.' Please remember the boys were only seven years old. Nearly every little boy had written that they wished that Daryl would get well. She told me she cried her way through marking their work and I cried as she told me. I never actually met Daryl personally but I often saw him when I and the other Mums picked up their children from the school gate at home time. Daryl was always picked up by his grandmother who was looking after him. It was much later that I found out that Daryl lived with his grandparents most of the time.

As 1984 progressed, Daryl's condition deteriorated and he was unable to attend school during most of the summer term. The boys kept in touch by writing to him and sending him pictures every week, letting him know what was going on in their class at school. When the children broke up for the summer holidays Daryl was dangerously ill.

Teatime on Friday the third of August 1984, as I was making our evening meal, our telephone rang. It was a friend of mine who also had a son in the same class as Daryl and she was crying. She told me that she had just heard that Daryl had died and the funeral was to be on the following Tuesday. Then she asked me if I would be going. I said no, as I didn't know the family and I didn't want to intrude because I was very aware the church would be packed to the rafters. I put the phone down and burst into tears.

This was all so close. A child the same sex, the same age and, more importantly, a friend of our son had died. I managed to finish making the family meal between my tears, by which time Alexander found me crying.

After telling him as gently as I could that Daryl had gone to Heaven, I was amazed by his response. "He'll be safe now, Mummy, and he won't be in any more pain. His tummy hurt, but it won't now." Out of the mouths of babes... he actually made me feel better. He did have a few tears but, looking back, I'm sure he was upset because I was upset.

It was normal for me to be up late at night as I had paperwork to do and the best time for me to do it was when everyone had gone to bed and the house was very quiet. This night was no exception. I sat down beside the fire with the coffee table in front of me all ready to do my paperwork but I couldn't get Daryl out of my mind. As the night wore on I became more upset. I remember thinking to myself that I was being totally irrational; I didn't even know him but that didn't help and it didn't stop me from crying. Words kept going through my mind. A little soul went home today. The words kept repeating themselves over and over and over again. What made me write them down I honestly couldn't say, but I did and as I kept looking at them a thought came into my mind. Perhaps I could write some words of comfort for Daryl's family, as I had done for someone else the year before (this might come later), but the harder I tried to write the more confused I became.

By this time it was about three thirty in the morning and, even by my late hours, this was way past my bed time. But something was keeping me up. I was absolutely exhausted. I had cried more than I had in years, yet there was no real logical explanation. My mind was now completely worn out, almost blank. That's when the words started to flow. It was as if I were plugged into a dictating machine. Each and every time the 'I' in me had tried to write, the words just wouldn't come. But once I stopped trying to write myself, the words flowed. I soon realised that the words were being given to me from somewhere in the spiritual realm, but from where exactly I wasn't sure.

It was about six o'clock in the morning when the poem was finished. I was physically and emotionally exhausted. I read through the words many times; they were so simple and beautiful. The poem was not for me, but clearly for Daryl's family. But what could I do? Should I try and get it to them? Was I being presumptuous in thinking I should even try?

What a night.

I knew if I gave myself any time to think, the logical side of my nature would take over and the poem would end up in the bottom of a drawer in our home, never to be seen or read again. So at nine o'clock in the morning (I never did get to bed) I rang our son's school. Even though it was the summer holidays and Saturday, there was a good chance the headmaster would be in his study, as he lived on the premises. It was the only way I knew of getting Daryl's family's address. My luck was in or, as I'm now sure was the case, the powers-that-be made sure he was there for me. The headmaster answered the telephone. I didn't want to go into the real reason for wanting the address, so I told him that we had just heard about Daryl dying and we wanted to send a card to the family from

Alexander. He was more than happy to oblige as he knew that Alexander had been a friend.

Having checked my A/Z of the area to find the street where the family lived I got into my car. I must have looked like last week's dinner! I could hardly see out of my eyes, they were so puffed up, but I was determined to deliver the poem before I gave myself a chance to change my mind.

You can't begin to imagine how I felt. What right had I to presume the family would be interested in the poem? They might be very annoyed and angry with me. They might think me a total crank. All these thoughts and many more were pouring through my mind as I drove to their home. It didn't take me long to find the street and the house, but I was so nervous I parked the car on the opposite side of the road and sat shaking for ages, before I gathered up the courage to walk up the path to their front door.

Having knocked on the door, I was about to leave when an older gentleman answered it. All I could say was, "I'm so sorry," as I handed him the envelope in which I had placed the poem. I turned around and walked away.

Well, I'd done it now. At least (I thought) they don't know me, so if they were angry they wouldn't be able to find me. What a muddled mess I was in.

Having spent what I can only describe as a lost weekend, I decided to have a few days off work. I was shattered. Monday came and went but on Tuesday, while I was sitting having a cup of tea late in the afternoon, the telephone rang - my friend again. She had been to Daryl's funeral. The telling was as I expected, the church had been packed out with family, friends, parents, teachers and the headmaster, who apparently stood with tears streaming down his face along with everyone else during the service.

But the next thing she told me made my heart miss a beat.

After the opening hymn the Vicar had stood up and then he picked up an envelope, explaining to the congregation that a lady had hand-delivered it to the family. He said he was going to read the poem instead of the usual funeral service, as the family felt it said everything they wanted to say and that there was no need for any other words.

My reaction? Firstly great relief (at least they weren't annoyed with me) and then, I think, pleased, at first with myself, but after a few seconds thought and remembering that I knew I hadn't written the words, just pleased I had been able to hear the words and secondly that I had the courage to follow my instincts and deliver it to the family.

The summer of 1984 was a time I'm never going to forget. I was very pleased the rest of the year came and went without any more unusual experiences for me. In fact, so did most of the following year but the story doesn't end there.

Christmas time 1985, seventeen months after Daryl passed over, my husband and I attended our son's school Christmas dinner dance. During the evening one of the other mums said to me, "Did you know Daryl's grandparents are here this evening and did you know that he lived with them most of the time?"

'Well no, actually, on both counts."

She pointed Daryl's grandmother out to me.

What made me go over to her I really can't say, but she did look very approachable and cosy. I apologised for bothering her and then I said, "I know you don't know me, but I'm the lady who handed..." She didn't give me the chance to finish my sentence. She took hold of both my arms just below my elbows, as tears started to gently fall down her face. "You'll never know. You'll just never know what that poem meant to us all." She let go of my arms, opened her handbag and pulled out what was by now a very crumpled looking envelope. "I carry this with me always. I read it every morning and every night; it's the one thing that has helped to keep me going."

By this time the tears were streaming down my face. She tried to thank me but I stopped her and tried to explain to her that the words were not mine; they had been given to me because her need had been so great. After a lovely cuddle I wished her well and left her side.

I wasn't much good for the rest of the dance, but I had the most wonderful warm feeling deep down inside me. For once in my life I had done something very worthwhile. Not just the writing, but following my intuition in taking the poem to the family when the logical side of me had desperately not wanted to.

Over the next few years I was to visit the family with messages from Daryl for his grandparents and his mother. It was the most wonderful comfort for them all.

The only reason I have been able to scribe this with so much accuracy is because I wrote this all down in longhand in 1986. I took it to Daryl's grandparents in 1992 to let them read through it all and asked them that if, in the years to come, I was ever to write a book, would they like me to include Daryl's story. They both said they would. I was to write the story with their blessings. I promised I would; I have now kept my promise.

I'm sure a few of you are wondering what the words were so I am going to include them for you to read.

3rd August 1984 for Daryl

A little soul went home today
To peace and rest and love.
His Heavenly father welcomed him
To his Heavenly home above.

The pain he felt, confusion too,
Have all now gone away
And we are left to mourn our loss
On this, our saddest day.

Lord, please be with his family.
Let them lean upon your arm
And help them through the coming days
With peace and love and calm.

Be with them Lord and let them know
That you have got him safe
Until the day when, one by one,
They shall see his smiling face.

CHAPTER TWELVE

During these and the next few years I built up a business. A colleague once said to me, "Great oaks from little acorns grow," and he was right. From working alone I ended up with six employees and me. Who would have thought? My staff used to jokingly say I should put a sign on my office door with the words, 'Marjorie Proops'. Everyone would come to me with their problems, clients and staff alike. I guess it was partly because I was such a good listener and I would always get them to look at their problem from lots of different angles.

This, of course, came from all that good training a few years earlier.

It always takes something dramatic to happen to turn our lives around and move us in a different direction and I was about to be hit with two tidal waves. Both events would test my faith in the Universal energy to the limit and then some.

It would be very easy for me to skip over what happened all those years ago but, truth be told, they are two of the reasons that I have spent so many years now working (that's not the right word) as a healer.

Everything happens for a reason but these were very hard lessons to learn. But I'm hoping that by my sharing my own lessons with you, it may help someone reading this, now or in the future.

I have skipped over and missed out so much of my own life in the fear of boring you. I will just have to trust that I don't put boring things in and I don't leave important things out.

My father meant the world to me. He was my best friend for many years until, as rightly should be, my husband took his place.

During my earlier years he was almost a stranger to me. Father worked all day and I was usually in bed by the time he got home from the office. He had set up his own business when I was a child. Back in the 1950s this could not have been easy. But as his business grew and he had more staff, he would give himself days off, mainly to tend to his beloved garden, go fishing or write his sermons.

Not only a business man, my father was also a Methodist lay preacher, but a preacher that very much lived in the world and was very aware of everything going on around him, both at home and abroad. I'm telling you this because my very strict Methodist upbringing obviously played its part in shaping me at an early age. I was brought up on God and Jesus love you. I knew they did. But I didn't believe everything I heard in Chapel, even when I was young.

Over the years, as I got older, my father and I would spend hours talking and discussing spiritual things and things not of this Earth. We had many talks on the possibility of life on other planets. I can even remember a conversation we had about the possibility that the whole world was actually a pin point on the end of some being's, or somebody's finger. Well, it stretched my mind as did many of our conversations. I guess as he grew older he also opened his own mind up to the great mystery we call life. He wasn't the narrow-minded Methodist preacher that he used to be when I was very young.

Because I had a few very strange and wonderful experiences during my late teenage years, travelling out of my body, I was able to tell him about them and, by this time, I wasn't told I was being stupid. He didn't tell me to keep quiet as he had done when I was a child. He did say to me that he didn't understand why these things should be happening to me but he said he had a strong feeling that one day I would.

He was the one at my side when my first marriage went very wrong. Sad to say, my first husband was abusive. But Dad was there, helping me in any way he could. My father told me when I was in my late teens that he only wanted his three-score years and ten because he didn't like the way the world was going. I kept that one to myself. He had been diagnosed in his late fifties with diabetes and at the time he refused medical help because he wanted to walk by faith. That was his way.

Unfortunately, many years later, he had to relent, partly

for my mother's sake, but also because he was beginning to find it difficult to read his Bible and his other treasured books. This meant a few days in hospital for his blood sugars to be balanced.

As the hospital was some thirty miles from our home I could only go and visit Dad after I had done my day's work and then fed and watered my own family. By the time I reached the hospital, the rest of the family had left and I had time on my own with him. Time with my father was always precious to me. He told me while he was in the hospital that if he ever had to come back in again it would be to die. There was no way he would agree to, as he put it, "enter these premises otherwise again."

Needless to say I also never repeated this to anyone.

As I was leaving to go home, on the night before he came out of the hospital, Dad insisted that he walk with me through the hospital's miles of corridors to the main entrance where I had parked my car. As he was up and dressed, I agreed.

When we reached the front door he stopped to give me a cuddle. I always felt so safe and secure in my father's arms. I may have been a married woman with a family of my own but he was still my Dad and I loved him.

While he held me in his arms that night, he said to me I would never know how proud he was of me. He said that, against all the odds, I had accomplished much. He also said for all the ups and downs we had while I was growing up, they meant nothing compared to the strength and trust he said he knew I had now.

"You're my daughter and I love you. I'm so proud of you."

I told him how much he meant to me, how he'd been my strength so many times in the past and without his love and encouragement I might not be here now. This sounds a bit melodramatic but after a broken marriage because of physical abuse, a breakdown and an operation for suspicious cells, as well as being told I would probably not be able to have children, all by the age of twenty-two, without his love and support, I may not have been here.

We said all these things with our arms tight around each other.

Unconditional love. What a wonderful thing.

What we both felt deep inside and wanted to say was said. I never forgot that night because I knew, whatever happened to either of us, we would never have any regrets.

How many times does life give us the chance to say how we feel?

How many times do we take that chance and say them?

How many times do people say, if only?

If you are lucky enough to be presented with a chance of telling someone how much they mean to you, how much you care, please take it. It may be the only opportunity you are ever given. Believe me, I know.

If we could all remember this, when we do lose someone we love, be it friend or family, at least we will know that they knew we loved them. I've seen far too many people over the years with so many regrets when they lost a loved one, just because they never told the person who died how much they cared.

This is another lesson worth remembering.

CHAPTER THIRTEEN

Summer 1987. I remember very clearly being out in my father's garden talking with him, when I looked at him and suddenly had the feeling I wouldn't have him for much longer. I couldn't have explained the feeling to anyone even if my life depended on it. It was just a knowing.

It was no use worrying anyone else at the time because, of course, I could have been wrong. So I kept my thoughts to myself. Even though I now knew I was going to lose him sometime soon, I didn't feel too dismayed because I knew he would not be too far away from me and that he would always be watching over me.

At least I had been given some time to prepare myself, or so I thought.

But at the beginning of 1988 I was feeling very uneasy and I began to think that it must have something to do with my father. That's when my thoughts went back to last summer. Perhaps something was trying to tell me that the time was fast approaching for Dad to leave us?

January turned into February and the uneasiness was growing stronger so, at the end of February, I decided to seek the help of a clairvoyant because I couldn't get the thought of my father dying out of my head. I had only ever seen a clairvoyant once in my life, many years earlier in 1972, just after I left my first husband for the second and final time; a friend had given me her address and said how good she was.

That little old lady had been so accurate with the information she had given me and had been so very sweet and kind, I felt quite confident in seeking help from another clairvoyant. Unfortunately, this time I didn't have anyone to ask for a recommendation. The only thing I could think of doing was to go through the local telephone directory to find a clairvoyant in our nearest town. I found myself making an appointment with a lady I didn't know.

When I was sitting in her waiting room waiting for my

slot, her receptionist was on the telephone and I was a bit unnerved by the one-sided conversation I was hearing. The receptionist was telling whoever was on the other end of the phone that she would get the 'spell' she urgently needed to sort out 'that man' as soon as she could speak to ... (the lady I was about to see). This did not bode well for me. I was sitting there wondering if I should get up and leave when I was asked to go into her room. When I walked in I was met by a woman in her fifties and she was dressed in black from top to toe. Oh dear!

She told me to sit down on the chair at the other side of her large desk. She looked at me and said, "So you want to know what's going on?" and I said, "Yes."

"Your grandfather is here. He's come for your father."

I felt as if I was sinking.

"Your father is going to die very soon and your grandfather has moved in close."

I asked her which grandfather. "Your father's father, of course."

My memory of him was very faint. I had only been about four years old when he passed so I could barely remember him.

Then she said to me, "You won't see him you know. I know you can see and hear things but you will never see your father again." I crumpled and started to cry.

"Is there anything else you want to know?"

I said, "No," and left her office.

Oh how I wished I'd never seen her. But in the years to come I would remember this and make sure that any messages I may get would be passed on with love and care.

The thought of never being able to see my father again was so upsetting to me, my mind couldn't take it in. In one fell swoop I began to realise why my father was so against anything to do with Spiritualism. If this had been my only experience I would have felt the same. This clairvoyant had upset me beyond words. Her words were going to haunt and upset me for a long time. I needed to go home. I needed a cup of tea and a good cry. She might be wrong but I didn't think so. Perhaps we would have him for a few more months. I needed to hang on to that thought for now.

I'm sure you will know, if you've lost a loved one, no matter how well prepared we think we are, when it happens it hits hard. I think you can see now where I'm going with this.

My precious father died suddenly in March 1988, only five days after I had seen the clairvoyant. I must give the lady her due. She had known he was very close to leaving the planet. Yet the week before when we had visited my parents he seemed fine.

It would be so easy for me to skip over my father's passing but I was given such wonderful help from unseen forces. By me writing this all down it's my way of saying thank you to all the unseen souls involved in helping me and my family. I'm not sure if I'm making any sense but I would like to relate the happening. Part of this is going to be easy for me, as I wrote the beginning of this tale down in longhand in 1991 and I'm sure I'll remember the rest.

Springtime 1988, my husband, myself and the children had been to my parents for tea the previous weekend and my father was fine. I visited that clairvoyant the following week on the Friday. The following Monday morning while I was at work, my receptionist put a call through to my office and said to me, "Your sister's on the line." My sister had never rung me at work in the whole twelve years I had been in business so I knew something was very wrong.

"Dad's in hospital. He had a slight heart attack during the night but don't worry, he's doing fine." My heart sank. She said she was going into the hospital that afternoon and so was my brother. Would I please go up tonight to the hospital and join Mum and then take her home?

After tea with my family I rushed off. When I arrived, Mum was in his room talking to him. My father was propped up on his pillows looking amazingly well. He gave me a big hug and I felt greatly reassured. Because he couldn't see very well he was a bit unsure of his surroundings, but he was chirpy. The monitors he was attached to seemed reasonably stable and I breathed a sigh of relief. My mother said the doctor had told her he would be home by the weekend. I wasn't so sure.

The following day we followed the same routine. The family visited him during the day and I went up to the hospital in the evening. My mother stayed with my father when the rest of the family had left, waiting for me to arrive so I could take her home again. When I entered his little room I felt most uneasy. The monitors he was attached to were going haywire. I asked the nurse what was happening. She said, "Don't worry. Your father has had a busy day. Your sister and brother and their children have all been in this afternoon and he's very tired." I'm afraid I wasn't convinced.

We talked for a while, but he was very restless. First he wanted the television on, then off, then he wanted to sit up and then lie down; he was all over the place. The final straw came when he tried to take his pyjamas off. He said he wanted to be free of everything constricting him. I actually said to him, "If you don't lie still Dad, I'll dig a hole and put you in it. But I promise I'll line it with cotton wool." I've thought about the way he behaved that night quite a lot over the years and I honestly feel, in his way, he was trying to 'get out of himself, free himself from this Earthly coil.'

The nurse came into the room at this point and told us she had been watching through the large glass window into my father's room. She said we could stay until he went to sleep if we would like to but my 'voice' in my ear was telling me, in a very commanding tone, to get Mum out of the hospital now.

One half of me desperately didn't want to leave him. I actually told Mum I didn't want to leave and, bless her, she said, "Then don't. We'll stay." But something far stronger than me took over. I picked up my mother's bags and said to her, "Come on, Mum. He'll settle much better when we've gone." I gave him a cuddle, told him I loved him, Mum said her goodbyes and we left.

As my mother and I were walking down the long corridors to the car, I had a flashback to the year when Dad and I had walked arm in arm down the very same path. What stopped me from running back to him? I will never know.

When I got Mum home I suggested she rang the local taxi firm, to make sure she could get a taxi in the middle of the night if necessary, as I lived twenty miles away and it would take me over half an hour to get to her. She did this before I left to drive myself back home. I told her I was only taking precautions, just in case she needed a lift quickly. Mum, bless her, was okay. The doctor had just told her again that Dad would be home by the weekend. What could I say?

How I got home that night, only God knows. As I was driving away from my parent's home I was trembling. I knew my father was dying and I'd left him. If 'I' had been driving my car, I would have driven straight back to the hospital. But the car seemed to be in someone else's hands. I may have had my bottom in the driver's seat, my hands on the steering wheel, but my thoughts were most definitely not in control. I'll never forget the drive home that night.

The sky was very dark but clear and the stars were shining. Part of my drive home was on very quiet country roads and, as I was driving up a hill, the full moon was shining in the sky right in front of me. It was one of those magical nights when everything around me was clear and bright. I had the feeling that the car could lift off the road and head straight for the moon with complete ease.

It was at this point in my journey home that I started to shout out loud to God and I mean shout.

"Please Lord?

Don't let him suffer. You mustn't let him suffer. He doesn't deserve to suffer.

I'll never forgive you if he feels any pain."

Over and over I repeated these words, screeching at the top of my voice between my tears. When I reached home I was in a terrible state. I had gripped the steering wheel so tightly I had broken all the small blood vessels in each of my fingers and my hands were throbbing with pain. Yet while I was driving I had not been conscious of this at all.

There was no way I could go to bed, I was far too restless. I was going to sit up and wait for the phone call that I knew was coming. My husband sat up waiting with me until one-thirty in the morning, trying to reassure me, but it was no use. I knew the phone call was coming and I was determined to stay up all night waiting if I had to. My husband said he would have to go to bed as he was so tired, but not before he gave me a glass of whisky to try to calm me down.

I was going to pray all night if necessary. Pray for my father to pass over gently. I have often wondered since, why I didn't pray for him to live. I can only assume my higher self knew it was time for him to go home.

At three thirty in the morning I was desperate to ring the hospital. I went to the telephone in our hall, knelt down and dialled the number, when I clearly heard my 'voice' very loudly say, "No, go to bed. You're going to need your sleep." I replaced the receiver and like a zombie did what I was told. I must have hit the pillow and gone out like a light.

The next thing I remember was the telephone ringing. My husband was already up getting ready to go to work. He told me afterwards that on the first ring he knew it was the hospital and my father had gone. He answered the phone in the hall downstairs. I could hear him saying, as if in a dream, "Yes, yes, she's here." It was like a distant voice, from a faraway place. The second phone was on the floor next to our bed. He shook me and handed me the receiver. I was still half asleep.

"It's the hospital," said a man's voice.

"I'm your father's doctor. I'm so sorry to tell you, your father passed away at three-thirty this morning." (The exact time my 'voice' told me to go to bed). It was now two minutes to seven. You'd think somebody had poured a bucket of cold water all over me and I went numb.

The first thing I managed to say was, "Does my mother know?"

"No, I thought it would be better if you told her."

"Does anyone else know?"

"No, we thought it best to tell you first so that you could break it to your family."

Dear God, why me?

The doctor then said, "Why don't you go and get yourself a cup of coffee before you ring your mother. Give yourself a chance to feel calm." I told him I would. He said that I could bring my mother up to the hospital for her to say goodbye if I would like to. I said, "Yes, I'm sure Mum will want to."

"Your father is in the same bed and room that he was in last night when you were here. We will leave him where he is until you and your mother have said goodbye to him." I thanked him. He also said that he would like to speak to us when we came. I thanked him again and said I would be there with my mother in about two hours' time.

By this time Marie and Alexander were both up and crying. Alexander was inconsolable.

David had to take the day off work to stay at home to be with him. Marie said she thought she would be better off at school with all her pals. It's so much easier for a girl to cry and be comforted by her friends than it is for a boy.

I did exactly what the doctor had suggested. After lots of cuddles with my husband and the children, I had a cup of hot tea, then a coffee and then I rang my mother. That was the hardest phone call I've ever had to make. It was about eight-fifteen in the morning by the time I had pulled myself together enough to ring her. When she answered the phone I said, "Mum, it's me. I'm so sorry Mum but I'm ringing to tell you that Daddy died during the night." I explained to her that the hospital had rung me first because they thought it would be easier for her to hear it from me.

"I'm coming straight up to be with you, Mum and I'll take you to the hospital to see him. I'll ring the rest of the family and tell them what's happened and then I'll come straight to you." My mother kept saying, "But the hospital said he would be home by Friday."

"Mum, I'll be with you as quickly as I can. If you can be ready to leave when I get to you, we can go straight to the hospital and I'm sure they will explain to you what happened."

She kept saying to me, "But they said he would be

coming home."

I told her to get herself a hot cup of tea and I would be with her as soon as I could. I rang both my sister and my brother to let them know what had happened. I asked them if they would like to go to the hospital to say their goodbyes to Dad but they both said; "No."

I can't explain the feeling of calm that came over me. I knew I was getting help.

I drove to my parents' home on autopilot. It didn't seem to take any time at all. One minute I was at home and the next I was with my mother in her home. I gave her a cuddle and told her how sorry I was. She already had her coat on ready to leave. Then she said something that surprised me. She said, "I'm pleased it's you with me." So perhaps it had been right that the hospital had rung me, instead of my sister or brother. They both lived much nearer to Mum. That's why I thought it strange that it was me that got the call and not them. But somehow the Universe had this all worked out; we were all in far better hands than I could have ever imagined.

She was very quiet during the twenty minute drive to the hospital. We walked again along the miles of corridors, back to the ward where we had been just hours earlier. Only this time we walked with very heavy hearts. When we went into the ward together the sister met us straight away. They had closed the blinds on the room Dad was in. Mum and I went in together.

My father looked very peaceful, just as if he were asleep. I said goodbye to him and then said to Mum I would leave her so that she could say her own goodbye to her husband. Poor Mum was in shock; she had not expected this. It was the only time I felt badly about not warning her, but I was sure if I had said something she would not have believed me.

When Mum came out of the room she was in floods of tears. The nurse asked us to come into the waiting room. She said she would get someone to get us a cup of tea while she went for the doctor, as he wanted to talk to us. The staff could not have been kinder.

The doctor came into the room after just a few minutes.

He explained to us both that they had started losing him at about three o'clock in the morning when he had a massive heart attack. They had tried to stabilise him but then all his other organs started shutting down.

Then he turned and looked directly at me and said, "I've got to tell you this, but I don't understand. Just before your father died I said to him, "Mr. Armstrong, you must be in terrible pain. I will give you something to help you." But your father said to me, "I'm in no pain whatsoever." Those were your father's dying words. A minute later, at three-thirty, he was gone. In all my years working with people who have died of a heart attack, that's the only time anyone has ever said to me that they were in no pain. I don't understand. He should have been in terrible pain but he wasn't. I just thought you ought to know."

I sat there for a few moments, taking in what he had just said. I thanked him for telling me and told him that his words meant more to me than he would ever know.

As my mother and I walked back down that long corridor all I kept saying over and over in my head was, "Thank you Lord, a thousand times, thank you." My pleas for him not to suffer had been heard. My prayers were answered in the most wonderful way and God made sure that someone was able to tell me.

We hadn't been back at my mother's house very long when my sister arrived. We were going to have to help Mum organise Dad's funeral because she was too upset to sort things out herself. Unfortunately, over the years my father had done everything for my mother. She didn't even know how to write a cheque or pay bills, so organising a funeral was beyond her at this point. It all got sorted and we did manage to have a few giggles along the way.

When the undertaker came and asked Mum to choose a coffin, Mum and I both looked at each other and said Dad would be happy with a cardboard box so there was no need for any expensive casket. Dad would be cross if we spent money unnecessarily. He knew exactly where he was going when he died and he would not have cared two hoots what happened to his body after he left our planet.

My sister would be the one to stay with Mum. She had gone to my mother's every day for her tea with her two little ones, as her husband worked away from home. This was going to prove to be a blessing, as Mum would very much need her company and support. I could now go home, knowing my mother would not be alone.

I promised her I would ring her every night and I did, for the rest of her life here on Earth.

The events and goings on in the family are not important for my tale. But there was something that happened for Mum that I thought was wonderful. From the second day after Dad passed over, my mother's telephone rang at seven o'clock every morning for about six months. She never did manage to get to it before it stopped. My sister asked BT to check the phone line. She also asked them to try and trace where the calls were coming from but, guess what, no one ever found out or solved the mystery.

I am absolutely sure it was my father's way of saying good morning to her and she agreed with me.

CHAPTER FOURTEEN

As you can imagine, I was very upset but I did manage to go back to work on the second day, as I felt it would help keep my mind occupied and it did.

But at night when all the family had gone to bed, I sat downstairs crying. Not because I had any regrets, but because I realised how much I was going to miss him. Miss his love and miss his support in so many ways. On the third night after his passing I was sitting on my own crying and asking him over and over, "Are you there Daddy? Are you anywhere near me? Can you hear me?"

To my complete amazement I heard his voice answer me back. There was no mistaking it. He told me he had a message for my mother. He asked me to get a pad of paper and a pencil so that I could write his words down and I did, just as he gave them to me.

What a state I was in, a complete jumble of emotions. My father had just died three nights ago but I could hear his voice. I was going to miss him so much, but he was here with me now. Even though I couldn't see him I could hear him clearly. Could this be right or was I imagining it?

Then he was gone.

I just sat there and read and re-read, over and over again, the words he had given me. It was like a letter, or perhaps you would call it a poem, but it was most definitely for my mother. I just sat there that night in complete and utter amazement.

Then I remembered something. My parents had lost a very dear friend of theirs in a tragic accident on a cold frosty November night in 1983. They were there with Mary and her sister when the accident happened. As Mary, her sister and my parents left the little chapel in their village after a Bible class Mary dropped her Bible on the pavement and, as she was kneeling down to pick it up, a car skidded across the road on the black ice, mounted the pavement and knocked her down. The car crushed Mary's head and neck and she had died instantly. My father had been the one to find Mary under the car and I don't think he ever forgot that tragic scene.

The reason I'm mentioning this is because I knew how upset my parents were and how devastated Mary's sister was when the tragedy occurred. A few days after the accident happened I was sitting late one night on my own when I got a very strong urge (that's the only way I could describe it at the time) to write something down. What I wrote was a poem for Mary. Where the words came from to be honest I didn't know but, at the time, I thought 'I' had written them. I remember taking the poem to my parents for them to give to Mary's sister.

The words were so beautiful, they described Mary to a tee and I realised it would be something that her sister would be able to treasure and find very comforting. My father read it and re-read it. He must have asked me at least half a dozen times if 'I' had written it. He kept saying to me, "Are you sure? Are you absolutely sure you wrote it?"

"Well, of course I did, Daddy. No one else was in the room at the time."

I think my father realised far better than me at the time that the words had been given to me from what he would have called 'Heaven'. Then he said that perhaps there was something going on that we didn't understand. He went on to quote from his beloved Bible. I can't quite remember the exact quote but it was something about testing the spirits. He was trying to tell me to be very careful about trying to push or ask for things that I didn't understand. To be honest, at the time I didn't really understand why he was even bothering to mention this to me.

Now, somehow, it was my father sending his words to me. Being a Methodist lay preacher, my father was very against Spiritualism. He believed there was a gulf that could not be crossed between our world and the next. Well, I guess it hadn't taken him very long to figure out that the gulf could be crossed with ease.

As soon as I was up and dressed the next morning, after Dad sent Mum her letter, I rang my mother. I tried to explain to her what had happened and then I read it to her. I'm not sure what my mother must have thought. I told her I would be coming to see her in a couple of days, so I would bring the poem for her to read and I would give it to her for her to keep.

About half an hour later my sister rang me and asked if I'd just rung Mum and read something to her. I said, "Yes."

"Well, Mum thought she had dreamt the whole thing somehow."

On the fourth night after he passed, I was sitting downstairs on my own again, crying and asking him where he was. I kept saying out loud, "Where are you Daddy? Are you alright? I just need to know that you're okay."

To my complete amazement he answered me again. I could hear his voice so clearly. What was happening was beyond my wildest dreams.

Bless you Dad, a thousand times over. You weren't in the ground yet. We hadn't had your funeral and there you were talking to me and reassuring me. How blessed was I? How fantastic that I could hear him so clearly, but what amazed me the most was that my father was such a good communicator.

Someone once told me that love builds the bridge between this world and the next. Well, if that was the case, I could easily understand how we could talk to each other because there was so much love between us.

He said to me, "I knew you would be able to hear me because I realised you were hearing 'things' years ago and I knew you would write my words down for me."

"But where are you Dad?"

"Get your pad of paper. I have something for you."

And here are the wonderful words that he sent me that night in March 1988.

The grass is green, much greener
Than the brightest green you know.
The colours are more vivid
Than a picture postcard shows.

You ask me to describe to you
The colours that I see.
Have you ever seen the colour blue
Much deeper than the sea?

A rose so perfect one would think
The painter's brush you'd missed.
Gardenia and petunia and begonia stand in line,
The colours of the rainbow.
There, that describes it fine.

I'll give this garden all the love
I gave to mine on Earth.
I'm happy just to potter on
And sit and watch the Earth.

Now don't be sad.
Your eyes are filling up with tears, I see.
You should be very happy
Because you can hear from me.

Even now all these years later, I still have tears in my eyes
when I read this. It's just so special to me. In a few simple
words he was able to portray to me exactly where he was. No,
he hadn't suddenly sprouted wings when he passed over four
days earlier and no he hadn't been changed; he was still just my
Dad.

He was always good with words when he was here on
this planet. After all, he had his sermons to write and they were
always worth listening to. So he had had thirty-five years to
practise his preaching. I can remember when I used to work for
him many years earlier, if a business owed his company money
and he was having difficulty getting paid he would sit at his
desk and compose a poem and send it to the offending
business. It never failed. The cheque would appear a few days
later. The poems he wrote were often very humorous, but the
words were always very apt. Now I had two poems to take to

my mother to show her.

She sat with me and read them both over and over again. Then Mum looked at me and said, "They really are from your father, aren't they?"

"Yes Mum, of course they are."

Mum then told me that she had been writing something herself.

"I've been sitting for the last few days worrying that I won't recognise him when it's my time to go so I've written a letter to Billy Graham." She showed me her letter; it was about four pages long. Poor Mum; she was worried about so many things.

I then said, "Look Mum, why don't you wait a few days and see if Dad can answer your questions for you? He may be able to help."

"Do you think so?"

"Let's give Dad a chance, Mum. You've seen what he has managed to write so far, so let's both wait and see if he has anything more to tell us." Bless her, she said she would.

This was all so very hard for her to comprehend. The Methodist Chapel preaches that death is final, that there is no communication between Heaven and Earth and that's what she had believed all her life. So there was no way that my father should have been able to communicate with me. But she was holding her letter in her hand saying, "This really is from your father."

That very same night, after the family had all gone to bed, I was sitting downstairs on my own, but this time I was actually waiting for Dad to come to me and it didn't take him long, just a few minutes.

I asked him if he knew about the letter Mum had written to Billy Graham. He said he did and he had already prepared an answer for her. As I was sitting all ready to write with my pad and pencil, my father started to dictate his words to me. I could hardly write his words down through my tears. The words that he was sending were so beautiful and so meaningful. He was answering all my mother's questions in the most wonderful way imaginable. This poem was three pages long and, over the years, this particular poem has turned into a few of my closest friends' favourite poem of all, out of the hundreds he was to write. All my father's poems or messages deserve to be written down and all the stories behind them, but now is not the time.

My mother was overjoyed when I was able to give it to her. She sat quietly reading through his words (twice) and then, without a word, she got up from her seat and went to find her handbag. Mum pulled out the stamped letter she had ready to send to Billy Graham and, with a smile on her face, she tore the letter up. As she said, there was no need to send it now because Dad had answered all of her questions in the most wonderful way.

"Why can you hear him, Isabella, and I can't?"

"Mum, I've been hearing voices since I was a little child." That's what I wanted to say to her but I didn't. I didn't feel she would understand, not yet anyway. And, to be honest, I don't think I did either. So I said to her, "I think perhaps it's because I am his child, Mum. You were married to him but I'm a part of him, just as I am a part of you." This seemed to help her a little bit but then she said, "But how can he talk to you Isabella, when we are taught that there is a huge gulf between this world and the next, that death is final?"

"Mum, do you remember when I wrote the poem for Mary's sister? Dad made a comment about 'testing the spirits'. I think he was quoting from his Bible. You didn't take very much notice at the time Do you remember?"

"Yes, I do."

"Well, I think Dad realised then that I was hearing from the spirit world and it made him question all that he thought he knew."

"I don't understand this, Isabella."

"Never mind, Mum. Is the poem from Dad?"

"Yes it is."

"Then Mum, that's all you need to understand at the moment."

I did say to her, "Do you realise how blessed you are?

How many people do you know who have such wonderful words from their husband? Let alone before his funeral."

She said, "You're right. I feel very blessed."

My father's funeral was obviously a sad day for all concerned but I felt lifted. In fact, I wasn't the only one feeling it. My mother said she had a very calm feeling inside. Our son told me he thought he would be frightened when the coffin came into the chapel but he said he wasn't. My sister came up to me and said she felt as if something had been lifted from inside of her. It seemed as if Dad's passing was creating a wave of love and support that we could feel but we couldn't see. He was having a very positive effect on his loved ones and it showed. All our family were smiling at his funeral tea, not crying.

Two days after the funeral my sister rang me unexpectedly. She said she wanted to apologise to me for the mean things she had said and done to me over the past few years. She asked me to please forgive her. She said that she had been very jealous of me all of her life because I had done something with my life and she felt she'd done nothing with hers.

I think it would be fair to say this was a most unexpected phone call.

I told her if she knew half the things I'd been through over the previous years there is no way she would be jealous. But I thanked her all the same. We both agreed that Dad's passing was certainly bringing things up to the surface in a positive way.

Mum didn't tell anyone that I could hear his voice, let alone about the wonderful words he was sending. I told my sister and, of course, my husband and children and one close friend but that was all. No one would have believed us.

Our two children asked if Granddad could please send them each a message and, of course, he did. They were over the moon with the words he sent them. I can't begin to tell you how this helped us all.

My father may have passed into the spirit world but he

was still very close to all of us and the fact I could hear his voice was a comfort beyond words to me.

Life went on and my mother got all the help she needed from all the family.

But my life was beginning to change and I wasn't quite sure which way I should be going.

CHAPTER FIFTEEN

For the first few weeks after my father passed over, my mother felt the need to visit his grave at least once a week. Unfortunately, the graveyard where my father was buried was at the top of a very steep hill and not an easy walk for anyone, let alone my mother. She found it quite a struggle. I told her that I wouldn't be going to visit his grave because Dad wasn't there. But I did say to her that Dad would go with her every time she went because he was very close by her at the moment. So if she went to visit his grave, Dad would most definitely be by her side.

After about four weeks of her struggling to climb that hill, I just couldn't stop myself from telling her I thought she was being silly because I felt Dad would much rather visit her in the home they had both shared together, rather than go with her to his grave every time and watch her struggling to get there.

But no, she felt she had to go.

Then, wonder of wonders, my mother rang me after what was going to be her last visit. She said to me, "Isabella, you won't believe what happened to me this afternoon. I had just got to his grave but my hands were so cold I put my handbag down on the frozen ground to enable me to put my gloves on. Then I heard a voice clearly say to me, "Why seek ye the living amongst the dead?" " She told me she picked her handbag up, turned and walked away.

"You're right Isabella, he's not there."

"Yes Mum, I know he's not there and I do believe you."

My mother never did go back.

Even though my father had not stopped talking to me since he passed over, at least twice a week and sometimes more, dictating his wonderful words to me, I was missing him so much it hurt. It was so selfish of me because Mum would have given her right arm to have been able to hear his voice. But it's the physical presence that we all miss when a loved one dies. It's not even right for me to use the word 'dies'; Dad wasn't dead. Just like the voice had said to Mum at the graveside, "Why seek ye the living among the dead?" – Dad was alive and very well on the other side of life, in another dimension. He was in the spirit world. Or as I prefer and in time will explain to you, he was in Heaven.

I was still occasionally having treatments with Nansi. My sessions with her were very important to me. She was the one person I felt I could be completely honest with because she never judged me and she never told me what to do. She was the person I turned to after my father passed over, as I felt my husband had seen me shed enough tears. I was able to cry with Nansi, knowing it was not hurting her in the same way it hurt him when he heard me crying. She was separate from the family and not tied up with the loss I was still feeling. She told me that for every tear I cried a swan appeared in Heaven, just for me.

"Nansi, there won't be a lake big enough to hold them all."

"Oh yes there is," was her reply. It was a nice thought.

Just when we think we have cleared past hurts and forgiven and let go, up comes something else that we have hidden deep in our thoughts, hidden deep within our memory files. It happens to the best of us and I'm no exception. If my father had still been on Earth I might have asked his advice but I don't think so. For the past twenty years, while he had been here with us on Earth, I hadn't, not for this problem. You see, it involved my mother and I didn't want to hurt anyone's feelings.

That wave my father had created when he passed over was really doing a good job of bringing things up to the surface. It had opened up this old wound and a few more to boot. Over the years, I had talked to my husband about my problem but he always said to me, "You've got to forget it." Those were the wrong words to use because it's impossible to forget things that have happened to us; we're not meant to.

But we are meant to learn from them.

114

In fairness to him, he did say that if I ask my mother to explain herself she might not remember, or she may not know why she did what she did. But I desperately needed to be able to let go of the hurt I was still feeling. Knowing what I know now, I should have said something long ago and saved myself years of grief.

Let me explain.

In 1968, when I was eighteen years old, I was walking home from the bus stop on a showery summer's afternoon when I was attacked from behind by a young man. He grabbed me around my neck with one hand and his other hand went up my skirt as he tried to pull me backwards. I managed to turn around and I shouted at him. He backed away from me. I turned around and kept on walking.

Then he came at me again.

This time I hit him with my rolled up umbrella. With that, he ran off towards what all the locals called the 'dene', an area of woodland. It was broad daylight on a busy road and I was only about one hundred yards from our home when this all happened. I had left work early that day because I wasn't feeling very well and this made me feel even worse. It only took me a few minutes to get into our family home where I would be safe.

As I entered our hallway my mother was standing with her headscarf around her head and her raincoat on, with her shopping basket in her hand all ready to go out to the shops. She took one look at me and said, "What's the matter?"

"I've been attacked Mum. I've just been attacked, just up the street by the school gate."

"When?"

"Just now, just a few minutes ago."

"Well, I'm all ready to go to the shops. Ring your father and tell him!"

And with that, she turned and off she went.

I needed a cuddle. I needed my mother to say, "I love you. You're safe now," but she didn't. She walked out of the house and left me all alone. I was shaking like a leaf. I went into my father's study and rang his business and asked his receptionist to put me through to him. When he answered the phone I said, "Daddy, I've been attacked."

"Where are you?"

"I'm at home."

"Where's your mother?"

"She's gone out to the shops and left me on my own. She told me to ring you."

There were a few moments silence and then he said; "Tell me what happened to you," so between my tears, I did.

"Now Isabella, I want you to do exactly as I tell you. When you put the phone down from me I want you to dial 999 and tell the police exactly what you have told me. Can you do that?"

"Yes Daddy I can."

"I'll be with you as soon as I can. It will only take me about ten minutes to get home, I promise. Now, put the phone down and ring the police."

So I did exactly as he said. I dialled 999 and told the lady who answered the phone what had happened.

I think the simplest way to explain what happened next was that 'all hell broke loose' apparently. Obviously I was safe in the house but I was told there were police dogs, police cars, the main road was closed off and there was a full scale search on to find the male offender. My father closed his office and factory and had every one of his work-force out looking for the young man because I had seen the offender head for what we called the dene, about two miles from my father's business, which was next to the small infant school very close to our home.

My mother had left me all alone in the house. My thoughts were all over the place. Why had she left me? How could she? I just sat by the phone in Dad's study and cried.

My father was as good as his word. He was with me within ten minutes, but the police were with me within five so I wasn't on my own for very long. As soon as Dad saw me he wrapped his arms around me and gave me a hug.

116

"You're safe now; nothing can harm you."

"I'm okay, honestly Daddy, I'm okay. I know it could have been so much worse. He didn't hurt me. He didn't get the chance because I hit him twice with my brolly."

The policewoman had already started to question me as to exactly what had happened. She wanted me to describe the offender so she could relay his appearance to her colleagues who were out looking for him. I had given my father and the police a brief description when I had phoned them. He was about five feet ten inches tall. My boyfriend was six feet and he was not quite as tall as him. He was wearing blue jeans and a green top, scruffy and untidy with wild dark eyes. Everyone was being very kind to me but I was feeling very confused and hurt.

My father was very angry. He left me in our home with the policewoman because he said he wanted to go out and join in the search for the offender. But he came back quite quickly because there were so many police with their dogs all over the area. Well, that's what he told me anyway.

My mother came back from her shopping trip on our local high street after about an hour to find our house had four police officers inside and three police cars parked on the drive and she hadn't a clue what was going on. She had seen all the police activity on the high street when she was out shopping but didn't realise it was all because of me.

After what seemed like a long time, but it might have only been an hour after my mother got home, I was taken to the police station with my father and the lady officer. They had set up an identity parade. They wanted me to see if they had caught the culprit. It was horrible and very frightening, nothing like I had seen on the television. I was taken into a very large room, where there was a line of about fifteen young men, and I was asked to walk along the line very slowly to see if I could identify the man who had attacked me. I was no more than two feet away from them all. It was a very intimidating experience. It was 1968, but I'm sure they could have done it in a better way than they did. I was frightened. As far as I was concerned he wasn't amongst them. The police thought he was, but I said

I would always remember his wild eyes and I was sure he wasn't there. So that was that. They took us back home.

Unfortunately, or fortunately for me, I was due to go on holiday the very next day. I was driving to Fort William in Scotland on my own to join my boyfriend and his family. It was going to take me hours to drive there and my mother didn't want me to go. But my father said I could, providing I rang home every two hours to give them a progress report on my journey, to let him know I was safe. My father felt the holiday would be far more beneficial to me than staying at home and he was right. The following morning I set off on the long drive to Fort William. I did what Dad had told me to do and rang home every two hours. I made it and in good time. I loved driving. When I drove back from my week's holiday my boyfriend came back with me in my car to keep me company.

I was very quiet for the next few weeks and my father was obviously worried about me. I couldn't bring myself to tell him how hurt I was because my mother had deserted me when I needed her. Over the years in our home, I had watched when problems had occurred and recognised that things were not said, problems were pushed under the carpet in the hope that they would go away, but of course they never did. They just gathered more dust. No one asked me what was wrong. I don't think my father wanted the answer and I think my mother knew she'd let me down, so no one was talking about it.

My father told me he had organised for someone to come and talk to me, to see if this would help me with my obvious bouts of silence. There was no way I wanted to tell my father how hurt I was, not because of what had happened to me, but because of my mother's lack of love and concern. I didn't want to cause any problems between my parents, so I was hurting instead. Talking to a stranger would be good. I would be able to tell someone, anyone, how I was feeling and they might be able to help me.

I wasn't stupid. I realised he had organised for a private visit from a psychiatrist. The day came and I was actually looking forward to the appointment. What I hadn't counted on was my mother sitting in the room with me, listening to every word that I was to say. So I kept quiet. How could I sit there and say how I was feeling when the one person who was causing my problems was sitting there with me, listening to everything I was saying? I had the feeling, by the look on her face, but I could have been wrong, that she was willing me not to say anything. Or, if I had said she left me all alone, she would have pounced on me.

The 'gentleman' asked me quite a few questions about the attack. But I kept my responses to how I was pleased it had been me and not some older lady or younger girl. They may not have fought back and could have been in real trouble. I had a wry smile on my face when 'the gentleman' told my father that he thought I was a very well balanced, sensible young lady. If only he knew how I was actually feeling. I was very cross with my mother for not allowing me to see the 'gentleman' on my own.

Life went on and no more was said. Under the carpet, under the stairs, gathering dust and that's where it stayed until after my father had passed over.

One year after the incident happened, there was a very accurate photo-fit picture in our local newspaper of a young man who had attacked a lady. It was most definitely him. I would have recognised those eyes anywhere. I don't know if they caught him but they were on the case again and I knew he was definitely not in the line-up I had been subjected to.

It was time to put this to rest and the only way I could do this was by having a talk with my mother. Even though she was still grieving, I just had to speak to her. The next visit I had with her I was going to bring it up and I did.

"Mum, I need to ask you something. Do you remember when I was eighteen years old I was attacked?"

"No Isabella, I don't."

"Well Mum, it's been troubling me for years. You walked out of the house and left me on my own. You told me to ring Dad and then you walked out of the house."

She started to cry.

"I need to know Mum why you left me all alone."

She kept saying, "I'm sorry, I'm so sorry. Can you forgive me? I can't remember. If I did this to you can you ever forgive me?"

"Yes Mum, of course I can forgive you, but I'll never be able to forget. But perhaps now I can let go of the hurt that I've been carrying for all these years."

"I do love you, Isabella."

"I know you do Mum and I love you."

I left Mum's home that night feeling very peaceful inside. That memory would no longer have any hold over me. I'm not going to make excuses for what she did that day but, and there is a big but, as I have been going through the menopause myself (as she would have been at the time this all happened) it does throw a different light on how I look back on her actions. You truly think you are losing your mind at times and I'm sure most women going through the menopause would agree with me, it's not an easy time. We often do and say very strange and often daft things for no apparent reason whatsoever because half the time our brains are not connected to us in any way. I keep telling my friends our brains have gone to the Menopause Beach Hotel and they are having such a good time, they don't want to come back. My mother may not have been able to give me a reason. It didn't really matter to me now; the important thing was I had got it out into the open and let the air in, which made me feel so much lighter and peaceful inside.

I should have said something years ago instead of carrying the hurt. I can understand that at eighteen I was too young to realise that I would carry it for so long. But I honestly didn't want to hurt my mother's feelings. I didn't want to cause any problems between my mother and father. I loved them. But in doing so, I ended up carrying the hurt for twenty years. There never seemed to be a good time over the years to ask my mother why.

A friend once said to me that you can't make an omelette without breaking some eggs and she was right. Sometimes things need to be said but they can be said with love and not anger, caring and not bitterness. There is never a good time to say things that might hurt someone else but, God willing, there will be time.

If you find yourself in a similar situation, for your own sake, for the sake of your health, say what you are feeling. Tell the person who has hurt you exactly what you are thinking, say it with love and ask them to help you understand why.

Unto thine own self be true. This was probably the first time I could honestly say I owned those words.

CHAPTER SIXTEEN

Over the years I have never purposely hurt anyone's feelings with the spoken word. But I know I have been misunderstood many times because the words I have spoken have not been the words the other person has heard. Instead of them asking me exactly what I meant at the time, they have kept quiet and reacted later, or they have reacted in a way I did not understand.

Misunderstanding each other happens all the time. In just the same way, people have said things to me and the words I have heard have not been the words that they said.

It's so easy for us all to let little misunderstandings go by which, in turn, allows little unnecessary hurts to build up inside of us. What a mess we sometimes get ourselves into during a simple conversation. If we could all remember to ask each other what the other person was really trying to say, we could save ourselves a lot of upset.

Not only was I hearing my father's voice so clearly at night I was also hearing other voices. This was very confusing for me because most of the time I didn't know who the voices belonged to. I could easily distinguish between male and female but I was finding the whole experience a bit disconcerting. My father's voice was a wonderful comfort to me but strange voices I wasn't so sure.

I happened to be out shopping the day after one of my nightly 'events' when I passed a bookshop and before I knew what I was doing I found myself inside without knowing why. It was as if I had been 'guided' by unseen hands. My 'voice' directed me through the shop straight to a shelf full of Mind Body Spirit books. I was then directed to look down at the books on the bottom shelf. And there on the shelf, right in front of my eyes, was a little book with the title 'Voices in my Ear' by Doris Stokes. I couldn't believe it. This was me, voices in my ear. Without hesitating, I picked the little book up, took it to the cash desk, paid for it and left the shop, smiling from ear to ear. I couldn't wait to get home to read it.

But of course the family came first.

As soon as everyone had gone to bed that night I started to read it. It made me laugh and it made me cry. I loved the way she wrote.

I was sitting on the settee, saying out loud to myself, "I wish I could have met you, Doris," when I clearly heard a woman's voice answer me. (Crumbs)

The voice said, "It's me."

"Who?" said I.

"Doris."

Was I going bonkers or what?

"It really is Doris, dear," was her reply. I had said I was going bonkers out loud, but I don't think it would have made any difference whatsoever. She would have heard me anyway. Doris came to visit me for the next few nights as I read her first book. She was such a help to me. I'd never read anything like it before. She explained bits of her story as I was reading it. She was so gentle and kind.

Doris helped me to understand that hearing voices was no big deal, just a very natural thing. As she said to me, I should be really pleased that I could hear so clearly and not to ever be frightened or worried by it. What a lovely soul. Not only did she help me, Doris gave me a beautiful poem that she had written for me to write down; this was in August 1988. The poem she gave me is called 'A playground far from Earth' and it's precious. I thanked her numerous times for helping me, especially for giving me her poem and then she was gone. Bless you Doris, wherever you are now.

That wave of clearing energy was still working for me. In the same month that I heard from Doris I was visiting a close friend for a chat and a cup of tea when another of her friends came to call unexpectedly. This lady was introduced to me and she told me that she was a clairvoyant. My friend explained to her how I was writing poems that my father was dictating from the other side of life and the lady was very interested. She asked me if there was anything she could help me with. It was just a chance meeting but as she had asked me I said yes, there was something she might be able to help with. Would she please ask my father why he had stopped speaking to me when he found out I had MS years earlier. I explained to her that we had always been close and I had found it very hard at the time because his silence had lasted about six months. He never did explain why, when he was alive, and I didn't have the heart to ask him but perhaps now he could explain himself.

We sat together for a few minutes. I was beginning to think my father wasn't going to be able to respond to my request. I knew he would find it difficult to communicate with a stranger; this was Spiritualism and in life he was dead (no pun intended here) against it. But he did respond and what made it so special for me was that I could hear his voice as he was talking to the lady. He explained to her that he had been very worried about me. He had been worried that I would not be able to cope and he couldn't understand at the time why this should be happening to me.

He said this had been the first time in his life he had been lost for words to try and reassure me because he was frightened for me. He didn't realise at the time just how strong my trust in God was. He also said that was why when I was a child, suffering from migraine headaches, he would appear to be angry with me because I would lie in bed moaning, caused by the pain in my head. His anger was because he felt helpless to help me.

I used to moan so that I could hear the sound in my head. It helped take my mind away from the pain I was in. I think my mother realised what I was doing at the time so, as she went around the house doing her housework, she would sing. I used to love hearing her. It may have all been hymns she was singing but it was very comforting to a seven year old and, actually for the few years that I suffered from all the migraine attacks, it always helped distract me from my pain. I still love those old hymns.

Thank you, Mum; I haven't forgotten.

When I thought about what he had said, I realised that

124

during all the years I could now remember, my father would always find a way to help when things went wrong. He would put things right, not just for our family, but for friends and colleagues. He was rarely lost for words. One of his many sayings was, 'Where there's a will, there's a way' and he would always find the way. My illness was something he couldn't find a way out of for me. Because he didn't know what to say to me he kept his distance and silence for six months.

So now I knew why.

I had been able to hear most of the words my father was speaking to the lady myself but it was obvious to me that he had struggled with the connection. Everyone vibrates at a different wave or energy band and everyone's auras are different. My father was used to communicating with me alone; our energies were compatible. This lady was a stranger to us both and her energy was very different from ours. But thankfully the few words I missed she managed to pick up. I was very grateful to both her and my father for being able to give me the answer.

Some of you must be wondering why I just didn't ask my father myself. This was all so new to me. Yes, I had heard my 'voice' since I was a child and I had seen things and yes, I had written words that were given to me from my father, but only three times in thirty-eight years from 'other' voices that I could identify, so I wasn't exactly an expert. There had also been a few times that I had talked with what I described as ghosts at the time because I didn't know any better. I was also hearing other voices but I was keeping that one close to my chest at the moment.

I felt that I was a complete novice and a novice with very little faith in my own ability. I trusted God, I trusted my father, but I didn't trust myself. And being very honest with myself, I think perhaps the main reason I didn't want to ask him was because I was worried in case I misunderstood what he might try and tell me. That's why I asked her.

But this experience had been a good one, thank goodness, because I was still carrying the hurt from the other lady clairvoyant I had seen and the thought that I would never see my father again was still troubling me beyond words. This lady couldn't have lied to me if she'd tried because I had also heard the conversation almost word for word. I understood what my father was trying to say.

Those migraine headaches had reappeared again, so I will tell you the story now so they never need to be mentioned again.

Nansi had helped me find the trigger for my MS. I was able to find the trigger myself for my migraine attacks. To be honest, it was as clear as the nose on my face when I had thought about it a few years earlier. They had started when I was six and a half years old, about six months after my sister was born. From being a small child I have always loved babies. If any of our neighbours had a little one I would be there wanting to rock the pram, play with the baby, hold and cuddle the baby. Just be with them. Unfortunately, when my baby sister was born I wasn't allowed to touch her.

There was one particular day that I remember well. My mother, grandma and I were going to take my sister for a walk in her pram. Grandma was pushing the pram when I got a hold of the handle and asked if I could help push. My hand was immediately removed.

"You must never touch the pram, Isabella. You are not allowed to."

This went on until my sister was walking and even then I was often told not to touch her. It doesn't take a genius to see why I developed migraine. But that was many years ago. I forgave my mother and grandmother in my heart a long time ago. They were being over-protective of my sister and didn't give a thought to how that might affect me.

That's why, whenever I see a patient who is about to have a new baby, if they already have little ones I always suggest to them that they find some special time each day for the older child or children. It may only be for a short time, ten or fifteen minutes, but this special time will benefit everyone. Your older child or children will not feel as if they have had their noses pushed out when a new baby arrives on the scene and harmony will prevail.

I have mentioned before that the best time for me to do any of my office paperwork was when the rest of the household had gone to their beds and it was proving to also be my special time for my father to communicate with me. But during those summer months of 1988 other souls started to want to be heard and it didn't have to be late at night. It was getting very confusing for me. I could be cooking the tea when I would hear a voice speaking to me and I would have to say, "I'm sorry but I'm busy. I really have to finish cooking the meal for the family." I didn't really know how best to deal with this. I felt badly about not being able to respond straight away. It got to the point where I asked the spirit world to please just let souls come to talk to me when I could respond, not when I was cooking or having my bath or even while I was sitting on the loo!

One particular night, I was sitting doing some paperwork, with papers strewn all over the coffee table in front of me, with our local radio station on tuned to a phone-in programme. People would ring in and chat about anything they wanted to. I wasn't taking very much notice but it kept me company, providing background chatter and some light music while I was working. I was only half aware of a lady talking to the radio host about her recent bereavement. She was explaining all about it to the listeners but, as I said, I wasn't really listening, when a lady's voice in my ear kept saying to me, "That's my daughter, that's my daughter."

This voice wasn't going to go away.

By the time I had put two and two together, the lady who called into the radio had finished telling her sad tale and I had no idea what on earth had been said. I had to stop what I was doing and put my paperwork to one side because this voice in my ear was so persistent. She kept saying to me, "I have a message for my daughter. You must write it down and give it to her." As I had pencil and paper in front of me I was able to scribe her message straight away. When I had finished writing it

127

for her, I just sat and cried when I read the words she had sent.

Now what was I going to do? I had been in a similar position once before but at least the last time I was able to find the correct address and deliver it to the family in person (even though I made a very quick exit after handing it over) but this was not quite the same.

As I was going to see my mother the following night, I had a thought. I'll show Mum what I had written and ask her what she thought I should do with it? When I arrived I explained to her what had happened the night before and showed her the message. She also cried when she read it.

"You must somehow pass this on if you can, Isabella. Why don't you ring in to the radio station and explain to them that you have a message for the lady who was so upset, about two nights ago. They may be able to help."

Trust me on this one. If you had known my mother, this would have been the last thing you would have expected her to have said. She was a very reserved, very old-fashioned lady in a nice way and, of course, the wife of a Methodist lay preacher, who up until very recently did not believe in this sort of thing. This was not the response I had expected but it was the response I needed to hear.

"You're right, Mum. If this is meant to get to the right person, it will."

If any one of you out there still thinks I may have an ego, forget it! I was so unsure of myself (still am most of the time). These are not the actions or thoughts of someone full of themselves; they're the actions of a woman who thinks she may be wrong and doesn't like to intrude.

There was nothing for it. I was going to have to ring the radio station. When I got home that night I waited until the same programme was on air, at about the same time of night, and I rang the radio phone-line. I asked the receptionist if she could remember the lady in question. She said she could. She told me she knew the lady's name and phone number but obviously she couldn't give the information to me. But she promised me she would ring the lady and let her know that I had a message to pass onto her. I hadn't told the receptionist what the message was, or who it was from, just that I had one.

Four nights went by and no phone call came. Now what was I to do? The voice in my ear was still telling me to please pass on the message. There was nothing for it. I was going to have to go onto the radio phone-in programme and hope and pray that the lady in question would be listening. I was going to have to read it out over the air waves. This now seemed the only way I could deliver the message.

Back to the telephone, the same phone-in programme, at the same time of night. I rang the telephone number. Apparently, it would normally take about twenty attempts before you could get through to the receptionist because of the number of people calling the number and then an age before you could get on air (so I was told afterwards). But guess what, I got straight through without any bother. The lady receptionist had remembered that I had rung a few days earlier, so this time I explained to her that I would like to read the message that I had for the lady over the air waves, in the hope that she would hear it, as she hadn't rung me. The receptionist assured me that the programme had passed my message on, but obviously I had had no response.

If you could have seen me, my legs were knocking, I was so nervous but there was nothing for it. I had to pass this message on no matter what. Then a recorded voice said, "You are the next in line to speak on air." I took a deep breath and prayed I would be able to read it without making any mistakes.

The radio host asked me what I would like to talk about so I explained to him that I had a message for the lady who had rung into the show about a week previously, after her mother had died. He said, "Yes I remember. That was Edna. She is a regular on my show. What's the message?" After I had finished reading it, he said, "That was lovely." I said goodbye and put the phone down. Well, I'd done it now, no going back. About three minutes later our telephone rang.

It must have been about two o'clock in the morning. I just prayed it wouldn't wake the family up but it hadn't. When I answered the phone a lady's voice said, "Please read the poem again," then again. She actually asked me to read it to her about five times before she explained the whole story to me.

Apparently her mother had been ill for a long time and she had been looking after her but in the process she had made herself ill. Her doctor had told her that if she didn't take at least a week's holiday to rest and recharge her batteries she was heading for a breakdown and then she would not be able to look after her mother. She reluctantly agreed to go away for a few days holiday with her husband. The sad thing was, she went away on a Friday and her mother died on the Saturday. She said she couldn't forgive herself for leaving her and not being there when she had died. So that's what the message was all about. Her mother telling her from the other side of life that she had nothing to feel guilty about. She must have thanked me half a dozen times for passing on her mother's message. I promised her I would put the message into the post for her the next day, if she would give me her address which, of course, she did.

I must be honest and say I was pleased that I had taken the time to help. Very little effort on my part had meant such a lot to someone else. In fact, it had meant the world to her and had probably stopped her from spending years blaming herself for not being at her mother's side when she passed over which, in turn, would have caused her aura to have gone out of balance and we all know now what that can do.

Thank you Lord, for allowing me to help in such a simple way.

CHAPTER SEVENTEEN

The year was now drawing to a close. It had been an emotional roller-coaster of ups and downs and very confusing for me in so many ways, but a year I will always remember. The year my life started to change in more ways than one.

The first Christmas after we lose a loved one is never an easy time but it was going to be doubly hard for my mother, as my father's birthday was and still is Christmas Eve. My mother was still struggling with the loss of my father so I suggested that she came to stay with us over the Christmas holidays. That way she would not be on her own and she agreed. It was also going to be hard for me but I was determined to try and make it a happy time for all of us.

I was not going to forget Dad's birthday just because he wasn't here on Earth with us. I bought him a card and a small bunch of flowers and put them beside his photo in our home. To be very honest, I did this for the next ten years. I still blow him a kiss to this day and wish him happy birthday. Just because he's not here in the flesh, doesn't stop the fact it's still his birthday. If there is a rose flowering in our garden at Christmas time I pick it and put it by his photo.

Christmas is a time for children and ours would certainly help to lift the mood. Our two loved their Christmas stockings filled with little presents. I filled a stocking for Mum too, so she could join in the fun. Just like all Christmas mornings, even though Marie and Alexander were now young teenagers, they still had us all up early to see if Santa Claus had brought them the gifts they were hoping for. Mum, bless her, joined in the fun. After we had all opened our presents I said I was going back to bed for a couple of hours as I was still tired. Dawn had not broken yet. Then I would get up and prepare the Christmas dinner.

As I was walking out of the lounge door I heard my father's voice clearly say to me, "Now you will get my present to you." I can still remember thinking I wonder what on earth he means. I had all my presents, or had I?

I went up the stairs and climbed back into bed feeling very peaceful, happy and relaxed because my mother seemed to be enjoying her grandchildren's and our company. I drifted off to sleep very quickly, in a blissfully peaceful state.

What happened next was so wonderful for me, that I would like to share it with you. As strange as this will all sound, it's the absolute truth. I felt myself being lifted up out of my bed and, before I had time to think, I floated through the ceiling in our bedroom and then up through the roof of our house. It all happened very quickly but not so quickly that I didn't know what was happening or able to see everything around me. Going through the ceiling was like passing through a thin layer of soft dust and then I was in our roof void which was quite a big space. Even though it was dark in our loft I could still see the beams and roof trusses quite clearly because there was some sort of spectral light shining everywhere. Then I flew through the roof itself. Again it felt as if I was passing through a dark cloud of mist, then I found myself outside, above our home, flying up into the air.

The strange thing was, I wasn't frightened. It felt quite normal in one way but very surreal in another. It's not every day you find yourself being able to pass through walls. But that's exactly what I had been doing. It was just starting to get light as I floated and hovered about one hundred feet above the roof of our house. Just like Superman, I felt myself turn towards the city.

I floated over the tops of houses and roads until I reached the river, when I heard a voice say to me, "Follow the river to the sea and you can watch the sunrise over the water."

And that's exactly what I did.

I hovered above where the river met the sea and watched the sky turning a myriad of golden colours, as the sun rose above the water on that Christmas morning. I must have hovered there for quite a while because I saw the whole sky light up as the sun rose to its full size above the horizon. It was one of the most beautiful sights I have ever seen.

Then I found myself turning and I flew back home slowly, taking in the wonder of what I was seeing in every moment of my journey. I floated gently down above our home, down through the roof and ceiling and back into my body lying on our bed, with a light thump.

I woke up immediately feeling in complete awe at what had just happened. Very happy just doesn't come close to how I felt. Ecstatic would be more like it. Sometimes I feel I can't find the right words to use to describe the things I see because the right words don't exist in our language. But my father has used a word quite a few times over the years in the poems he has dictated to me. Wonderment, sheer wonder. That comes somewhere close. I was grateful beyond words for the experience and very thankful. It goes without saying I blew my father lots of kisses.

I have seen many sunsets over the years, but never before had I seen a sunrise. And I don't suppose many of us can say they have seen a sunrise from a floating position one hundred feet above the water. This had to have been one of the most unusual Christmas presents anyone has ever had.

Pure magic.

I think it would be fair to say I had a smile on my face for weeks afterwards. When I explained to my husband what had happened he said. "The next time you go flying out through our roof, you can check the roof tiles to make sure they are all in place!" But he did believe me.

I can't remember the exact time David told me, whether it was after I had told him about my adventure this time or perhaps it was after another one of my travels. He explained that he often knew when I had been travelling out of my body because he said it was as if he had been put into a very deep sleep so that he didn't turn over in bed and wake me up. If he had done that, I would have been pulled back into my body with a shock but he has never disturbed me during any of my travels and now I know why. It's wonderful the way this all works. And even he knew it.

Nansi had once said to me, "The more grounded you are,

the higher you can rise." Well, I'm not sure if she meant I would rise up through the roof! But I was well grounded; both my job and my husband did that for me.

This was not the first out-of-body experience I had had. But for me, this was the most special because it was a gift from my father. Or at least he knew I was going to have the experience and was able to tell me. It didn't matter to me, how or why. I was just very thankful.

One day I would love to write about all the other times I have travelled outside of myself, both before this one and after, but now is not the time. I need to keep on track.

CHAPTER EIGHTEEN

Not long after my father passed over I employed a new cleaning lady. She was a gem. We affectionately called her Mrs.T. I would come home at teatime from the office to freshly cut flowers from our garden and a lovely smell of cooking coming from the kitchen. She was worth her weight in gold to me because she took a load off my shoulders.

My business was growing rapidly, through no effort on my part and knowing there was someone at home doing the cleaning and occasionally preparing our evening meal was a godsend to me. Most evenings I would have paperwork to do after the family had gone to bed (yes I did find time for my husband). I loved the peace and quiet in our home late at night; for me it was the perfect time to do my work.

But many a night, just as I was about to start my paperwork, either Dad would drop in to say hello or give me a poem to dictate, or some other soul would want me to write something for a loved one. So it was no surprise to me when Mrs. T's son dropped in with a message for her. It turned out that he had passed over about fifteen months earlier, just after Guy Fawkes Night.

Again, I was a bit apprehensive about giving her the message but I was beginning to learn that if a person from the spirit world could somehow find the right energy to communicate with me here on Earth, the least I could do was to pass the message on. It wasn't for me to decide who should receive a message and who shouldn't. So I gave it to her when I came home from work that next day.

Mrs. T read the message. She was quiet for a few moments and then she began to cry. She had been with me for quite a few months when this happened but she had never told me what had happened to her son. This message was an opening for her to be able to tell me her own sad tale. Apparently her son, who had been in his late twenties when he passed over, had been at home alone watching television. He had been drinking from a can of beer and eating pizzas, all at the same time, when he choked on his food and died. All I could say when she told me was, "I am so sorry." After I had listened to her story, I gave her a cuddle and then I explained to her that I had been writing messages from the spirit world since my father had passed over; she was very pleased that I had received one for her.

We are all, unfortunately, very human and often forget lessons learned and I'm no exception.

In the springtime of 1989, almost a year to the day after my father had passed over, a client visited me at my office to go over his final accounts. This gentleman had sold his business due to ill health and was retiring. After I had gone over all his paperwork with him he thanked me for a job well done. He then said that he could now go home, relax and forget all about the business world that he was very happy to leave behind. We then sat and had a lovely chat. He told me all about the holiday he was about to go on the following week with his wife. They were going to go to America for a second honeymoon. Although he was in his early sixties, he explained to me that he had remarried the previous year, after both he and his wife had been widowed and alone for a long time. He was like a teenager in love, full of happiness and excitement. When I walked him out to the front door of my office to say good bye to him, I had such a strong urge to put my arms around him and give him a hug and wish him and his wife Godspeed but I didn't, I held back.

That evening my client went home a very happy and content man, knowing his affairs were all in order and greatly looking forward to the coming holiday. (His wife later told me.) In the evening he enjoyed helping her with the final preparations, getting their case labels ready, making lists etc. He apparently was always well organised. She told me she retired to bed to read, followed shortly by her husband. When she woke the following morning he was lying dead beside her. She said he hadn't made the slightest sound or movement. I don't think anyone can begin to imagine the shock she must have received, unless of course you yourself have had a similar experience. I thought I had learned to follow my instincts but, because I was worried in case he thought I was being forward or just daft, I had gone against a very strong feeling and I didn't give him the cuddle I was meant to.

I've promised myself I won't do that again.

On a lighter note, the few friends I told the story to soon after it happened said they'd be frightened to let me ever give them a cuddle again, just in case it was their time to leave the planet. But you know they all soon forgot. I pray I never do.

This is yet another lesson worth remembering. This gentleman's wife was obviously very upset but she had no regrets. Her husband had gone to bed that night a happy man.

The words that I am reminded of with this story are never go to bed on an argument because none of us can ever know what the next few hours may bring. We all need to try and remember this.

1989 was turning into a very peculiar year for me. Thankfully, I had very good staff at work. If I was late getting into my office in the mornings because I was up half the night writing from the spirit world, each member of staff knew what had to be done and my senior assistant was a wonderful lady who ran things in my absence. So if the boss was late in it was no big deal.

All my staff knew about the poems that I was writing. One member of my staff had typed each one of the poems onto the word processor for me. I didn't like computers myself (they were a relatively new invention) but I realised they were the way forward for any business. So I employed a young lady to be trained in how to use one. My husband taught her. She was then able to do all the accounts, letters etc. and, of course, the messages and poems from my 'witching hour.' She could be found crying over her screen as she was typing them. After the first few had come from my father in 1988 she asked me what she should put as the title for each of them, as I hadn't given a title to any of them. I said to her, "I haven't got a clue. Why don't you give them each a title as you're typing them," so she

137

did.

And to this day I haven't changed a single one.

It didn't take very long for quite a few of my clients to find out that I was writing from the spirit world. They kept finding my typist crying over her computer screen and they wanted to know why. As word spread, quite a few people, from my staff to my clients, started to ask me if I could get a message for them. More than one of my clients said to me, "If you can write like this, why the heck are you doing accounts work?" It was a fair comment but, like all of us, I needed to earn a living to help the family.

But something was going to have to give.

In the summer of 1989 my mother told me about a family tragedy that had just happened. I hardly knew the relative involved but I had met some of the family many years earlier when, as a child, I was taken to a family wedding. My mother attended the funeral along with her cousin but I didn't go because I hadn't known the family personally. It was about a week later at my 'witching hour', while I was trying to work, I heard a young girl's voice. I instinctively knew who it was.

She dictated a beautiful, very descriptive and happy message in poem form for me to send to her mother and father. She explained to me that she was the teenage daughter of a cousin of my mother's and she was out for a walk with a friend when a car knocked her down. The emergency services and her parents had been called. As the accident had happened quite close to where her parents lived, they had been able to get to the scene almost as fast as the ambulance. She had still been alive when her parents and the ambulance got to her but she told me she died soon afterwards at the roadside. Her words told her story of what happened to her, not the accident, but how she had stood outside of herself watching the paramedics trying to revive her. How she saw her parents and had tried to speak to them to let them know that she was okay.

Well, I had been here a few times before so the next time I went to my mother's I showed her the poem. She agreed it was lovely and should be sent to the family. She gave me the relatives' names and address so that I could send it to them, in the hope that it would bring them some comfort in their time of sorrow. I sat and wrote them a long letter, explaining to them how I had been hearing from my father, how he had sent me, my mother and other family members some wonderful words of comfort when we needed it. Then I explained that I had also been hearing from other souls. I tried to explain all of this in the hope that it would help them understand how I had been able to hear their beloved daughter's voice and dictate her words for them.

We all know in this life we can't win them all.

The response to my letter and the enclosed poem was horrendous. My mother received a visit from her cousin about four days after I had sent the letter. She told my mother that the family had been in touch with her and they were furious with me. How dare I send them a poem supposedly from their daughter; their daughter was dead. I was cruel and obviously not right in the head. I felt sick when my mother related this to me:

"You shouldn't have sent it, Isabella. You really shouldn't."

"But Mum, you were the one to give me their address. I don't think it was our choice to make. Their daughter would not have given me the words if she hadn't wanted the message to be passed on, surely."

"You've got to stop doing this, Isabella."

I was very confused and very hurt. All I had tried to do was help. All I kept thinking was I hope and pray they don't tear it up and throw it away. In the years to come they may come to understand and realise that it really was from their daughter.

For the next few weeks I tried to ignore any voices in my ear other than my father's. There was no way I ever wanted to be told that I 'wasn't right in the head' and that I was 'cruel'.

It was probably about three months after this that my mother said to me, "I've been thinking about the poem you wrote from Lisa (that was the young girl's name who died). I think you were right to send it. It wasn't for you or me to decide not to give it to the family. So I don't think you did anything wrong."

Now she tells me!

Everyone deals with the loss of a loved one differently and that's as it should be because we are all different. Even though I was hearing my father's voice, I think in some ways it was making me miss him even more and I couldn't get the thought of not being able to see him out of my mind. That lady clairvoyant's words had really gone deep when she told me I would never see him again. I'd never thought of myself as any sort of psychic. I found out that the word for being able to hear from spirit people was clairaudient. I had seen spirit people as a child but that seeing had left me as I got older because I suppressed it. So when I was told I would never see my father again I assumed that meant I would never see spirit people ever again. (Wrong.)

I just wanted to see my father one more time, one more cuddle, just one more hug so when he was talking to me at night, I've got to be honest, I kept saying to him, "I want to see you Daddy. I just want to see you," and I'd been doing that for well over a year now. He never really answered me. He would tell me he loved me and then he would dictate some more of his beautiful words.

I would like to tell you about an event that happened in my life that means the world to me and I'm *never* going to forget.

It was one of those magical, almost unbelievable events that if we are very lucky will happen to us once in our lifetime. And I think I would like to share it with you now, as it was at this point in my story, in the autumn of 1989, that it happened.

If I was to say to you that I've been to Heaven and come back to tell you the tale, what would you say to me? What indeed would you say? You're crackers, you must be mad, you're out of your mind, and goodness knows what else without swearing at me. But the truth is I have.

I have been to Heaven and come back to tell the tale!

If you know me you will know I would never lie to you but if you don't know me you will have to decide for yourself whether you want to believe me or not; the choice is yours. But what I'm about to tell you will certainly give you food for thought.

One autumn evening in 1989 after I had gone to bed and had fallen asleep I was 'woken' by the most horrendous noise. The best way I can describe the noise to you was as if I was standing at the tail end of a jet fighter, as it was powering up its engines to take off. Or the noise we hear on the television when we sit and watch an Apollo rocket taking off from Cape Canaveral. So powerful, that the sound of the wind noise itself could knock you into next week by the sheer ferocity of it. That's exactly what it sounded like. I was frightened, but only for a split second.

The next thing I knew I was being pulled head first out of myself. It felt as if I was in a tube of some sort protecting me from the power of the noise that was surrounding me and then I became the rocket. There was nothing physical protecting me that I could see as I was being pulled upwards by a power that could have sent a man to Mars. I knew I was in a tunnel of protective energy, travelling at a speed beyond my comprehension, with the roaring noise all around me and I had no idea why. I can remember saying to myself, "Don't be frightened. Keep calm," because somehow I was aware that something very special was happening to me. But I had no idea what.

As I was travelling at the speed of light in my 'tube' with the noise of the hurricane force winds surrounding me all the time, I could see lights outside of my tube, beautiful coloured lights flashing by so fast it would have made me sick if I'd tried to concentrate on them.

On and on for what seemed like an age then, in an instant, the noise stopped and I stopped. It took me a few moments to realise that I was standing on grass. The most beautiful green grass that I had ever seen. The colour was so bright. I stood there trying to get my bearings. Where on Earth

141

was I? But I guess I kind of knew I wasn't on Earth. It seemed to me that I was in a large meadow and, directly in front of me and a bit to my right, the ground rose up into a mound or small hill of grass that I couldn't see over the top of. There were trees of every colour of green you could think of then some dotted about quite a distance from me and I could hear birds singing. The whole scene was so peaceful and calm as I stood there in absolute awe and amazement.

Then I noticed the light that surrounded me; it was like sunlight, but I didn't see any sun's rays. It was a very gentle light, but just as bright as any summer's day here on Earth. Everything seemed to glow with a faint light of its own. I took in the whole scene in a few moments.

As I was looking towards the small hill I saw someone walk over the top and come towards me. As the person came closer to me I couldn't believe my eyes; it was my father and he was smiling. He looked amazing, so well and healthy, just as he had in the prime of his life when I was young. He was dressed in casual summer trousers with an open-necked checked shirt.

I ran to him shouting, "Daddy, Daddy, is it really you?"

I threw my arms around him as he put his arms around me and I cried, yes I cried and cried. As he was holding me I can remember thinking, "Dear Lord, I can 'feel' his arms around me. I can really feel his touch."

What I was experiencing was so much more than I could have ever wished for. Tears of pure joy were running down my cheeks. I think that's when I realised that I must be in Heaven, but I didn't think there were any tears in Heaven and I told him what I was thinking as he hugged me.

"Am I in Heaven, Daddy?"

"Yes you are. You wanted to see me so much that it was arranged that you could come for a visit and I couldn't be happier for us both."

"But I'm crying Daddy and I didn't think there would be any tears in Heaven."

Holding me at arm's length and smiling, he said, "But you don't live in Heaven. You are a visitor so you can cry as

142

much as you like because they are happy tears."

"Oh Daddy, I can't believe this is happening to me."

Then my father said, "Well it is, it really is."

Hugs, hugs and more hugs. I didn't want to let him go. Being able to 'feel' his arms around me as he cuddled me was overwhelming. In my wildest dreams I could not have imagined this. This was real! He took me by the arm and walked me up over the little hill and the sight that met my eyes when we reached the top 'blew me away'. It was incredible.

I truly was in Heaven. The Golden City. That's what met my eyes. There in front of me in the distance was the Golden City. Everything about it shone, from the city walls to the roof tops of the buildings. It was probably about half a mile away from us as we started to walk towards it. I was going to visit the Golden City that was talked about in the Bible.

"Is this where you live, Daddy?"

"I have a place inside the city walls where I can stay but I prefer to live most of the time in the countryside outside of the city walls, where I can tend my beautiful garden. We are going to go into the city so you can see it for yourself."

And that's what we did.

Even the streets were paved in gold. This was the city that my father, while he was here on Earth, had expected to see and live in when he passed over into the next life and so many thousands of other souls must have thought the same thing. And here it was.

Remembering that 'thought' is a very powerful energy I could well see how the Golden City had been formed. (I've got to be honest it would not be on my 'thought' list because I wouldn't like to live in a city, even a city in Heaven.) I was pleased that my father was not living there permanently because I knew that, like me, he didn't like city living. We both loved the countryside and wide open spaces, so I was glad that he had a home outside the city walls with a garden of his own.

With every step we took my father was talking to me explaining so many things and, all the while we were walking, my hand was firmly in his (because I didn't want to let go. I didn't want to stop feeling the 'feel' of him).

I kept saying to myself over and over, "I must remember everything he is telling me. Somehow I must remember. He's explaining so many things that I've always wanted to know." But it was hard for me to concentrate on his words because the streets we were walking along were so full of people happily chatting to one another. As some of them walked by us they turned their heads in our direction and smiled at me (as if they knew I was just visiting). I was desperately trying to listen to my father as my eyes were taking in the diversity of the colours and styles of the clothing that people were wearing. It was then that I noticed a group of about seven ladies all talking and laughing together just a few yards in front of us. It was the way they were dressed that caught my eye. It was as if I'd stepped back into my childhood. Every Sunday, when I was small, we all got dressed in our Sunday best to go to Chapel. In the summer time, that meant Mum would wear a pretty summer frock, complete with summer hat and white cotton gloves (and me looking like a miniature copy of her). Well, that's what these ladies had on, right down to their sparklingly clean white gloves. As I was watching them, they all turned off the street, climbed some steps and entered a building. Yes, a church or it could have been a chapel.

I turned to Dad and said, "Daddy, why are they going to church? Surely there's no need for them to go. They are already in Heaven."

"You're right," Dad said. "They don't need to go. They don't have to go. They go because they like to. This is Heaven and if anyone wants to worship in the same way they did on Earth, then that's what people do. There are buildings of worship for everyone."

Because there had been so much going on around me, I hadn't noticed that the pavement beneath my feet and the buildings around me were subtly changing colour from gold to the most beautiful golden sandstone and, as we walked on, the gold completely disappeared and all the streets and buildings were now a fresh, clean, stone colour. (Please don't ask me how and please don't ask me why because I don't know and I didn't think to ask; there were far more important things for me to talk to Dad about.)

Not long after this Dad said to me that it was almost time for him to leave me. My heart sank and I became upset because I didn't want to leave him. Then he said to me, "Your journey is not over yet. There is more for you to see and there is someone who wants to talk to you."

We seemed to have walked for miles yet we were still inside the city walls. I have no idea how big it was but we came to a gate in the wall and my father took me through it. I was now looking out over a beautiful lake that seemed to go on forever. The colour of the water was an indescribable sparkling blue. And there on the water were hundreds of beautiful pure white swans.

"This is where I have to leave you, Isabella, but you will see me again sometime in the future so there is no need for you to be upset anymore."

He hugged me for the hundredth time and just as he was leaving me I found myself flying off to my next stop on my journey. But wherever I went, and I know I went somewhere to speak to someone, I can't bring back into my consciousness what was said to me, or who it was that I had been speaking to. But I know I was with the person or soul for quite a while; that I do remember. God willing, when the time is right, I will remember this bit of my journey but until then I am sending love to the Universal energy for allowing me to visit Heaven.

The next thing I knew I was back in my bed.

Now the choice is yours.

This experience was so special for me that I'm not even going to try to put my feelings into words because I haven't and never will have the right words to use.

Have I been back since? Yes I have, but that's not for this story.

CHAPTER NINETEEN

Not long after my amazing event, towards the end of 1989 I found myself organising a very sad event for me.

Just to add to my workload at work, my right-hand person was retiring. She had told me at the beginning of the year that she wanted to retire on her 60th birthday in October. The memory of the first time I met her still brings a smile to my face. I had advertised for a book-keeper and she responded to the advert. She walked into my office and said to me, "I'm probably not what you're looking for because I'm sure you'll not want someone of my age."

I looked up and smiled at her and said, "You're exactly what I'm looking for and your age is an asset to me." We both started to laugh. She turned into the best assistant and member of staff I could have ever wished for.

We had laughed, and cried, together over the previous ten years and I knew I was going to miss her. She was much older than me, excellent at her job and always there for me, supporting me in everything I did and I loved her for that.

I organised a leaving party for her without her knowledge. Her family were all in on the surprise as well as most of the clients that she had been dealing with over the previous ten years. We were having the party in our home. Our children put balloons up all over our house for me and I somehow managed to organise all the food and drink. A great time was had by all and I still have the photos our son took.

But I can remember feeling very sad after everyone left our home that night because I realised things at the office would never be the same again, no matter how good her replacement might be.

Towards the end of 1989, Nansi had asked me if I would please do some treatments with one or two of her patients because she felt I may be able to help them more than she could. "Crumbs", "What?" and "Don't be daft" came to mind but I agreed to give it a go. Nansi had been so good to me I hadn't the heart to say no to her, even though I wanted to.

An evening and a time was arranged for me to go to her home and meet with whoever she had invited. I was to treat a very dear friend of hers first. Imagine my surprise when I was introduced to the lady I had met from the Samaritans, who had given me Nansi's address years earlier. I hadn't realised they were such good friends.

Nansi asked if she could observe me as I worked. "Yes, of course you can, as I haven't got a clue what I'm going to do or how I'm going to do it." But the strange thing was as soon as I began by raising my hands above this lady's head, I just instinctively knew what to do. This was the very first time that I had ever worked with anyone lying on a healing bed and this was the very same healing bed that I had lain on many times myself over the previous eight years. Wow! I simply allowed the healing energy to flow through me and out through my hands with absolutely no thought on my part. I honestly felt as if I had been doing this all my life, it felt so natural and normal. My hands were moving in a wave-like manner from the top of her head and down over her body. I had no idea how long I worked with this lady, but there was a point when I felt that I had done, or I should say the energy had done enough, so I stopped.

Nansi said to me, "Where did you learn how to do that?"

"I haven't got a clue Nansi. It just happened."

"Good," was her reply. "I have never seen anyone work like that before but, I can tell you now, if you keep working just as I have seen you do now, you are going to be amazed at the healing that will be done. Don't ever let anyone tell you to do it any other way."

The lady I had worked on said she felt wonderful. The pain she had been experiencing had disappeared and she said she felt very relaxed.

To this day I often say to people, "Don't ask me what I do because I haven't got a clue. Please remember it's not me doing it. It's the wonderful healing energy running through me."

I was to see two more of Nansi's patients that evening and all of them said it had been a very worthwhile experience. That was my very first taste of things to come. I was just pleased I was able to help and very pleased that Nansi had been by my side.

About eight days before Christmas I had a most unexpected visitor at my 'witching hour'. Daryl. It had been five years since he had passed over and I'd never actually heard his voice before, but he was very clear and very excited to be talking to me. He had come to me to ask me to take a message to his grandparents. He said they had been very down during the past year. They were still missing him and were worried in case he was not alright. He then told me he had tried to let them know that he was okay but they didn't seem to be aware of him, but his little brother was. Apparently he was also living with his grandparents, just as Daryl had done. His brother had only been one year old when Daryl had passed over. He said he often went to talk to him. He then told me that his brother could both see and hear him. Would I please write the message down and take it to them? I said of course I would.

The words he gave me to write were very funny. I had almost forgotten he was just twelve years old. I finished writing his words down, he thanked me and then disappeared. Typical. Just like my own son; they get what they want, say thanks and are gone. Even though it had been five years since I delivered the poem that I'd written for Daryl's family, I could still remember where they lived. Their house was only two streets away from where Nansi now lived. So after tea the following day, once again I found myself knocking on their door, but this time I didn't make a quick exit when Daryl's grandfather answered it. I explained why I had come and he immediately invited me into the house and into their lounge. Grandma came into the room from their kitchen and gave me a big hug. She recognised me immediately. While I sat and explained to them that Daryl had come to me the previous night and given me a message for them all I hadn't known that his little brother was in the next room listening to me from behind the door.

Halfway through me reading them Daryl's message, his little brother ran into the room shouting, "That's from my brother, that's my brother."

I said, "Yes, your brother gave me the words last night."

"He comes to talk to me when I'm in my bedroom."

I said, "That's wonderful for you. He's around you all a lot."

"I know he is."

I asked his grandparents, "What does he mean about making you jump?"

His grandfather said, "We often know when he's about because he makes cups, dinner plates and all sorts of things move across the kitchen bench. We were worried in case he was upset about something. We kept asking ourselves, is he alright?"

"I think you've got your answer. He was concerned enough to come to me and give me the message for you because he knew you were worried. I just think this is so lovely."

His grandparents both sat beside me and cried with joy. They said it was the best Christmas present they could have wished for. After lots of hugs from them all, I left. For me writing the words from Daryl and delivering it to his family had been a small thing. But for his family, it had meant the world.

It was getting harder and harder for me to do my work because by night I was using much higher energies than during the day and it was starting to affect me. I was beginning to realise the time would be coming very soon when I would need to choose between the world of finance, the world of spiritual things or perhaps even heal.

No contest really, but I was earning a good living and being able to contribute to all the family finances meant a lot to me.

CHAPTER TWENTY

At the beginning of 1988, about two months before my father passed over, my husband had decided to go into business with a member of my family. David had been unhappy at work for quite a long time and when this opportunity presented itself he felt the idea was worth running with. It would mean he could be his own boss. After spending years working for other people he wanted the chance to try. As I had been self-employed quite successfully for years it seemed only fair that he should also have the opportunity.

My brother had developed a product for the DIY market and we all agreed as a family that it was worth trying to turn it into a viable product and market it. It wasn't going to be easy and it wasn't going to be cheap. He needed both financial help and someone with business acumen. My father also lent his wisdom, having spent many years running his own successful business.

It would take two years before the new business could actually start trading. Months of talks and discussions and time to find and source the company to make the special tooling to manufacture the product. My husband was able to organise most of this while still keeping his job but there came a point when it was time for him to leave and set the new office up with my brother.

The only way we could raise the finance to produce the product was to put our home up as security. The bank took hold of the deeds of our house. I can still remember how my heart sank on the day David and I signed the papers, but David wanted to do this so I felt I needed to let him have the chance. My brother had no money to set the business up on his own. He had no equity in his home but we had. My brother proposed that he and my husband would run the business together and share in the profits fifty/fifty. Because he had come up with the idea, it was only fair that our part to play would be to guarantee the bank overdraft that was needed for the set-up costs, until hopefully sales would start being generated, putting money back into the bank.

Setting up any new venture takes time. From sourcing materials to finding the right manufacturer and much more, this took all of 1988 and most of 1989.

One good thing that happened was that because the product seemed so good we were awarded a grant towards the cost of tooling up the new machine that was needed. It had to be specially made to make the plastic mould.

David had to start working full-time at Easter 1989 because he was the person that was dealing with the manufacturing and all the paperwork side of the business. He was also handling and dealing with the patents. My brother started a month or so later. He was to design and source the packaging, which all took time and, of course, time is money.

It was spring 1990 before the first samples rolled off the production line and then it was all systems go to get the product marketed. But, as the summer progressed, they had only managed to sell a few hundred. The business plan had shown they would have sold thousands by this point. It was turning into a very difficult year for many businesses, as the bank interest rates were going through the roof. This was stopping a lot of the large DIY stores from taking on any new products. So where, nearly two years earlier in 1988, when my brother had done his market research and quite a few of the large DIY stores had said they would be very interested in taking the new product, now they were all saying that, due to the financial situation, they were pulling in their purse strings and reducing their product ranges.

It had taken a full year to find the right company to make the moulds and produce the tooling equipment so that the production could start. The business world was now a different place. The bottom had fallen out of the DIY market and, by late summer 1990, it was obvious that they had reached the end of the road. At the same time, the bank holding our property deeds called a meeting and told us, with regret, they were calling in the overdraft and putting a stop on the account. I had to agree; the situation could not go on.

I think you can now see where the second tidal wave came from. We were going to lose our home, everything my husband and I had worked for over the previous fifteen years. It was heart-breaking. The bank called in the loan, which meant our home had to be sold to pay off the debt.

Telling the children was the hardest. But God bless our daughter. She sat there and said, "It's only a house, Mum."

"You're right, sweetheart. If we can pull together we can get through this." We had only just recently decorated our son's bedroom so his input was, "When we move and find another home, can I please have my bedroom decorated with the same colours and wallpaper?"

"Of course you can."

But I just didn't know if we would have any money left to be able to buy another home. I even wondered at the time if we would ever be able to own our own home again. I can remember sitting at our kitchen table and saying to the family, "A house united stands but a house divided falls. If we can all pull together we can get through this." The only way I could reconcile myself with what was happening was to accept that I must have owed my brother the money from a previous life.

The poor bank manager who was handling the bank account for the business was very upset for us, genuinely so. When he came to visit us in our home he was almost in tears because we were going to lose it. He wanted to try and get some of the money out of my brother. But I told him you can't get blood out of a stone. There was no way my brother was going to try and help us and that had to be alright. Our financial advisor and our solicitor asked me to ask my brother if, in the years to come, when he came into money when my mother passed over, would he please give some money back to us because, of course, this was now two years after my father had passed over. I didn't want to ask him but they insisted. When I approached him with this he said there was no way he would give us any money in the future and that was that.

We had effectively paid his wages for eighteen months

and provided him with a car but he refused to ever help by paying just a little bit back. That's why I somehow felt I must have owed him this from a previous lifetime. It helped to stop me from being angry. I didn't want to be angry and thank God I wasn't. But I was devastated.

I just wished my father was still here to be able to advise us; we really could have done with his wisdom. All I kept hearing when I asked him was that everything would be alright, whatever that meant.

I wasn't cross with my brother. We all have choices in this life and my husband and I had both chosen to do this, so there was no one to blame. It would have been nice however if my brother and his wife could have said just once, "I am sorry you're losing your home," but they never did.

Our lives were going to change and change drastically.

Even though David had no income now, I still had a thriving business. Such a lot had happened over the previous two years. I realised that I was much happier sitting late at night writing messages from the spirit world than I was going over a set of accounts that I had prepared for a client. My heart just wasn't in my business anymore. But now, more than ever, we needed my income.

I was still trying to balance the two worlds, the two different energies. When I went into my office the following day, after I had been writing during the night, I was never quite with it. It took a huge effort on my part to pull myself back to Earth, to be able to handle my clients and my own office work.

Should I stop writing from spirit? I didn't think so, but what was I to do?

Somewhere from deep down inside of me I knew all I needed to do was trust. Trust that I would be guided so for now all I needed to do was take one day at a time. One day at a time, simple words but, oh boy, they were going to prove very hard to follow.

It was important that we got our home onto the market as quickly as possible because, as each week went by, the interest on the money we owed to the bank was building and that meant we would owe more than the original overdraft. To say it was a difficult time would be an understatement.

I sold my expensive car and we bought a much cheaper vehicle for both my husband and I to drive around in. Thank God my business was doing well and we could have some semblance of normality in our lives until our home sold. Our home was put onto the market and the estate agent's 'For Sale' board went up outside. This meant that I needed to be at home on the days there were viewings. It was very hard letting people into our home knowing that one of them may be buying it and we had to move out. Let's be very honest here, none of us wanted to leave our home but we had to. We had no choice.

This home had been very special to us. My husband found it in the spring of 1983 after the house we originally wanted to buy fell through one week before we were due to sign the contracts. We had our house sold and were ready to move when the whole thing went pear-shaped. It left us with two weeks to find another house to buy or we were going to lose the sale on ours. We had both spent an age looking for the right area to live in. Then we narrowed our search down to one street of houses. We both felt we had found the perfect place because it was halfway between our daughter's and son's schools.

When I got the phone call telling me our house purchase was off, I went into a panic. I put the phone down and said, "Please Lord, help us. We need to find a home and we need to find it fast."

When my husband came home from work that evening I told him what had happened. He said, "Now what are we going to do? We'll lose our sale if we don't have somewhere to move to."

I asked him to please go out that night after tea when it was dark and walk the moor behind the street of houses where the original house was that we had wanted to buy, to see if he could find one in darkness that might be empty. He looked at me as if I'd lost my marbles.

"Please do this for me."

So bless him, he did. He came home that night a bit confused. He told me there was a house in darkness. It did look empty from the outside but there was probably someone living there because we couldn't be that lucky! I said I would drive past the house after I had taken the children to school the following morning and have a look in daylight to see if I could see whether it was empty.

Lo and behold not only was it empty, there was a 'For Sale' board outside (no surprise to me). I made an appointment for us to view the house three days later.

In the previous few weeks nine couples had looked at this particular house. It was up for sale because the old lady who had lived there had just died and the family wanted the house sold as soon as possible to close the estate. Nine couples. I was so worried because the asking price was more than we could afford and if there had been so much interest we didn't stand a chance of buying it. We would be outbid.

The day came for us to view. After looking around the house we both agreed it would be ideal for us. It was very old-fashioned inside but well maintained. It was actually in a far better position than the original house we were going to buy and in much better condition.

As we'd been walking around the house I had been aware of the presence of a lady. I told my husband the old lady who had lived here was still here. I could feel her. I said to him, "She's been watching us as we've been looking around her home." There was only one thing for it. I sat myself down on the low window-sill in her lounge and in the peace and quiet I began to talk to her. Firstly I explained what had happened with the house further down the street that we had wanted to buy. Then I explained to her how much better her home was than our first choice because hers was much further away from the main road, so it would be much quieter for us to live in. I then said to her that I could see how much she had loved her home and garden, so I promised her that I would take care of her home and fill it full of love and I would love the garden and feed the birds, just as she had done. Finally I asked her to please help us. Her home was just out of our price range. My parting words to her were, "We will only be able to buy your home if you help us."

Guess what? She did. Nine families were more than interested before we came on the scene but none of them put in an offer. Our offer was the only offer they ever received.

My husband has since told me that he was very cross with me because I put our offer up by five hundred pounds without asking him first. Sorry, David. But I received a telephone call at my office from the estate agents saying if I could put our offer up the house would be ours. I had to think on my feet. Finance was my business and I knew it was well worth it. We did get the house for a lot less than the asking price.

The old lady stayed in the house for a few weeks after we moved in. I thanked her many times for helping us. Then one day I realised she was gone. I never saw her. I didn't hear her, but I knew she had been helping us.

"How?" you might say. I don't know. I just don't know. So to the lady who owned that home of ours, whoever you are and wherever you are now, thank you.

Having to sell our home was heart-breaking, but what was making things worse for me was I had no idea where we were going. I was beginning to picture a tent big enough to take the four of us plus the dog and the three cats. It would have to be a very big tent! I didn't know how much we were going to get for our home. We had the selling price but everyone knows a house is only worth what someone is prepared to pay for it. So until it was sold we had no way of knowing how much money we would have left, if any. The bank would take what they wanted first. The longer it took to sell, the less we would have.

Like any good mother, I have always been a home-maker. Our homes have always been a place of safety, a sanctuary from the world around us, a safe haven for all the family. The picture of the tent in my head wasn't helping me in any way.

I was so desperate one day I decided I would go and see

a clairvoyant. I was a bit apprehensive because of my past experience but I was desperate for some advice. And the one person I wanted to get the advice from was my father. If my father could manage to communicate that would mean the world to me. We are all products of our parents until we learn, as we grow older, to think for ourselves, make our own decisions, make our own minds up on how we view things and I was no different. My father had always said that Spiritualism was a dangerous thing to get involved with. I remember him telling me when I was in my early teens about an aunt of my mother's who became very unstable. The family blamed her involvement in the Spiritualist Church. It must have been sometime during the 1930s or 40s. Goodness knows what happened. My father had no real understanding of what Spiritualism was all about; he didn't want to know. That's what I was told when I was young and it had stuck. But it was me who could hear the voices and see things. It was me who could now hear my father. I hadn't tried to do this myself in any way; I just could. I had never been into a Spiritualist Church in my life. I had only met three mediums in my life. Two were good and one that I wished I had run away from. And, of course, that wonderful book by Doris Stokes and the words of love and support she gave me.

My father had always said to me, "Don't go looking for things, Isabella. If you're meant to do something it will come to you." Well, hearing voices had been with me from being a child without me ever trying. And of course it was only a few months earlier that my father had managed to answer my question through the medium at my friend's house. So it didn't seem wrong to me anymore (I don't think it ever did) but I had learned not to go to a medium unless the person had been recommended to me.

I can't remember where I got the contact from but someone gave me a phone number of a clairvoyant who worked full-time helping people and they told me this man was very good. I rang and made an appointment to go and see him.

To be honest, I do remember being very nervous but

determined at the same time.

I was looking for reassurance and I was praying that my father would somehow be able to help me. All I had been able to get from Dad over the past few weeks was 'not to worry'. As I was waiting to go into the clairvoyant's room I kept asking Dad to please be there for me, please try and help.

This was going to be an experience I would never forget.

I can't remember the clairvoyant's name, so I will call him Tom. He invited me into his lounge which was quite a large room. He told me to sit down on the chair facing the settee, which he then sat down on.

Tom told me a little of his own story. I realised afterwards he did this to allow himself time to pick up on any souls that might have been around me wanting to communicate. Then I noticed he had tears in his eyes and I had no idea why. This was the conversation as near as I can remember.

"I have a gentleman here with me and an overwhelming love coming through for you. I am sure it must be your father. Has your father passed over?"

"Yes."

"He's showering you with love. That's the only way I can describe it to you. I haven't felt this much love coming from the spirit world for years, if in fact I ever have. It's so strong it's making me cry. Do you realise how loved you are?"

By this time I was crying.

"Your father is telling me that you are very worried about something. Can you tell me what it is?"

So I explained to him as quickly as I could what had happened and what my main worries were.

"Would we have any money left?"

"Your father is saying, yes, there will be some money left after the bank have got theirs."

"Will we be able to buy another house? What type of house should we be looking for, Dad? Where do we look?"

"Your father says to tell you that there will be a light shining above the house." Tom said to me, "I know you can

158

see things, so you might see an actual light shining above it or there will be something about the house that you will recognise, just as if a light were shining and that will be the house you are to buy. That will be the home that's meant for you. Don't worry. Your father is saying I must tell you not to worry. You will definitely know the house when you find it."

Then he said to me. "Do you realise how well guided and guarded you are?"

"Well no, not really."

"I'm sitting here looking at you and I see the figure of Christ as clear as day behind you."

I was flabbergasted. I asked him how he knew it was the Master.

"Because I can clearly see a huge cross behind him; that's His way of letting me know who it is."

"Dear Lord."

"Trust me. You have absolutely nothing to worry about. You are being protected and guided better than the Queen of England."

"Gosh," was about all I could say to this.

"Your father loves you so much. I only wish we were all loved as much as you are."

I was in bits by the time the interview with him was over. He was genuinely moved himself by what he had seen and heard. There was no way I was ever going to forget my father's words. I thanked him and left. Dumbfounded, speechless and wiped out was how I felt. I needed time to sit quietly and think about what had been said.

CHAPTER TWENTY-ONE

As I was driving back home in my car, I kept going over in my mind all the things that my father had managed to relay to me. The love that he had passed on to me was tangible. I could still feel the glow surrounding me. To be told that the Master Himself was guiding and protecting me, I honestly couldn't take that one in. I not only felt blessed, I was blessed. There are just no words in our language to be able to explain to you how I was feeling as I drove home in my car that afternoon with tears falling down my cheeks. Remembering how my father had felt about Spiritualism while he was here on Earth, I was completely overwhelmed. What had just happened was beyond my wildest expectations.

It must have taken a gigantic effort on my father's part to have been able to communicate so well with a stranger. The fact Tom was practising a religion that was completely alien to him and against everything he had ever believed in, this thought was blowing me away.

His love for me was more precious than gold.

As I was driving home I was sending my father a blessing, a thousand blessings. He would never have done this in life so I could only surmise that his whole attitude towards spirit communication had changed since he passed over. He must be learning so much that he hadn't known existed while he was here on Earth and I was very happy for him.

I couldn't wait to tell my husband what had been said at my reading. When I arrived back home I was able to relay my father's words through my tears of amazement and joy. David agreed that I had had a most unusual afternoon. But he also wondered what my father had meant about 'the light'. We were both going to have to trust that we would understand at the right time.

We had no choice but to put the failed business into voluntary liquidation but everyone was going to have to wait to be paid until our home was sold. Because both my husband and

I didn't have the heart not to pay everyone that was owed money, no one was going to lose out. We would pay all the bills from the failed business once our home was sold and our secured debt to the bank was cleared. This was probably very naive of us but that's the way we had both been brought up. You pay your debts no matter what. I don't think either of us could have slept in our beds at night if we had caused another business any financial problems.

We needed to find somewhere to live. My father had said there would be some money left and, with that information, we both agreed that we should start looking. We would try the best we could to be prepared to move out of our home. Neither of us was very sure about what sort of house to look for, or where to look, but we both thought we had better start looking now. We didn't want to be homeless when our home sold.

I was often out and about because of my work, visiting clients at their place of business. This particular day was no exception. The business I was visiting was only about a mile from our home. As it was late in the afternoon when our meeting finished I decided I would go straight home instead of going back to my office. Because I knew the main road would be busy at this time of day, with commuters going home from work, I decided to take a short cut through the side streets to avoid the congestion.

As I was driving in a thirty mile an hour zone and driving slowly, I was able to take notice of everything that I was passing, and I noticed a 'For Sale' board outside a house with a very overgrown garden. The board was almost obscured by the hanging branches and ivy on the walls. I stopped the car and got out to have a look. The house looked deserted and extremely neglected. All I could see was the number on the gate post but it looked as if it might be an interesting property for us. I could enquire the following morning on the way to my office. The house was only three streets away from our home, in a good area, and still near to the children's schools.

During the past few months my husband had set himself up as a computer consultant so I would have to wait for him to come home for his evening meal before I could tell him about the house I had just seen. He agreed with me that it was worth enquiring about as, because of its neglected condition, we might be able to afford it. But we still didn't know how much money we were going to have left from the sale of our home.

The following morning I went to the estate agent's office to pick up the details and arrange to view the property. When I walked in I asked for the details of the house by the number that I had seen on the gate post, number six, and of course the road it was on. The lady in the office said to me, "Oh yes, number six. That house is called Ravenswood House."

I said, "Pardon?"

She repeated the name, "Ravenswood House."

"Dear Lord, I don't believe it." The words were out of my mouth before I had time to stop myself. She asked me if I was feeling alright and would I like to sit down. I just stood there with my mouth wide open staring at her. All I could bring myself to say was, "I don't believe it. I really don't believe it. That was the name of the house I lived in with my parents before I got married."

"My goodness, that must be a sign," and that was the lady in the office, not me! I did sit down. I was feeling positively wobbly.

I said to her, "Yes, you're right. It is a sign."

She gave me the details and asked, with a smile on her face, if I would like to go and view with my family. We made an appointment for that coming weekend. I left with the written details in my hand, smiling from ear to ear. It felt as if I had entered the twilight zone. If I'd heard the theme tune from the old television programme I wouldn't have been in the least bit surprised.

My father had said there would be a light shining over the house. But this was a beacon, and a very large beacon at that. He had been right. There was no way I could have missed this. I was so excited. I couldn't wait to tell David. When I showed him the details and he saw the name of the house, even his face lit up. "My God," he said. "We couldn't miss this if we tried."

162

The price was a bit high, but the details did say there was a lot of work to do to the property, so perhaps this would put a lot of prospective buyers off.

The weekend came and off we all went to have a look. We were going to have to have hearts like lions to take this old house on because it was in a terrible state. But David and I could both see its potential. There was ivy growing in the upstairs toilet. It had come in through the rotten window frame, grown around the toilet bowl and then it was winding its way in and out of the floor boards as it headed out along the corridor. The whole place was a mess.

There were great big mushrooms growing out of the walls on the first floor landing and we knew what that was a sign of. The smell in this area of the house also gave us a clue. No mistaking it, it was dry rot. The downstairs kitchen smelled of damp rotten wood. There was an old metal bath under a broken wooden bench in one corner and a very old, dirty, cracked, smelly sink with one tap in another. The window was so small there was virtually no daylight to be seen. That was the kitchen. The whole house would need gutting, but, and it was a big but, there was the most amazing staircase, curving up the full three floors of the house, with the most beautiful wood banister and spindles in perfect condition. The walls also curved, mirroring the curve of the staircase, and at the beginning of each corridor were the most beautiful angel faces in white plaster. It was obvious they had been there since the house was built in the eighteen hundreds and would need to be kept intact if possible, allowing for any damage the dry rot might have caused. We'd never seen anything like this before, or since. Oh boy, I think David's heart sank at the thought of all the work that would need doing but even he could see that it could be made into a lovely home.

The children went around the house with us and were very excited by the prospect of having the whole of the third floor all to themselves, their very own domain. They would each be able to have a very large bedroom and there was also a separate long narrow room that could be turned into a toilet and shower room; all this on their own floor of the house.

It took us all of five minutes to decide to put in an offer on the house because we all liked it so much, even though there would be a massive amount of renovation work that needed to be done and we hadn't a clue how we were going to be able to afford to do it, but that didn't put us off. My father had been right, it would make us a lovely home.

Thinking back, putting the offer in was a bit daft because our home wasn't sold yet. But this house was meant for us and hopefully it wouldn't be too long before ours was sold. After all, we had a lovely home.

I must have gone back to walk around the outside of the empty old house at least half a dozen times. This was my way of getting the feel of the place, even though I needed my wellies on because of what might have been lurking in the undergrowth. Each time I visited the house I fell more in love with the place.

About six weeks after we had put in our offer we received a phone call from the estate agents to say there was a cut-off date on all offers received for the purchase of the property. All prospective buyers were being given seven days' notice to put in their best and final offer, and because we couldn't proceed we would have to withdraw.

I was devastated, and that's the understatement of the century. My father had said the house with the light over it was meant for us; this would be our new home. And with every fibre of my being I believed him. I didn't understand what had gone wrong. We had done everything we could but we lost Ravenswood House. Someone else bought it. The estate agents did inform us after the event that the purchaser had paid the full asking price. Even if we could have proceeded we could not have afforded to pay the full price.

How could this be? I had simply trusted all the words my father had said to me without question. Every part of my being had told me he was right. Now what were we supposed to do? My direction had disappeared and I was floundering in very deep water.

Do you remember what the Professor had told me years earlier? Avoid anyone with the flu, avoid stress and keep out of the sun. Well, let's be honest here, I was stressed to hell and very upset. Not just because we had lost the house but because I now had absolutely no idea where we were supposed to live or what I was supposed to do or think. My trust in God and my trust in my father were both still intact, but any trust I had in myself had gone out the window. Perhaps I had misunderstood. I was beginning to think I had dreamt everything that my father had said to me.

It was starting to rain cats and dogs again.

CHAPTER TWENTY-TWO

We lost Ravenswood House in July 1990. Our home sold in September. We did receive a good price which meant we would have some money left but we were going to have to move and we had nowhere to go.

It seemed to me at the time as if the Universe was conspiring to work against us. If only our home had sold a few weeks earlier, we might have stood a chance of buying Ravenswood House. My father had been right about some money being left over. Not a lot but enough for a small deposit on something else, but the something else we wanted was now gone. At least we would be able to pay all our debts due to the collapse of the business and our mortgage but that was not making me feel any better.

The couple who wanted to buy our home told us they were in no hurry to move in. It was now September. As they were moving back into our area and were able to complete on the purchase of our house without selling their existing home, they said they would like to sign all the contracts ready to exchange them in the New Year.

We agreed because this would mean that we could have Christmas in the home we all loved. We now had to find somewhere to live. As we had just over four months to do this I was quite confident that we would be able to find somewhere reasonably convenient for both the children's schools and my office. I couldn't have been more wrong if I'd tried.

There were plenty of houses to rent, but we had a dog and three cats that we all loved very much. They were part of our family and every time I rang the agents about the prospect of renting a property on their books and I mentioned that we had animals, time after time I was being told that animals were not allowed. It was now the beginning of November and in about ten weeks we would be without a roof over our heads. This was making me feel ill. If you have ever been so far down and confused that you weren't thinking straight. If your thoughts have ever been in such a muddle and everything seemed to be conspiring against you, then you will know how I was feeling and understand when I say I didn't have the sense to go and see Nansi.

Over the many years that people have been coming to me for healing, I am often told by new patients that they have had my phone number for months, and in some cases years. They tell me that they wished they had rung me when they were first given my name and number, because they felt so much better after their treatment and if they'd come sooner they could have saved themselves months, and in some cases years, of pain and stress. Like I always say, "There is always a right time and the right time for you is now." But I still had this lesson to learn the hard way.

Not having something to hold on to was a new experience for me and I wasn't coping very well. In fact, I wasn't coping at all. It felt as if the rug had been pulled out from beneath my feet.

The mother in me didn't know where her chicks were going to rest their heads and that hurt me badly. That tent kept reappearing in my mind, but it would have to be a very big one to get us all in. My thoughts kept turning to the possibility that my father might have been wrong. But that just didn't feel right or make any sense to me. My brain was in such a muddle it felt as if I'd lost my connection, lost my sixth sense.

I found myself making an appointment to see a doctor and, to be honest, even at the time I was not sure why. We were still with the same practice we had been with since I was diagnosed with MS. We had moved house but we were still within the radius the surgery covered.

I rang the surgery to make an appointment and was told I would be seeing a new lady doctor. This did not bode well for me. At the appointed time I was sitting in the waiting room, feeling very uneasy, but I needed help and advice desperately. It had been years since I had been in the surgery and I was worried about how I was going to be treated. But this was a new doctor and attitudes must have changed and moved on since the last time I had been there.

It dawned on me that there was no way I could explain about talking to my 'dead' father and the real reason I was so upset. The doctor would think I was 'losing it' big time. But I was fairly sure if I just explained about losing our home and having to pay most of the money back to the bank and not knowing where we were going to live, that in itself should be enough for her to understand why I needed some help.

It was raining cats and dogs, but it was about to start raining down hailstones as big as bricks. After I told her about losing our home, I explained to her that I was worried in case my stressed state brought on my MS symptoms. That's when the hailstones started to fall.

"You haven't got MS."

"Pardon?"

"You haven't got MS. The new Head of Neurology at the hospital has written to me, telling me that anyone diagnosed by Professor Branson is to be told his findings were all wrong; therefore you don't have MS."

This was all too much for me. Talk about the worm turning. For the first time in my life I wasn't going to let a doctor walk all over me. I told her that was ridiculous. How could someone that had never met me turn around and say there was nothing the matter with me, after everything I'd been through.

Then she said, "Well, you've never come to me with any symptoms of MS."

"No, I haven't, because I'm well aware there's nothing you can do, other than give me drugs and I would not agree to this, so there was never any point in seeing you." I couldn't tell her about the fact I had been so well for a few years because I had seen a healer. She would have had me committed.

"Would you like me to make an appointment at the hospital, so you can see the Head of Neurology?"

I said, "Yes, as soon as possible." (I didn't even say please, I was so cross.) She said she would write straight away and I was to wait for a letter from the hospital with my appointment. Then I left her surgery.

Not only did I not get any help, she had managed to make me feel even worse. I went home and sat and cried. When I told my husband what the doctor had said, he said, "Does it really matter if you are now being told you haven't got it?"

"Yes it matters. It matters to me. If you had walked in my shoes for all those years and had gone through all the things I had gone through, trust me, it would matter to you. I'm going to prove 'that lot' wrong." As bad as that sounded, that's how I felt.

That night, when I went to bed, I was an emotional wreck. We were losing our home. We had lost the house my father said was meant for us. The doctor told me I didn't have MS, and never had, and we had to move out of the home we loved in the next few weeks but we had nowhere to live. And my husband didn't understand how I was feeling.

Boy, was it raining hailstones!

As I was lying in bed, wondering how on earth I was going to get to sleep because my mind was in such turmoil, the most wonderful smell of perfume began to fill our bedroom. I just lay there trying to figure out where it was coming from. It was nothing that I had ever smelt before. I could have lain there all night just breathing in the wonderful fragrance.

Then I started to hear music. (I know one day someone will lock me up, but I have a promise from some friends they will find the key and let me out). This was truly an out of this world experience. I was wide awake by now, lying there listening to what I can only describe as a Heavenly orchestra playing the most beautiful symphony. All the while the music was playing I was still being surrounded by the most wonderful perfume. Okay, so I'm a bit slow. It did take me a few minutes to realise it was Heaven sent. Truly Heaven sent. I fell into a deep relaxed sleep and drifted away.

When I woke up in the morning, try as I might, I couldn't bring back into my conscious mind the fragrance that had permeated our bedroom, or the sound of the music from the night before. They were truly out of this world. I'd never smelled the perfume or heard the music before and I've never had the same experience again.

But by God's grace, perhaps one day I will.

Each time I lost my way, or more importantly for me, I forgot to trust, the Universe stepped in and gave me something to hold on to and made me realise yet again just how blessed I was. It was no wonder God or, as some people might prefer, the Universal energy, had come to my rescue last night. I had asked my doctor for help and had got none. Even though it had been years since I had been in the doctor's surgery, the memories of how badly the last doctor had treated me came flooding back into my mind as if it were yesterday. I'm sure part of the reason for this was because this new doctor was sitting in the same room, behind the very same desk, where years before I was told, "We take no notice," and you know the rest. Not only had I been refused help yet again but I had also been made to feel ten times worse. To say I was getting fed up with the way doctors treated me would be an understatement but I don't think I ever felt that they were in the wrong, I should have done, but I didn't. What a roller-coaster ride I was on.

We were still desperately trying to find a house to rent but all our pets were causing us major problems. No one wanted to let a house out if you had animals. We were turned down time after time.

My world kept being turned upside down. But my wonderful experience had reminded me to simply ask for help from Heaven, so I did. "Please Lord, help us find somewhere to live."

Trying to raise the energy to go into my office was becoming harder by the day. Over the previous year my business had grown considerably and I was missing my dear friend and right-hand person. Her support and love had been the one thing that had kept me on track at my office over the previous years. I didn't have the heart to continue my business without her. To me she was irreplaceable. I had interviewed one or two people to fill her place and I'm sure they would have been good at their job but I realised things could never be the same again. I wasn't the same.

The spirit world and hearing voices; writing my father's and other souls' wonderful words of love and reassurance down on paper; helping Nansi with her patients. All these things were becoming far more important to me than sorting out people's finances and preparing set after set of year-end accounts. The difference in the energies was so great, this was also adding to my confusion. The gulf between my two, for want of a better word, jobs was huge. One job was dragging me down and the other was lifting me up, and I was floundering somewhere in between.

It had seemed to me that when Doris retired last year I had had three options. I could employ a new senior staff member, I could go into partnership with someone or I could try and sell my practice. But I had no idea if my business was worth anything.

Option two was a 'no go'. I had seen far too many partnerships go pear-shaped over the previous fourteen years. Option one had been a possibility then, but not now. I was very tired of the financial world. My heart just wasn't in it anymore. Everyone in the business world seemed to be out for number one, not giving a care whom they trampled on in the process. It hadn't been like that when I started in 1976. But I honestly didn't think option three was a viable proposition. I didn't think my business was worth very much, certainly not enough to make any sort of difference to the position we were in. Or was it? There was only one way to find out. I needed to ask someone in the know. I was fast realising that I no longer wanted to work in the world of finance and it dawned on me that, actually, it didn't really matter what it was worth; it had to be worth something. I was at the point where I just wanted to get out.

We were friendly with most of our neighbours and I knew that one of them was a partner in a very large accountancy firm so I took it into my head to go and ask his

171

advice. He was very kind to me and very helpful. He explained that any accountancy firm would normally sell for about one and a half times turnover. But, because my business was part book-keeping and part accountancy, he explained it would depend on the size of the practice wanting to purchase my fee base. They might not want the book-keeping side of my business but, on the other hand, a small firm might. At least now I had a rough idea, and I must admit I was quite surprised, nicely so. But I wasn't going to get my hopes up. It made sense to sell out now if I could, while I was still on top of things.

But this could take months if not years. I would have to advertise and that would mean my staff would find out and this could cause problems, problems that I just could not have coped with. So I did what I should always do (when I have the sense to remember). I asked the Universal energy to show me the way. I simply asked for help. That was me asking for help for the second time in the same week.

It was the following week, after asking for help with the sale of my business, that I happened to buy our local weekly business newspaper, something I hardly ever did. In fact this was the first time in about nine years and, as I was skimming through the 'Business Wanted' section, an advert caught my eye and I couldn't believe what I was reading. There was an advert asking to purchase a small practice with a turnover of fees exactly the same as mine. After I had read the advert about three times, just to make sure I wasn't imagining things, I put the paper down and rang my solicitor. I asked her if she would please act on my behalf and find out for me if the advert was genuine and, if it was, to let the person know that my practice may be available to buy.

Within two days she was back in touch to tell me that a local chartered accountant was seeking to purchase a small business such as mine to build up his client base, and he would be very interested to meet with me. I asked her to arrange a meeting at her office so that it was on neutral ground. I didn't want anyone coming into my office to alert my staff that I might be selling my practice. Not yet anyway.

Within days she was back on the phone. She had set up a meeting for the following Monday afternoon, as the accountant was very interested to meet with me as soon as possible. She asked me to come to her office half an hour sooner, because there were a few things she wanted to go over with me before our meeting with my prospective business buyer started.

When I arrived at her office for the meeting her main question to me was whether I was sure I wanted to sell my business. I assured her I did.

"How do you want me to play this?"

"Let's just take the meeting one step at a time and see what he has to say." I explained to my solicitor that he may not want the book-keeping side of my practice. We would just have to wait and see.

He arrived for our meeting on time. He was very friendly, pleasant and professional. He explained he had heard of my practice and he knew my business had a good reputation, so that was a good start. As it happened, his office was only about one mile away from mine. Then he explained to us both that he was interested in my business as a whole. He wanted to buy both the book-keeping side and the accountancy work, as he was looking to expand his fee base. He said he was aware that the book-keeping could be just as profitable as the accountancy if worked properly and yes, he would pay me one and a half times my turnover. The gentleman then asked if he could come and visit my premises as quickly as possible to look over my client list and some sample files. Because it was getting very close to Christmas, I asked him if he could come during the Christmas holidays, when my staff would be on holiday. That way they would not be alerted in the event he decided not to proceed. So the meeting was arranged for between Christmas and New Year and he left.

My solicitor and I just sat and looked at each other in stunned silence.

She broke our silence when she said, "If this goes ahead it will be the easiest business sale I've ever been involved with, and I've a good feeling about this."

I said, "I know. So have I." I couldn't believe what had just happened. With no effort on my part whatsoever I might have found a buyer for my business.

No one outside of my own family, other than my solicitor and the prospective buyer, was aware of what was happening, and that was the way I wanted it to stay. It was very important to me that neither my staff, nor my clients, would be told anything until a contract had been signed, and even then not until the last minute. But my thoughts were jumping ahead. This all needed to be taken one step at a time.

A lot of thanks were said skywards by me for the rest of the day.

Obviously my husband was delighted for me and so were the children but we were all going to have to keep this a secret.

"It's not over 'til the fat lady sings."

At almost the same time, in the same week that I spotted the advert the accountant had put in the newspaper for the purchase of fees, we found a house to rent. Things were happening so quickly we hardly seemed to have time to draw breath. I honestly can't remember whether it was my husband or me that found the advert in the papers: a house to rent no more than two miles from where we lived now within days of me asking for help. We arranged to go and see it that day in case someone else got in first. It was horrible, and I do mean horrible. Each room was painted a different colour. Bright blue, purple and red and all the skirting boards were painted black. The last tenants had been students and they had painted some of the rooms themselves. Black seemed to be the new white. But when we asked the letting agent if the animals could live with us the answer was, "Yes." We asked if we would be allowed to paint some of the rooms the colours that would be more suitable to us and they agreed. We could have the keys three weeks before we were due to move in.

As the completion date for the sale of our home was not until the beginning of February 1991, this gave us the time we needed to organise the work. I asked one of my clients who had a painting and decorating business to go into the house and paint the hall and landings white and white gloss all the skirting boards. We also asked him to paint what would be our dining area, kitchen and lounge. He was able to book this into his schedule of work, to be finished a few days before we were due to move. We could live with the colours they had the bedrooms painted, but the rest I could not have managed to live with. This would clean and brighten the house up no end. It would be a roof over our heads. As horrible as I thought it was, at least we would all be under one roof, pets and all.

The same week we found the rented house, just three weeks before Christmas 1990, I received a letter from the hospital with an appointment to see the Head of Neurology. The appointment was for the following week. At least I wasn't going to have to wait months to get this sorted out. There was so much going on, my head was in a spin.

Thursday arrived. Time for me to go back to the hospital for my appointment with the new Head of Neurology, and I was not looking forward to it. I had a knot in my stomach. It had been nine years since I'd been shouted at by the doctor in the hospital, who had demanded that I did what he told me. It had been nine years since I turned my back on him and walked away, as he screamed after me, "You'll be back!"

Well, I was going back but not because I was asking for help, but because I wanted to prove to this new doctor that my diagnosis by Professor Branson had been correct. When I walked into his consulting room he was sitting behind his desk. He looked up at me and, without even saying hello, he said, "You haven't got MS." I'd never met such an unpleasant man in all my life. Unknown to me this doctor had a reputation for being completely devoid of any bedside manner.

I said to him, "How can you say that?"

"You walked in here. If you had MS you would be walking with difficulty, if at all."

He raised his left arm and with a flip of his hand he pointed to all the MRI head scans on his wall and said, "If you had MS your brain would be showing scar tissue, just like these scans."

Then he proceeded to explain some of them to me, giving me a running commentary on just how badly each of his patients was affected by their scars. Some of the scans each had a few small areas of scar tissue, and other scans had one or two bigger ones.

"But you haven't got it. Your brain will not have any scar tissue. You're wasting my time."

"You don't know that because you haven't scanned my brain, and you have completely ignored Professor Branson's own findings. How can you ignore the findings of someone who spent his whole life working with and researching MS?"

"I have seen many of his so-called patients over the past few years and not one of them had MS. He had misdiagnosed in every case I've investigated, and I'm not wasting my time on anyone else."

"So please explain to me why my legs almost gave out on me when I competed in races, when I was at school. Explain to me why I had a net curtain across my eyes for so long. Explain to me why I kept dropping things, breaking things and walking into walls as I turned a corner. If it's not MS then what is it?"

"Do you have seven and a half thousand pounds?"

"No I don't."

"Well if you want an MRI scan, that's what it will cost you to have it done privately."

"There is no way I can afford that."

"Hmmm, I could put you into my research programme and you can have your MRI scan, but you will have to wait about a year before you will get an appointment. But I'm telling you now, you haven't got MS and I'm the expert."

"I'll wait," said I.

He put his head back down and started to read the papers on his desk. Apparently my appointment was over.

As I was walking away from the hospital my thoughts were jumping from what had just been said to me and the memory I had from nine years earlier. It seemed almost impossible to me that this particular department in the hospital could produce two doctors that were so unpleasant. Well, that was over. I was just going to have to wait a year before I would have the MRI scan, but that was okay.

I was, and still am, a very patient person. It would be worth waiting for, because I knew this new Head of Neurology was wrong in my case. He may be the expert but he was just a man, and men make mistakes. His attitude towards me was so arrogant he was discounting out of hand my diagnosis, and at least now I knew why. In fact, I now had the answer to a lot of questions that I had had from years earlier.

Professor Branson had fallen out with the health authority over his diagnostic research and left his post as Head of Neurology. That was why he set up his own private clinic to continue his research work. It made me stop and wonder how many other people had their medical records changed without anyone taking the time to check. Mine had now been wiped clean. As far as the medical profession was concerned I never had MS. The old Professor had been wrong in his findings, all because this doctor said so. No checking, just a wave of his hand. But this expert hadn't walked in my shoes. I knew beyond a shadow of doubt that I had MS. And of course my 'voice' had told me something was very wrong with me many years earlier and that was 'The One Voice' that I trusted beyond words.

I would look forward to the day I could prove this doctor wrong.

CHAPTER TWENTY-THREE

Knowing it would be the last Christmas in the home we all loved I was determined to make it a good one for all of us. I'm sure I did.

To be perfectly honest with you, I can't remember very much about it, other than an afternoon I had all to myself. I spent time putting up all the Christmas cards, decorations, lights around the windows and lots more. I wove fir tree branches through the spindles on the staircase. Then I wove lights up among the smaller fronds of the branches. The house looked and smelled the best it ever had. But it was all done with a very heavy heart.

I'm not sure if my mother came to stay with us again or if we went to David's parents for Christmas lunch. I honestly can't remember. I can't even remember Christmas Day so I'm not going to tax my brain trying. I promised myself when I started writing my 'tale' that everything I wrote would be the truth, the whole truth and nothing but the truth (sorry, I just couldn't resist that one). My mind was in such a muddle at the time, nothing much was registering in my mind. I'm sure we all had fun. Even the dog and cats would have had their stockings filled with treats as they all had each year. But Christmas 1990 is mostly a blur to me and that's a shame.

Except of course there was one more appointment that I had to keep before the year was out and this one was quite exciting for me, the possible sale of my business. David came to my office for a couple of hours with me the day before the meeting was to take place to help me compile a client list, because I had no idea how to work my office computer. But thankfully he had been the one that set the whole system up for my staff so it was no problem for him to find and print out all the information I needed. After I made sure I had everything I would need and all three of my offices were nice and clean and tidy (I had done this while he had compiled and printed everything for me), we both left and went home. I'd done all I could to be well prepared. The only thing left to do now was to say a prayer and ask for help.

The office was warm, the Christmas tree lights were on and my rooms were ready for my visitor. All I needed now was for the gentleman to actually turn up for our meeting. The doorbell rang right on time and I invited him in. We spent time going through my client list. Then I allowed him to look through a sample of my client's correspondence files and one or two client accounts files. It hadn't taken very long for us to do this but he said he'd seen enough. He told me that he knew I would have a well organised office and he said that he wasn't disappointed.

"My mind was made up even before we went through your files. I want to buy your practice. I'm going on holiday with my family for two weeks but as soon as I come back I will arrange another meeting with you and your solicitor. We can then finalise everything and arrange a date for completion. You have just sold your business. Have a good Christmas and I'll see you in the New Year," and with that he left my office.

Unbelievable.

The New Year was upon us and it was 'all systems go' to have the family ready to move house. The only thought that I do remember having was the worry that the rented house we were moving into was so horrible the children would not want to bring any of their friends home for tea or to play, as they had since they were both little. They were used to being able to have friends over whenever they wanted to.

Our home had plenty of space to play both indoors and out. Our garden was not very big, but it was a lovely place to be able to sit and relax, and our animals loved the garden more than the children. They often preferred to be outside on the street playing on their bicycles, skateboards or roller boots and as the road we lived on was very quiet they were both perfectly safe. But there was no outside space, no garden and the road outside where we were going to live was not a safe place for children to play. It wasn't unusual to have at least one extra child for tea, which was always a home-cooked evening meal when David came home from work; that's the way we liked it, all of us together around our kitchen table eating and talking.

I had a lovely big kitchen to work in, with plenty of storage cupboards and lots of bench space, which made it a pleasure for me to prepare food. But the rented house had what would have been described as a 'back scullery.' This was a very small room with an old gas cooker on one wall, the sink, with a cupboard underneath, on the other wall, the back door in front of you and no room to swing a cat, or anything else for that matter.

The room before this would have been called the breakfast room so at least there was a room we could eat in. Most people, when they modernised an old terrace house like this one, often knocked these two rooms into one to make a decent-sized kitchen but, of course, this house had not been modernised. Where on earth was I going to put all our everyday kitchen crockery for four people, let alone my pots, pans and cooking utensils? I had a picture in my head of having all our food stuff in boxes on the floor and where the fridge would go at this point in time was way beyond me.

It was no wonder I was having problems trying to think straight. Our home had always been filled with friends. It was very important to me to have a home where all were welcome. It still is, and there has been a good reason for this for a very long time. Life is forever teaching us lessons, but I learned many years ago that sometimes the lessons come from the most unexpected places and not always from something that we ourselves have said or done.

Remembering that there are no mistakes in this life, only lessons, and the bigger the 'mistake' you think you've made or someone else has made towards you, the bigger the lesson there is to be learned. The nice thing is, if we learn from these 'mistakes' or events, then we will never have to repeat them; the lesson will be learned. When we experience an event in our life that causes us immediate hurt and makes us feel small, lonely and left out, we aren't going to forget it in a hurry. After this incident happened to me I realised, after I stopped crying and had time to think about it, what an important event had just occurred. In all honesty, I don't remember thinking the words, 'This is a lesson,' at the time it happened but, because it had left me so upset, I can clearly remember thinking I must never do this to anyone. I told myself I must never forget in the years to come because I must never hurt another soul in the same way as I had just been hurt.   And may God forgive me if I ever have.

When David and I were first married we were fortunate enough to be able to buy our own home with a five hundred pound deposit, our wedding present from David's parents. Because I had been married before, I was still waiting for my money from the previous house I had owned with my first husband. How things have changed! We bought a small new two-bedroomed semi-detached house on a new housing estate. We were both a bit unsure if we would take to our new home, as we would have preferred to have bought an older house with lots of character. Unfortunately, our budget wouldn't stretch that far. Mortgages were hard to come by in 1974 so we were very grateful to have our own roof over our heads. Also neither of us was sure if we would take to living on a new estate. Well, we would soon find out.

Within a very short space of time of moving in we both knew we would not be staying very long. I'm sure you will know what I mean when I say if you didn't put up new curtains and talk about your new washing machine you were thought odd. So I guess we were the odd couple. We had turned two bedspreads that had belonged to my mother into curtains and hung them at the lounge/dining room windows. We had no curtains or carpets in the bedrooms and the carpet on the floor downstairs came to us because someone was discarding it. The settee we had in our little lounge was a spare one from my father's office. We had very little money when we were first married to buy new things so we made use of whatever we were given. We managed to get a new cooker on interest-free payments over two years. Otherwise I would have had nothing to cook on.

Over the first few months after we were married, while I was still working, we were able to save and buy bedroom carpets, curtains and a washing machine and fridge but we did without until we had saved the money. But those bedspreads were still at the lounge windows on the day we moved out and the old carpet was still on the floor.

We moved into our new little home on our wedding day. There was no honeymoon for us; we couldn't afford one. We had one little single bed between us. My husband slept in his sleeping bag on the floor next to me and I slept in my single bed from home. (My husband was much too big to get into the bed on his own, let alone beside me.) That was until our new king-size bed arrived courtesy of my parents as a wedding present. They had already paid for one wedding for me four years earlier so our wedding was a quiet family celebration with a few friends but we were happy and that's all that mattered.

When Marie was born she had her own little bedroom but when Alexander arrived he slept in his pram at the bottom of the stairs (he loved that pram). That was his bedroom. We had been constantly on the lookout for somewhere else to live before Alexander was born but we kept being gazumped, mainly because the housing market in 1976 was very buoyant. We were looking for a home a bit bigger and not on a new housing estate because we just didn't fit in.

There was no way we were interested in, I think the term was and probably still is, keeping up with the Jones's. Even though I was struggling to cope on a daily basis, with no help from anyone, I would try to take the two little ones out for a walk every day. Alexander would be in his pram with Marie sitting in her pram-seat on the top. Two babies under two years is hard work for any young mother but, of course, I had all my symptoms to cope with even though I had no idea what was wrong with me. As soon as Alexander was born I would have a sleep for an hour when he and Marie had their nap time. This was sometimes late morning or after lunch.

I can remember I used to put a note on the outside of the front door. It read, 'Please do not knock. We are all asleep.'

That way no one disturbed us. I think all my neighbours around me thought I was crazy. No one realised just how tired and exhausted I was. No one understood the waves of tiredness that would come over me. I just had to hang on and try and keep on my feet until the children had a sleep. But, somehow, on most days I managed to force myself to go for a walk with the children, weather permitting.

I had made a few friends, not real friends but other young mums like me. The housing estate was full of young couples with babies and young children. In the house attached to us were a couple about our age and their children were also the same age as ours. Most afternoons some of the young mums on our street, and sometimes from other parts of the estate, would gather together in each other's houses to keep each other company. All the children would play or sleep, while the young mothers would spend time talking over cups of tea and coffee.

This particular late summer afternoon, when Alexander was about ten weeks old, I had gone for a walk with the children to the local shops and on the way back home I decided we would see which house all the mums were in and join them for a chat and a cuppa. It was always easy to find where everyone was because of all the prams or pushchairs parked on the path outside and, on this particular day, all the prams were outside my next door neighbour's door. I parked the pram and walked the few steps to the front door and knocked.

"You can't come in. There's no room for you. Sorry."

Those were the words that greeted me when my neighbour opened her front door. She didn't say hello. She didn't say, "I'm so sorry."

"You can't come in," she said for the second time. "There's no room."

As I looked past her into her lounge I could see three of the other mums sitting on the floor talking and they were all looking at me. I had the feeling that this rather brutal little speech had been planned before I had rung the doorbell. My neighbour then shut the door in my face. I was crying as I turned and pushed the pram from her path to ours and made for our front door. If she had just been kind in her approach to me that day, or said she was sorry as if she had meant it, the whole episode may not have left its mark on me. But then, of course, I wouldn't have learned such a valuable lesson. Somehow I managed to get my two little ones into our home as I was crying. Marie could not understand what was wrong with her mummy so I did my best to reassure her that I was alright. The words that kept running through my mind that day were, 'No room at the inn' and they are still the correct words to paint the picture of that late summer afternoon.

Thankfully we found a new home after months of searching, quite by 'accident'. Our house sold very quickly and we moved within a matter of weeks. For those few weeks I kept myself and the children at a distance from our neighbours because I couldn't go through that hurt again. Now I'm sure you can see why it's so important for me to always welcome people into our home. I never want anyone to feel left out, the way I had been all those years ago. The valuable lesson I learned that day has never been forgotten. No matter how tired or stressed I have been over the years, I've never to my knowledge turned anyone away. From our children's friends to our family and friends and anyone else that comes to our door, a warm welcome always waits.

That's why I was so concerned about the rented house we were going to because I didn't know how I was going to prepare food and manage with the tiny space that was to be my kitchen. It hadn't dawned on me that, actually, it didn't matter.

My solicitor rang the second week in January to say my business buyer had been in touch with her. She told me he was in the process of organising his finances to allow him to purchase my practice and he was fairly confident that he would have everything in place by the end of February. My mind at the time was so full of trying to organise our move that I was very grateful that I didn't have to cope with my business sale all at the same time. I just prayed that it would go ahead.

The week before we were going to move out of our

home it started to snow, and it kept on coming. As moving day crept closer I was more confused than ever, remembering, always at the back of my mind, the fact that my business sale should be finalised within a few weeks. If this had happened six months earlier we might have been able to buy Ravenswood House.

What a muddle my mind was in.

CHAPTER TWENTY-FOUR

At my best, I was trying to keep the family working together because I knew how important it was for us all to be 'singing from the same song sheet'. It wasn't just me that was feeling lost and confused. My precious family were all confused as well by all the things that had happened.

Moving day came. It was very cold outside, with about a foot of snow on the ground. Not the most ideal weather to be moving house. We had all spent the previous two weeks frantically packing boxes. Thinking back, we were well organised.

Most things were packed, not to be opened until we found a home of our own to move into, whenever that would be. All the surplus china, linen, ornaments, everything that we could manage to do without, was boxed up for us to store. Every box had a list taped to the top so we all knew what each box contained. The children packed their own bedrooms with a bit of help from David and me when asked for. I made sure that I had just the bare essentials that I would need for the kitchen, and even then I wasn't sure if everything would fit into the small space.

The rented house had a lounge, dining room, breakfast room and that scullery. It was decided that we would use the dining room to store most of the boxes we would not be opening. The fridge and freezer would also go into this room but we needed to make sure that when the removal men put things into the house, we could easily access them. Having to climb over a box to reach a pint of milk would not be good.

We decided that David and the children would go to the rented house on the day of the move, along with our pets. They would all stay there and make sure everything was put into the correct rooms. There was a spare bedroom so the cats could be kept confined with their food, beds and litter tray. That way they wouldn't get under anyone's feet and they would be safe. The dog would be happy anywhere as long as the children were around. Once everything was transferred, David would come back for me.

I, in the meantime, would stay in our home and, as each room was emptied, I could vacuum, dust, wash all the kitchen cupboards and floor so that I left our home lovely and clean for the new owners. It was very important to me to leave the house beautifully clean because when we left our first home years earlier, I was so unwell I remember leaving that home in a mess and I never wanted to do that again. It wasn't fair on the new owners.

Have I mentioned before that our daughter once said to me, "Mum, are you sure you weren't adopted?" I'm just mentioning this because of what happened next. It's a very good example of why my daughter doubted my connection to the rest of my family and even I can see why. As I was washing the entrance porch floor, the front door bell rang. I knew it wasn't David coming back for me yet, so who the heck was it? I really didn't want to see anyone. I had been crying as I was cleaning and I was in no fit state for any visitors. When I opened the door, I couldn't believe it. There was my sister on the doorstep, with her car parked just outside our front door with my mother and my sister's two children inside.

"We just thought we would call and see if you'd moved out yet."

"No Claire, I'm still busy cleaning. All the furniture is gone. I have a kettle and a little milk but only one cup so I'm sorry but I can't even make you and Mum a cup of tea."

"Oh well, we just thought we would call. We are on our way to pick up Ian (my brother-in-law) from the station and then we are going to your new house so we'll see you when you get there!" With that she and the family drove off.

I was flabbergasted.

If she had called to offer me some help, that would have been good. If she had come to give me some emotional support, that would have been even better. After all, the whole of our extended family knew exactly why we were moving out and they all knew that we were very upset about it. I kept on cleaning but my mind was going over what had just happened. What I couldn't understand was why my family should have come to see us today of all days. Let's face it, if a friend of yours or your family were moving house you might ask if they needed some help with the move, or you might volunteer to make them some food, or help in any way that was needed but you wouldn't just land on their doorstep in the middle of them moving out!

By the time I'd finished cleaning, the house was spotless. Even though our home was now empty it still looked nice. The couple who had bought our home had also bought all the carpets and curtains, so the house still looked cosy.

There was one more very important thing for me to do before I left for the last time and, as I was on my own, I could do it in peace and quiet. I went into our lounge and sat down on the low windowsill that overlooked the garden, the exact spot that I had sat years earlier, when I had asked the lady that owned the house before us to help us buy it.

Do you remember? She was still in the house in spirit. I had made her a promise that I would love and take care of her house and I would love and care for the garden if we were able to buy her home and over the past few years I had kept my promise. It was now time for me to say thank you to that lady and to God for the years of happiness we had had. I also asked the spirit world to hold all the love that was in the house for the family that were going to move in. It wasn't their fault that we had lost our home.

I was 'in bits' to say the least when I had finished, just as my husband came through the door to pick me up and make sure everything was locked up. The new owners were taking possession the following week. Even David was feeling the sadness. We both made sure everything was as it should be, checking everything was switched off and secure and then we left.

It only took five minutes to drive to our new, temporary home but the drive was a tearful one. David said my mother and all my sister's family were in our house making something to eat. I was so hungry I could have eaten a horse. I'd only had a small snack all day and it was now 6.30pm.

When I walked into our new home it felt warm (I think I was surprised) then I walked into the lounge. David had put the fire on and it was positively tropical. Our old cat, Green (don't ask) was curled up asleep on the rug in front of the fire. At least she had made herself at home. I went through into the breakfast room to find my mother, my niece and nephew sitting at our dining table which was all set out for a meal waiting to be served. Then my sister appeared from our small kitchen with plates of food in her hand.

"That looks nice, Claire. Is there some for us?"

"No, I didn't bring anything for you. You should have thought of something for yourself. I've only got food for us!"

You could have blown me over with a feather. I didn't say a word. I turned and left the room. My room, my table, all set for a meal but not a meal for my family. Dumbfounded, I burst into tears. What the heck was going on?

I went back into the lounge to be beside David who I now realised was staying out of the way, as were our children. It turned out they had gone upstairs to their own rooms with our dog. I was very upset. I was so tired and hungry and an emotional wreck. I couldn't think straight. All my family had been working hard since eight o'clock that morning moving house. All we wanted to do now was to have something to eat, put our feet up and relax in our new space. The last thing we all needed was my mother, my sister and her family taking over our home and leaving us out.

Within a few minutes my brother-in-law (who I hadn't even realised was in our home) came into the lounge and said, "I'm so sorry, Isabella. I don't know what Claire was thinking of. Why don't I go and get you all a takeout?" Thank goodness someone was thinking straight. David said he would go with Ian after he asked our children what they would like to eat. So bless them, they did. I didn't go back into our breakfast room because I didn't want any confrontation and I didn't want to get any more upset on the first night in our new home. I was far too exhausted to find any words to say, let alone the right words.

To be perfectly honest I don't think I ever figured out what lesson I was supposed to learn from this experience. There had been numerous occasions over the years when my sister and my mother did things that seemed very strange to me. I love them both but I don't think I will ever understand them.

Do I accept people for what they are? I think I do. I guess I always try and treat people the way I would like to be treated, but not everyone does this. The incident was passed over and forgotten. I almost want to say, 'under the table and under the carpet' just as it was in our home for years as we as sisters were growing up. So even I can understand why our daughter said to me years ago now, "Mum, are you sure you weren't adopted?"

The hot take-out meal came, by which time our dining room table had been cleared and there was room for us to sit down and eat. Food at last! I thanked Ian for going with David for our meal. Ian then gathered together his family and my mother and left.

We were now in our new home, on our own, as it should have been as a family, with a hot meal and a bottle of wine. Peace at last. Well, we were in. I knew it was going to be difficult for us as there was no outside space, no garden for us and all the animals to go out into and nowhere for the children to play. We were warm and we had a roof over our heads.

But the most important thing of all, we were all together.

CHAPTER TWENTY-FIVE

When I opened my eyes on the first morning in our new home all I wanted to do was cry. Two of the bedroom walls that I was lying looking at were covered in drawings and paintings and they weren't very nice. I lay there in bed thinking the last occupier of the bedroom must have been an art student. Some of the drawing had been drawn in charcoal and others were painted in psychedelic colours. Not exactly the decoration you would normally expect to find in a bedroom and definitely nothing like the tranquil bedroom my husband and I were used to sleeping in. But then I turned around in bed.

When we had first looked over the house a few weeks earlier the door into this bedroom had been wide open and, as it opened into the room, the wall behind the door had been obscured. I hadn't noticed the coloured drawing on this wall. Actually, I hadn't really noticed any of the other drawings either but this morning I did notice and I couldn't believe my sleepy eyes. A lotus flower about four feet tall, painted in pretty pastel shades. The main stem of the lotus flower was just beginning to open but the top few leaves were fully opened to the rays of the sun streaming down from the sun that was painted on the wall above the flower. All this was perhaps a bit strange to say the least. But what was way beyond extraordinary were the words that were written on the wall directly below the flower.

I can't quite remember all the words used, and I could kick myself for not taking a photo of the whole wall, but as best as I can remember this is what the words said:

Just like the flower
Your life is unfolding ahead of you in a beautiful way
Just as it should.
You are exactly where you're meant to be
At this point in time in your life.

The twilight zone again. There was another line but I

can't quite remember what it said, something about the right space and time. I was blown away. It 'felt' as if the painting and the words on the bedroom wall were there for me and the rest of my family, for exactly now. They were so apt. Looking back, I'm so cross with myself for not writing the words down at the time or getting our son (who was and is the photographer in our family) to take a picture. My only excuse to myself is that I was not thinking straight and I was exhausted.

Yet again I had been given a most unusual sign and words to help and comfort me, and they did. I would like to send a big thank you to the person or persons who painted and wrote on that wall some twenty odd years ago now. May the Universal energy pick up my message and bless you.

That first morning I realised how hard my family had worked the day before, when I had been left to clean our home. They had all managed to put most things away in the correct place. They had made up all the beds for the first night, (I had been so tired, I hadn't even noticed that my bed was made when I fell into it), the lounge was completely clear of boxes, all our clothes had been put into our wardrobes; they really had done well. All I needed to do was to try and sort the kitchen things out. We had the weekend to organise ourselves and get used to where we were.

The animals took it all in their stride. We kept the cats inside for the first week but the dog was able to go out for her walks twice a day and it didn't take her long to get to know her new route. Our children had a longer journey to get to their schools. It was a bit too far for them to walk and an awkward bus journey so most mornings their father would give them a lift or I would if I was up in time. (Remember I don't do mornings very well)

I, on the other hand, was closer to my office, actually within walking distance, but it was still winter, snow and ice on the ground, therefore much safer to use the car. The strain of not being able to say a word to my staff about the sale of the business, and having to act as if nothing was happening, was definitely putting extra pressure on me. But it did make sense to keep quiet. If the sale had fallen through it would have caused me major problems, so 'Mum' was definitely the word.

My solicitor rang me the week after we moved to tell me there was to be a meeting the following week to finalise the business transfer and all the paperwork that this would entail. She also said that we were to agree a handover date, so would I please think about this and how and when I wanted to tell my staff.

My life was about to change dramatically. Had I made the right decision? Every fibre of my being said I had.

The day of the meeting came and I realised that this day was going to be the turning point for the rest of my life. Things would never be the same again. I was excited and nervous all at the same time. I arrived at the appointed time, just as the gentleman who was buying my practice also arrived. It turned out he was more excited than me. This was to be the start of him expanding his practice, but for me it meant retirement. He wanted the buy-out to happen on the 1st of May 1991. As this was only about nine weeks away, I agreed. He suggested that I did not tell my staff until two weeks before the takeover. His reasoning was sound. He was going to take some of my staff into his practice, but not all. He didn't need my receptionist, obviously because he already had his own, and my part-time staff would not be needed. It would mean I only had two weeks of my staff being upset or annoyed. It also meant I didn't have to cope with any irate clients for more than two weeks. I would be pleased when this was all over.

The best part for me was when I was told the exact amount I was going to receive. The amount was almost the same as the amount that we had lost on the failed business the previous year. In actual fact, I was going to receive just a little bit more. You can never get back what you have lost, but the sale would give me the means to be able to help us find another home and that was a great comfort. 'Great oaks from little acorns grow,' a business colleague once said to me many years earlier. My little business had grown and I was about to reap the rewards of fifteen years hard work. As I left my solicitor's office my mind was in a spin. If only. If only we had had this money last year.

I'm sure most of you will know the saying, 'If ifs and ands were pots and pans, there'd be no need...' and you know the rest. It was no use me going backwards with my thoughts. This was to be a huge lesson in looking forward and learning to go with the flow of life. In fact, if I'd known then just how many lessons were about to be shown to me in quick succession, I would not have been feeling quite so comforted.

The next few weeks passed by relatively peacefully. It gave me the time I needed to think about and then compose a letter to send to all of my clients, explaining to them why I had decided to sell my practice and retire. I wanted to make sure I had everything in place for D day.

I could tell my staff and then, on the same day, post out all the letters. My letter was going to be followed by a letter from the new accountant introducing himself and his practice.

Before I knew it D day had arrived.

All the family wished me well before I left the house that morning and tried to reassure me that I would manage to get through the day. I wasn't so sure. Two of my employees would still have their jobs if they wanted them. They would transfer with the business but my part-time staff and the two full-timers that had not long been employed by me were going to lose their jobs and that was a hard one. I had always tried my best to take care of everyone that had worked for me over the years and I knew they would be upset and so would I.

When I arrived I went straight into my office and made myself a cup of tea to try and calm myself down. I opened my brief case and there lying on the top of my papers was a handwritten, folded note. It was a note from my daughter. I still treasure it and keep it in my box of precious things. This is what it said:

Mum
Good luck today – don't panic too much
I'm thinking about you
Lots of love

Marie

PS. I love you

This of course brought a few tears to my eyes but it also made me smile. I've never forgotten her thoughtfulness. That little note meant the world to me. I needed to take a few more minutes to compose myself before I gathered all my staff together.

A silent prayer was needed. I asked God to please give me the right words and the composure I would need to see me through the meeting and the rest of the day.

My staff obviously all realised something was up, because in all the years I had been in business I had never before asked them all into my office together. Once they were all seated around my desk I said, "I've got something to tell you all," but before I could say another word the young woman who I had promoted after Doris retired said, "You have called us in to tell us you've gone bust haven't you, and we are all out of work?" I looked at her in amazement. She had assumed because the other business had gone into voluntary liquidation, then my business must be broke too!

"No, I haven't. I've called you all in to tell you I've sold my practice."

There was stunned silence.

After I explained why and how the takeover was going to proceed, the same young lady asked if I felt she had enough experience to set up in business on her own.

"Well actually, no I don't. The very fact you thought I had gone bust should be telling you that you don't understand enough at the moment. Give yourself more time, learn more and get a better understanding of how a business works."

I won't go into the tears and upset but it did all get sorted out.

After the initial meeting, I spoke to each of them individually and listened to their concerns and I tried to answer each of their questions. I also told the staff who had worked for me for more than two years that I was going to give them each a bonus for their loyalty and years worked. There was just one thing more. I asked them each not to say anything to my clients for the next twenty-four hours, until my letter had time to reach them all and be read.

Three days before all the office equipment and furniture were to be moved to the new practice, our home telephone rang. I was just about to walk out of our front door to go to my office. My husband was the nearest to the phone so he answered it. It was my office to tell me we had been broken into the previous night and a lot of things were missing. When my husband told me what had happened I burst into tears. The past few days had been very emotional and I just couldn't take any more upset. He said he would go to my office for me and sort everything out. He would ring the police and handle whatever needed seeing to. He told me to come to the office when I felt I could cope.

Why was this happening to me? This was the last thing I needed.

It took me about two hours before I could bring myself to go. All the office equipment had been stolen. The equipment that the new practice had bought from me was all gone. The telephone from my desk was missing, but not the staff's phones. My tea cup and coffee cup were taken, but not my staff's. My tea bags were missing, but not the jar of coffee. As I was the only one that drank tea and my staff all drank coffee, this all seemed very strange.

As the hours passed by that afternoon, it became obvious to me that this break-in had been a personal attack against me. When I told my husband what I thought, he said, "You can't be sure." He was right, of course. I couldn't be sure but I had a very strong feeling.

Fortunately, I was well insured and I had all the necessary paperwork to show proof of purchase for everything that had been stolen. It did all get sorted quite quickly. The insurance company sent a representative within an hour of my ringing them.

I had to ring the accountant to tell him what had happened. He was very supportive towards me. I was able to

196

reassure him that as soon as the insurance money came through for the items he had bought, I would give him the money. He was very happy with that because I was insured on the basis of 'new for old.' But why had this happened?

When things go wrong we can't always see the reason at the time. But this one didn't take long for me to work out. Three days later, as all the furniture was being moved out of my offices, the (borrowed) fax machine received a message. It was from a client that I had wanted to drop from my client list for a long time but because I knew I would be selling my practice, the more clients on the list the more saleable my business would be.

I should have followed my instincts long ago and parted company from him, but I hadn't. Here it was again, the lesson of following your own instincts. Follow it and you will never have any problems; go against it and trouble will ensue.

The message on the fax machine was very curt. He was demanding that I pay him back money that he had paid my business for work that my staff and I had prepared about three weeks earlier. I was dumbfounded, but I knew why. The message said if I didn't pay him back within twenty-four hours, he was going to sue me. I remember thinking I was not going to let him bully me the way he had bullied other people over the years, even though I was tired. I knew I had done nothing wrong and if he tried to sue me for the return of his money he would lose. He was hell-bent on making my life a misery and I wasn't going to let him.

One of my staff asked me what I was going to do about the fax. I said to her, "Absolutely nothing; I will sort this out another day." My instincts were telling me that she knew this fax was coming in but I could have been wrong.

The move happened, the staff left and I was left to sit and wonder. As I sat at my desk surrounded by silence the only thing going through my mind was the knowing that a mountain had been lifted from my shoulders.

CHAPTER TWENTY-SIX

I could write a whole book on the antics of this 'bully'. He had told me on numerous occasions over the previous eighteen months that if the people he was dealing with did not comply with his wishes he would, in his words, 'have them sorted'.

Over the previous pages I have tried very hard to make sure everything has been in the correct chronological order, or I have given you an example of an incident that would help clarify a situation. But just this once, I am going to relate the whole tale of this event in one go. The reason for this is that the case, through no fault of mine, dragged on over a two year period, as daft as that sounds. By telling the tale now, I will not have to keep interrupting the rest of my story.

Within a few days of me receiving the fax message, he apparently called in at our local police station and demanded they arrest me because I hadn't paid him his money back. The police rang me at home and told me what he'd done and then asked me if this man was right in the head! The lady police officer said to me she had told him in no uncertain terms that they would not be arresting me.

The reason he was being vindictive towards me was because my business had produced draft year-end accounts for him and, when he found out how high his taxable profit was, he told me in front of two members of my staff that he would 'get' some more purchase invoices, dated before his year-end, to reduce his profit figure. I explained to him that unless they were genuine we would not be changing his accounts.

He had called back a couple of days later with a handful of invoices from one company, totalling over forty thousand pounds, and told my staff that his friend had 'done them for him'! Had he bullied someone else? We can never be sure.

Unknown to me at the time, my senior staff member had redone his trial balance and draft accounts for him to show the much lower profit figure, on the day he had brought in the false invoices. Late that afternoon she came to me with his accounts for me to check over. When I looked at them I realised that she had handed me a redrafted set. She told me that he had demanded that she did this, and the new figures that she had prepared were the ones he wanted sending to the Inland Revenue as his year-end accounts. I told her there was no way I was sending in accounts that I knew to be fraudulent and that was that. I also explained to her that she should have asked me first if she should redo the accounts. Who was the boss here?

She had thrown the first set of figures (the correct ones) into her waste paper bin. I retrieved them after she left the office to go home that night. This all happened about three weeks before the takeover. He was invoiced for the time spent from my staff's time sheet, his job sheet and he had paid the bill. The stupid thing was he was trying to falsify his accounts to the Inland Revenue. If he took me to court I had all the paperwork to be able to show exactly what had transpired, including copies of the false invoices (silly man).

I instructed my solicitor to act for me. She wasn't going to go to court with me, but she would make sure the paperwork for the case was submitted to the correct court office at the relevant time. It took me hours to prepare the file with copies of absolutely everything that had transpired. As I still had my office for the next three months, because the rent and rates had been paid in advance, I was able to go into my office most days on my own and sort through all the old paperwork and files, most of which I was able to destroy. But a good clearing out does us all good and I had heaps to clear. I also still had my own desk and chair to work at because they had not been sold along with everything else. They meant far too much to me because I had bought them from my father's business years earlier.

Six weeks after the sale of my business the accountant who bought my practice asked for a meeting with me to discuss a very serious matter. I hadn't a clue as to what this could be about, so I asked my husband to come to the meeting with me for support. When we were seated in his office he pulled out a tape recorder from his drawer to record our conversation. He started talking to me but I was making no sense of anything he was saying. His conversation was really strange, almost cloak and dagger. He appeared to be accusing me of going behind his back about something. I just sat there looking stupid.

"You mean you don't know?"

"I haven't a clue what you're talking about. Please tell me what this is all about."

"You mean you don't know that Sally has set up in business on her own and taken some of your old clients with her. I thought you were backing her."

"I can assure you I'm not. I had no idea."

Then I explained to him about the conversation I had had with her on the day I told all the staff that I was retiring, and how I had told her she didn't have enough experience or understanding of the world of finance to be able to go it alone, that she needed a lot more experience before contemplating trying to run her own business. I also said to him that this explained quite a few things for me.

"During the last two weeks of my business there had been quite a few clients' work scheduled into the diaries to be done, but the work never appeared. She has not only taken revenue away from you, she has also taken some away from me."

I had given my full-time staff bonuses for their loyal service and she had received the largest amount. So much for loyalty. The new accountant now knew where she had got the money from to set up her new office - me (but not intentionally). This also explained how she knew the nasty fax would be coming into my office on the very last day, because she herself had taken the bully on as a client before I had closed my doors. She must have known he was going to send it. I had had a feeling on that last day that she knew more than she was saying, but of course I wasn't sure then, but I was now. She had gone behind my back. Good luck to her. She would need it. I'm sure she must have been laughing at me behind my back in those final few days. There was nothing that I wanted to do about the situation. It was past and gone. I wanted to leave the past behind. There was nothing I needed to do. I would let the Universal laws of Karma sort that one out. Obviously I could not be held responsible for the act of another person so our meeting came to an end. The accountant apologised to me for thinking I was involved and we said goodbye.

During the next few months I was given various dates to appear in court. The court cancelled two dates and I appeared twice but the two times I did appear the bully didn't turn up. The third time I appeared at court, about a year after I retired, he did turn up. He arrived with his father. As I was standing outside of the judge's chamber both he and his father verbally threatened me. The lady court assistant then appeared and asked me if I wanted the other gentleman (being his father) in the room with us. I said, "No," in a very quiet voice. She disappeared into the judge's chamber and when she came out she told my ex-client that his father would not be allowed into the chambers with us. He became very angry with the court assistant, but she stood her ground and demanded that his father leave immediately. I was shaking like a leaf when I went into the judge's room. This man looked like a thug and acted like a thug and yes, they had frightened me. The energy around both him and his father was very angry. Both their auras were very unpleasant to say the least. They would have stood out in any crowd and been avoided like the plague, without anyone really understanding why.

When I sat down opposite this man the Judge turned to me and said, "I don't want you to say a word." He then turned to him and said, "If I find out anyone has been threatened in any way with regards to this case there will be very serious consequences indeed." My ex-client then demanded that his father be allowed into the room. The Judge asked him if his father was involved in any way with the case and he answered, "No."

"Then no, he cannot come in, but you can have a solicitor with you if you so wish."

He said he did, so the case was adjourned yet again.

He may have frightened me in the court house, he had

actually frightened me once before in my own office, but I knew that under no circumstances was I to send bad thoughts to him. Somehow I had to send him good thoughts. "Why?" you will say. Because I knew how powerful a thought can be and I understood the laws of Karma.

For years I had been taught by my father that we reap what we sow in this life. Nansi helped me to remember and understand that we reap what we sow over many lifetimes. My father's words had come from his treasured Bible. Nansi's words were from an Eastern philosophy, the law of Karma. Doris Stokes, in one of her many books, wrote that her father had once said to her, "Cast your bread upon the water, Doris, and it will come back buttered." I liked that one. My father was convinced that the walls of Jericho had 'come tumbling down', not through the power of sound (a trumpet), but by the power of thought and we had discussed this on numerous times during our talks together.

Nansi had always told me, if I ever found myself having any nasty negative thoughts I must turn my mind immediately. Find something nice to look at, something nice to think about, anything, but turn my mind away from all things negative and never, under any circumstances, think bad thoughts towards anyone as I could cause them great harm. I've never forgotten that. Let's be honest, if I hurt someone on purpose what in Heaven's name would come back to me? Thought is one of the most powerful tools in the Universe that we can use and I knew it. There was no way I wanted any bad thoughts coming back to me that I had sent out. I'm sure this is what all of the wonderful Masters down through the centuries have tried to teach us, from Jesus to Buddha and many more. Love thine enemy. This I know is a very hard thing to do, and in some cases almost impossible, but that's where my thoughts were with this event. Trust me, it wasn't easy and most of my friends were telling me not to be so daft. They would have crucified him given half the chance.

This was a huge lesson for me. Turn the other cheek, pour cold water on a fire, blow the wind out of someone's sails.

All of these sayings, when you think about it, are saying the same thing. Don't retaliate with anger; it will only make a situation worse and the energy and thoughts you put out will, without fail, come back at you. All of my friends at the time, without exception, were telling me to retaliate and I was insistent that I was not going to. I had to keep doing and following what I knew in my heart to be right. It was a wonderful opportunity for me to try and teach or pass on the knowing that I had to my friends around me at the time. But I'm not sure if any of them took any notice.

Think about it. If you think nasty thoughts towards someone, if you are angry with someone even in a small way, those thoughts of yours will come back at you. The wonderful thing about all of this is, there's actually nothing that we need to do because the laws of the Universe, the laws of Karma come into play.

The Bible says, "Vengeance is mine saith the Lord."

The most perfect law in the Universe.

The law of Karma.

I'd never had anyone be so mean or vindictive towards me before, but I knew with every fibre of my being I must stay calm and clear and send him good thoughts. Thoughts of forgiveness, thoughts of love, for nearly two years, because I understood the Universal law of Karma. Yes I struggled, who wouldn't, but I kept true to myself.

The fourth court date came around, but this time I asked a solicitor who I knew to come with me, for my own physical protection. Not to help me with my case in any way, just to be there at my side to give me a sense of physical safety. I trusted that God would keep me safe in all other ways. I just felt that if I had a man at my side my ex-client would not get the chance to threaten me. I also knew my solicitor would be allowed into the Judge's chambers with me and I would be perfectly safe. As my solicitor and I were sitting talking in the reception area of the court chambers on the day of the hearing, if anyone had overheard our conversation they would have wondered what on earth we were talking about. Our conversation would have sounded quite funny and bizarre.

My solicitor kept saying to me, "What does this guy look like?" and I kept saying to him, "Trust me, you will know him when he arrives." I knew that my solicitor would 'feel' the bully's energy without even realising. As people kept arriving he kept saying to me, "Is that him?" numerous times. I kept replying, "When he arrives you won't have to ask me; you will just know."

Sure enough, when the bully came in with his father and his wife my solicitor said, "My God, that's him."

"Told you."

As we were called through from the waiting area to go into the chambers I could tell by the look on the face of the bully he was furious that before we started. Furious because I had someone with me but, of course, he didn't know who it was. When we reached the chambers, once again he tried to take his father in but the court assistant stopped him.

"In that case she (being me) can't have her friend with her." The court assistant turned to him and said, "Yes she can. She has brought her solicitor." At that he went purple in the face.

When we were seated before the Judge, the Judge again turned to me and said, "Don't say a word." (Very strange) And yet again the bully demanded his father be allowed into the room and yet again the judge told him no. It was the same Judge as the last time (thank you, Lord).

The judge then said, "I told you at our last meeting, the only people allowed into my chambers are the two people involved in this case and your solicitors. I clearly told you last time you could have your solicitor present with you if you so wished."

Then the bully started. "Did you know she had her office broken into on purpose to claim the insurance money? Did you know that? She will be able to get one over on me because her solicitor can speak better than me."

The judge completely ignored his last remarks and then explained to him that my solicitor was only with me for support; he would not be giving any evidence. He then turned to my solicitor and said, "That would be right?"

"Yes, your honour. I will not be giving any help in this matter. Mrs. Clarence will be presenting her own case. I'm only here to support her."

The bully continued, "I'm not having this."

The Judge remained very calm. "Then what would you like to do, Mr. Black?"

"I'm getting a solicitor."

The Judge replied, "Then, in that case, we will adjourn until you do."

I was speechless.

My instincts had told me on the day my office was broken into that the bully was the one responsible and now I knew I had been right. I just knew.

As my solicitor and I walked away from the court house I thanked him for his support. Obviously I would be getting his bill in due course but it would be worth every penny because I had felt safe.

Months passed by and then years and I never heard another thing. The Universe had taken a hand. I had not been allowed to speak. Not one word in all the times I had been in the Judge's chambers. I had been protected in more ways than one.

The bully? I left him to the wonderful law.

The Universal law of Karma.

CHAPTER TWENTY-SEVEN

Now let's go back to the first few weeks after we moved house and just days after the sale of my business had been completed at the beginning of May 1991.

David went food shopping to the local shops not more than two miles away. When he came back into the house he had a very strange and puzzled look on his face. He said to me, "After I got the shopping, I thought I would look in some estate agents' windows to see what was for sale, in the hope of perhaps finding us a nice house and you're not going to believe what I have just seen. Ravenswood House is back on the market."

"You're joking."

"No I'm not."

"Which estate agent? How much? I don't believe this."

He explained the house was for sale through a different estate agent than the first time and the rest of the story is a bit of a blur to me because I was so excited. The excitement spilled right through the house, as our children began to hear what had transpired. This was beyond belief. Even our children were amazed. We would need to find out as quickly as possible what the position was, how long it had been on the market and if they had any offers.

Dear Lord, what was going on?

The following day I went to the estate agent's office as soon as I could. I can remember explaining to the assistant how we had tried to buy Ravenswood House when it had been on the market the previous year. She then explained to me what had been happening in the intervening nine months. The purchasers of the house last year were property developers. They had wanted to convert the house into two separate units, to enable them to make money from selling the two. Planning permission had been refused by our local council so they had appealed against the decision to a London office which had taken a few months to process, but they lost the appeal. The house was not to be divided.

Consequently, the buyers were now trying to sell the property as it was of no further use to them. She explained that it had been back on the market for the previous two months and there were two other interested parties. They were selling the property for 'offers over', no actual fixed price. Would we like to go and look around the property again? She didn't need to ask twice.

May my father forgive me if I had even the slightest doubt that his words to me one year ago could ever have been wrong.

"The house with the light over it will be your next home, the home that's meant for you."

Within days we were all looking around what we now realised could be our home. As we walked around the house we could see that it had deteriorated substantially since we had last paid it a visit. The dry rot had spread and so had the damp. But if we could get it for the right price, it would make us a lovely home, after it was gutted and updated.

The 'offer over' price was a bit high. We were going to have to go in with a lower offer and pray that it would be acceptable. One thing I had not quite taken in at the time of the sale of my business was that I was to be paid in instalments. The first payment was on the day of the handover, the next in July and the final balance would be paid in September. Apparently this was quite normal practice. I have mentioned this because if we were going to purchase a house quite soon, I would not have all the money due to me. But at least I knew what I would be getting and, of course, we knew how much we had left from the sale of our home. When David and I sat and worked out our finances we realised we could just about make a cash offer for the house. This would help put us in a very strong position. We had no house to sell and could proceed immediately.

Our offer was submitted.

Just to put our minds at rest and to make sure we would

be able to offer cash for the house, I arranged an appointment with my bank manager. I'd been dealing with him for quite a few years and he knew me well, so I was hopeful he would be able to help us. To my surprise he told me he was also my business purchaser's bank manager. He knew that I would be receiving the outstanding balance on the sale of my business in two more instalments and, because he would be the one releasing the funds for my purchaser, he said that if I needed a short-term loan to be able to make our offer on Ravenswood a cash offer he would have no problem lending me the money.

We would now have to play the waiting game.

This was almost unbelievable. The home that my father had said was meant for us, the home all of us as a family liked and had wanted nearly a year earlier when we were in absolutely no position to be able to proceed, was now available again. Only this time we were in exactly the right position. In fact, it couldn't have been better.

But now we would have to trust that the Universe would take a hand once again because we were told there were two other families interested. We would have to wait and pray. Unfortunately, the old lady who had lived in Ravenswood House all on her own had long gone, so I could not ask her to help us the way I had done with our last home. If I had known then what I know now I would have sat down in the house she had lived in for years and asked her for her help, but I didn't realise at the time that I could do that. But I could ask God for help and I did.

It was now the last week in May. The estate agent rang us on a Monday morning to ask us to put our best and final offer in writing by Thursday, when all the offers would be put to the owners. They would make their decision as to which offer they were going to accept and everyone would be informed by Friday lunchtime.

It's such a long time ago now, but I'm fairly sure we put our offer up by five thousand pounds. This would have taken our offer up to the same amount that we had offered the previous year. Our offer was hand-delivered on Wednesday morning. We would now have to wait until Friday. On the Thursday afternoon when we were all at home, sitting in the breakfast room having a cup of tea, I was talking and said words to the effect, "What if we don't get the house?"

Our fourteen year old son was just walking out of the door as I was speaking, when he turned around, stopped in the doorway and said, in a very clear, very decisive voice, "O ye of little faith," before turning and walking away.

My husband and daughter looked at me in stunned, silent disbelief. We all looked at each other as if we had just heard words from another world.

Actually we all knew we had.

"Dear Lord, that was my father speaking."

"You're right," said my husband.

"Yes, Mum. That was Granddad."

Friday came. The children were at school but David and I were at home waiting for the telephone to ring. After hearing Dad's words (coming through our son) on the Wednesday, I was fairly sure when the phone call came it would be good news. That still didn't stop me from saying a lot of silent prayers, as I'm sure the rest of my family did. It wasn't that I had doubted my father's words. I was hurt and upset with a court case looming and spending time on my own in an empty office going through fifteen years of old paperwork, shredding as I went along, hadn't put my mind in a place for happy emotions.

The telephone started ringing and David answered it. I could hardly contain myself. I waited. If you had paid me a million pounds I couldn't have read my husband's face as he put the receiver down.

Seconds passed and he said nothing.

"Well? It's ours?"

"Yes!"

I actually don't think he could believe it.

As I'm thinking back to all those years ago, even now I can only shake my head in wonder and say, "That was the most amazing turn of events I have ever known."

CHAPTER TWENTY-EIGHT

For the rest of that day we were all 'on a high.' David and I couldn't wait for the children to come home from school so that we could tell them both the good news. It would be 'all systems go' for the next few months but it would be worth it. The end result would be a lovely home of our own for all the family. To celebrate we had a bottle of bubbly and food around our patio table. We were using this, along with our four plastic patio chairs, as our dining room furniture.

As I sat late that night thinking about what had just happened, still not being able to quite believe that Ravenswood was now ours, it dawned on me how something as simple as a phone call can change our lives. It could be a telephone call telling us a new baby has been born or that job offer we had been waiting for or a call to tell us a loved one has died, just like the phone call I received when my father left this life. That one simple phone call changed my life in so many ways. Each of these telephone calls, no matter what they are about, can and do change our lives in some way or another. The phone call we had just received answered so many prayers for us as a family that we would all be grateful for a very long time.

The last thing I want to do is bore you with needless details about the purchase and renovations of the house but there are a few things that happened during the next few months that are relevant to my story.

We needed to act quickly to arrange a mortgage. This would give us the funds we needed to 'gut' the house. My husband and I both knew enough about renovating properties to know that we needed professional help, as the work that needed to be done on Ravenswood House was way beyond our capabilities. We were fortunate enough to know a good builder, who just happened to be short of work just at the time we needed his help. He was an ex-client of mine who was prepared to work with us over the next few months. He also said he would act as our site manager if we would like him to.

"Yes please."

We were advised that we should use an architect to provide the necessary drawings for all the renovations. This would then give our builder a detailed list of all the jobs to be done and a plan to work from. Our builder would be responsible for organising all the different professionals needed to do the different jobs throughout the house. From the dry rot to the wet rot work, the decorative plaster moulds and the structural engineering for a steel girder that was needed where a structural wall was to be removed, to the plumbing contractors who needed to install the new central heating system and the electrical contractor that would install the new wiring throughout the whole house, his help would be invaluable and his support would take a load off our shoulders.

We later regretted employing the architect as my husband found quite a few flaws in his drawings, especially with where the pipework was to be run throughout the house. Also, the drainage was in the wrong place. If it hadn't been for my husband's vigilance when he went over the architect's plans and his understanding of plumbing and drainage, the renovation work would have been in a right old mess.

David had just started a new job. That's how we were able to negotiate the mortgage because, of course, I now had no income. The short-term bank loan was put into place immediately and this enabled us to make up our own cash for the purchase of our new home. It would only be needed for about eight weeks so the cost was negligible. Somehow we managed to organise all of this within a matter of days.

We took possession of our property at the beginning of July 1991 and work began on the house within a week, with the hope we could be in by Christmas. The week after we took possession, the estate agents rang us to say they had found another set of keys for our home. They said they would hold them for us until we could call into their office to pick them up. This would give us the extra set we needed for the builder. When we went to pick up the keys the following day the estate agent told us that we might be interested to know that our offer had not been the highest but, because we had no house to sell and the offer was cash, the sellers had decided we were their best option. They needed their money back as quickly as possible and we were the safe bet. But the most amazing information that the estate agents gave us that day was, we apparently bought the house from the property developers for thousands of pounds less than they had paid last year. They had paid the full asking price at the time, whereas our offer last year was substantially less than the asking price, but the exact same price that we had offered this time and it was accepted.

Incredible!

This might sound daft but I truly believe, because we had not been in a position last year to be able to buy the property that we all loved, the Universal energy (or God) had picked the house up and removed it from the market for us and then held it for nearly a year until we were in a position to buy, and at the right price.

It was unbelievable, implausible and impossible when you think about it. But to me nothing is impossible for God and we all need to remember that, including me at times. Anyway, those were my own thoughts on the matter.

It was now nearly the end of July and I only had one more week left to finally clear my office and that included finding a home for my desk and chair. I would have no more use for it but I didn't want to sell it as it was of great sentimental value to me. Selling it seemed the wrong thing to do. I decided to give it to a colleague who I had worked alongside for many years. She had, and still has, her own accountancy practice and as far as I'm aware she is still sitting at what were my desk and chair.

As I closed my office door for the last and final time and walked away I felt so much lighter. My step had a definite skip in it. It was going to be great being able to sit at night writing, not having to worry about anything to do with work (other than a looming court case) but I would also have time now to sit and think, something I had not had the time to do for a very long time.

Over the coming days and nights, I spent quite a bit of time debating with myself as to whether it was the right time to start healing. But my thoughts were still saying not yet. I would have felt comfortable healing my own immediate family if that had been needed. I almost felt comfortable healing my friends but the thought of having to deal with people who would be strangers to me, that thought was making me feel very apprehensive. It was clear to me that I still needed more time to think.

Perhaps some of the apprehension I was feeling was because one or two of my friends that I had helped up to this time had told me that during and after a healing session they had been a bit frightened by me. It was not the act of healing itself that had frightened them, but the fact they could feel heat (or cold) coming from my hands. So much so that they knew this was far more than what they would call 'normal'. Where was it coming from? How was I doing this? And why should I be able to do this and not them? And who was I now? Had I somehow changed from the friend they had known for years?

They also said they experienced feeling tingling sensations and waves of emotions. That was what my friends were telling me and the questions they were asking. And last but not least, the most upsetting words for me that they used were, I was not 'normal.' The simple fact was 'I' wasn't doing anything. But even when I tried to explain this to them, that didn't seem to reassure them. My own friends were now telling me that I was odd. There was nothing I could do about that but the words they used and the things they said to me, and the way they started to treat me, reminded me so much of my school days. I still didn't want to be different. If my friends were thinking this and saying these things to me how would I cope trying to explain myself to complete strangers? At least with my friends, they had known me for a long time and I felt that I could explain most of their questions, but that didn't stop them looking at me 'sideways'.

Perhaps I was just being a coward. Anyway, I reasoned with myself that there was no spare room in our rented house or space in the rooms we were using, for me to be able to work in peace and quiet so any healing work would have to wait until we moved into our new home when it was renovated.

Not long after buying Ravenswood I was walking past the estate agents that had sold Ravenswood House the previous year to the property developers and, without realising what I was doing, I found myself walking into their office. I had got to know the lady who worked there quite well during our dealings last year. As soon as I walked in she said, "Hello there, how are you?"

"I'm fine thank you."

She continued by saying, "You know, I was so sure you would get Ravenswood House last year. I just felt it was meant for you."

"Funny you should say that. We have just bought it."

"Never in the world! How has that happened?"

After I related the whole story to her she said, "I'm so pleased you called in to tell me. You have renewed my faith in the powers-that-be. I just knew you were meant to get it and I'm so happy for you. After you had to withdraw your offer last year I have doubted my own instincts. This is what I needed to hear to restore my trust in myself. Thank you again for calling into the office to tell me."

My calling in was obviously meant. This is just a small example of how each of us can help one another just by following our own instincts, however small and seemingly insignificant they may seem at the time.

Just when the thought of me starting any healing work had been safely put to the back of my mind, up popped something else to make me rethink.

During one of the warm sunny days in August a lady who I had only known for a short time called in to see me in our rented home for what I thought was just a chat and a cup of coffee. We did chat but the real reason she had come to see me was because she wanted me to heal her. I hadn't realised that there was anything the matter with her. She looked fine. She explained to me that six years earlier, when her son had been born, she had had to have a caesarean section and, ever since then, she had been having a few problems. From time to time she had a nagging pain and, at the same time as the pain, she experienced a slight discharge.

"I'm convinced they have left something inside of me that doesn't belong there. I want you to heal me."

I can remember saying to her that I had no idea what the healing energy could do for her but we could give it a try. As she was sitting on one of our plastic patio chairs having a cuppa, I said I would work around her as she was sitting, but would she please remember I had no idea if this would help her problem in any way. Her reply was, "It doesn't matter. Just have a go."

The minute I lifted my hands above her head, that wonderful something outside of me took over. My hands knew exactly where to go and what to do without any thought on my part. Just the same as it had done with Nansi's patients and the friends of mine that I'd helped up to this time. After a little while a voice in my ear said, "You can stop now," so I did.

I told her I hadn't a clue as to what had been done or if it would help in anyway but she assured me that she was sure it would.

Three days later she rang me to say, "Thank you."

I said, "What for?"

"For healing me."

"What do you mean?"

"Last night when I went to the toilet I realised that I had passed something, so I looked and there in the toilet bowl was what looked like a very thin piece of wire or thread with a knot in it and there was also a small amount of old blood."

"Yuck."

Then she said, "I'd felt for years that they'd left something inside of me and now it's gone."

"Gosh, I am happy for you."

"You've got to start healing, Isabella. You could help so many people."

I promised her I would think about it. It felt to me that

there was so much more that I needed to learn about dealing with people. The right words to use, what needed to be explained and what didn't. It hadn't dawned on me (yet) that the best way to learn how to deal with and speak to people I didn't know was actually to do it.

We had all been going to the house every week to watch the renovation work going on and also to try and do a few small jobs ourselves. We ripped all the old wallpaper off the walls and we swept and cleared the rubble that the builders were creating from the house, wherever we could.

Because the garden was in such a mess we had great fun building bonfires. There was so much rotten wood coming out of the house that I think we must have had a bonfire every weekend for weeks and, of course, lots of barbecues amongst all the building rubble. We did have fun and lots of our and the children's friends joined in.

The plasterer told me with a wry smile on his face that the house had not been plastered, it had been bomb-proofed. There had been so much plaster put on the walls, where all the dry rot work had been done, to bring the lower part of the walls up to the thickness of the cornices on the ceiling it was going to take a few weeks, if not months, for the plaster to dry properly before any of the walls could be painted.

We now had a beautiful new split-level kitchen and dining area with French doors out into what would be our garden. There were two new bathrooms, one on the top floor for the children and the other one was an en-suite for the guest bedroom. The main bathroom had been plumbed but not fitted out as we had run out of funds. This could be done at a later date. With no carpets on the floors it was going to be a bit noisy and 'echoey' but that didn't matter. They could come later.

The plaster angels had been saved and we had found a solid oak floor under the old hall carpet when it had gone into one of the many skips the builders used. I would spend many hours on my hands and knees cleaning and oiling that floor. Our builder had miraculously managed to keep the banisters free from damage during all the building work.

We planned to move on a Friday in the middle of November, as our builder had told us he would be finished the week before and all his equipment and tools would be cleared out of our home. That gave me about five days between the builders moving out and our family moving in. The whole house needed washing down. Every floor in the house had been affected in some way or other, lumps of plaster stuck to floorboards and plaster dust in every crack. It would take a lot of work to get it all cleaned in time and get the one carpet that we kept from the lounge, and stored in our garage, put back down and cleaned. I had also kept the old curtains from the lounge and dining room. If they were cleaned they could go back up at the windows until we decorated the rooms and then we could buy some new ones.

Moving day with one dog, three cats and six two-week old kittens was no joke, but we managed. The children had been at school on the day we moved in, with instructions to remember to come home to our new home and not the rented house. It would be fair to say we were all relieved and very happy that the last few months in the rented house had come to an end. In fairness, we had been warm but it had been difficult for all of us, including the animals, because of the lack of space both inside and outside the house.

Now in our new home there was space to spread out, a lovely big new kitchen that was going to be a joy for me to work in and lots of outside space that the animals could enjoy, particularly our cats. They had spent most of the past few months indoors. I could now leave the back door open and they could wander in and out, along with our dog, in complete safety to their hearts' content and so could we.

CHAPTER TWENTY-NINE

We had no sooner moved into our new home than a letter arrived from the local hospital giving me the date and time for my long awaited MRI scan. Included with the letter was a leaflet explaining what an MRI scan was all about and also enclosed was an additional appointment date for a special eye test that I was to have. If you remember, I was told I would have to wait at least a year, so this was really good. I had only waited ten months. My appointment was in two weeks' time, not long to wait, and it would be done before Christmas. I've got to be honest, the thought of being put into a tunnel was not filling me with glee but I was determined to have this test and show the medical expert that he was wrong in my case. I knew I had MS and this MRI scan would show that.

David came with me to the hospital for support, as I was a bit worried about how I would react when I was in the scanner because I'm not very good in small spaces. I'm not going to say I'm claustrophobic. I just like space around me. The nursing staff could not have been nicer; they were all lovely people. They explained to me what would happen step by step while I was in the scanner. Being told I would be in it for at least an hour was a bit disconcerting, but this was something I needed to do for myself so somehow I would have to try and cope.

My stomach was churning as I left my husband's side to walk into the room where the scanner was. I was to lie down on what I can only describe as a long narrow tray suspended in mid-air but attached to the inside of the scanner. It looked as if it was levitating. A nurse then covered my feet with a blanket which I was very grateful for. Then my head was put into a cage. I was told that I would need to keep my head as still as possible for the time I was in the machine. But the cage was in place to help me. At this point I was feeling very nervous. What if I got cramp in my feet? What if I needed the toilet? What if I started to panic?

A nurse then attached two small clamps to my fingers. She explained to me that these attachments were to monitor my vital signs. Then they placed an earpiece onto my left ear. This apparently was to allow the staff operating the machine the means to be able to speak to me and me to them, if needed. They had warned me about the noise the machine would make as the magnets slowly took images of my brain, as the machine rotated around my head. I think it would be fair to say, at this point, all I wanted to do was to run as far away from this room as possible.

As the drawer that I was lying on slowly entered what I can only describe as a massive tumble-dryer, I closed my eyes tight shut. I had made a pact with myself the previous week when I read the leaflet the hospital had sent me that I was going to keep my eyes closed the whole time I was in the machine. If I could see how close the walls were around me I might panic but if I couldn't see how tight the space that I was lying in was, then I would be okay.

What I hadn't bargained for was the horrible smell of warm rubber that filled the space I was lying in, within seconds of the machine being switched on. "Dear Lord, I'm going to be sick." No one had warned me that this might happen but even if they had, it wouldn't have made any difference. Apparently, the machine was new and the tubes that delivered the fresh air into it for the patient to be able to breathe fresh air were new rubber hoses. But I didn't find this out until after my scan was finished. I started to panic big time; the smell of rubber was overwhelming. My heart was racing, my stomach was churning and all I wanted to do was scream, "Get me out of here!"

But I so desperately needed to have this scan. "Keep calm," was all I could think of to tell myself. "Somehow, just keep calm." But that didn't help at all. I was convinced I was going to start retching, the smell was so horrible. I needed help and I needed it now. That's when I shouted or, let's be very honest here, I screamed (not out loud) but in my head. The exact words I screamed: "Lord help me. Please help me. Now Lord, not next week. Not next month. Now..... Please."

219

If I live to be a hundred I'm never going to forget the wonderful feeling of peace and calm that swept over me within seconds of me finishing my plea. The wave started at the top of my head and swept down to the tips of my toes and every inch in between.

It was miraculous. My very own much needed miracle. I was instantly in a state of blissful calm and I knew it.

A voice broke my euphoria with the words, "Are you alright in there?"

I replied, "Oh yes."

Then I heard my father's voice as clear as day. But of course no one else could hear him or the conversation we were about to have.

"Why don't you come with me and we can both go on an adventure together? Where would you like to go?"

"Dad, I've always wanted to visit the barrier reef off the coast of Australia. Can we go there?"

"We can go anywhere you would like to."

"Then let's go," and that's exactly what my father and I did. I flew with him out of the hospital, up, up and away.

The next thing I knew we were both on the most beautiful beach of pure white sand, looking at the most inviting azure blue water I'd ever seen. Without any thought or fear we both walked into the water and kept on walking until we were both sitting on a rock, about three metres down, for what must have been at least half an hour in real time. The water was lovely and warm and crystal clear.

If you have never travelled outside of yourself before, you may not realise that you can go into the deepest ocean or fly out into outer space and be perfectly safe. You can breathe with ease. You can see, hear and speak perfectly normally. In other words, you can literally go anywhere on or off this planet in complete safety. It's wonderful and the cheapest way of travelling that I know!

Dad and I sat in wonder at all the beautiful colours of the fish as they swam by us and the beautiful corals waving their fronds gently, as some of the smallest fish swam in and out among them. In all honesty I could have stayed there for hours, I was so happy. I hadn't appreciated or realised that there were so many brilliant, vibrant and varied colours in the sea.

After a while Dad said to me, "Why don't we go and visit your new home now. I would love you to show me what you have been doing." (As if he didn't know) "You can explain to me all the things you still need to do to finish the house and then we can plan the garden together."

So that's exactly what we did.

First we went round the house and I was able to explain to my father what we still had to do. Then we went outside into the area that was going to be our garden. It was just a muddy trampled mess at the moment. But, by the time we had finished, I knew exactly what I was going to do and where everything was to go, from small stone walls and patios to the lawn and flower beds. Together we planned it all. My father had loved all the gardens he had while he was here on Earth and he had passed his love of gardening on to me. Having planned and replanted most of them himself, his input for me was invaluable. With what was now an empty messy site around our home at the moment, I would be able to turn it, with the help of my family, into a tranquil haven for us all to enjoy.

As Dad was giving me a parting hug, the tray I was lying on was slowly moving out of the tumble dryer (scanner) and I opened my eyes to three nurses standing around the tray.

As one nurse removed the cage from my head another nurse said to me, "Where on earth have you been for the last hour and ten minutes?"

I just smiled and said nothing. Then the senior of the three nurses said to me, "We were monitoring your vital signs and were at the point of making the decision to pull you out of the scanner because of the stress you were showing, when all of a sudden your vitals returned to normal. That's when I asked you if you were alright. And you haven't moved a muscle since. Where have you been?"

"Far, far away."

"I believe you."

There was no way I was going to try to explain to them what had just happened. I was sure they would have led me away to a locked room. Far, far away was as much as I was going to share.

When I went through to the reception area to join my husband I was smiling. Once we were both out of the building I explained to him what had happened. He just smiled like he always does when I tell him about one of my travels. But he did say he hoped I would be able to remember the garden plan.

Three days later I was back again in the same building to have my eye test but this time I went on my own. I was asked to sit down in front of what looked like a large television screen, next to a machine that had about ten wires coming out from it. Each wire had a suction pad on the end. These suction pads with the wires attached were then stuck with some sort of gel onto my head in various places. I was to sit quietly and watch the screen in front of me. There was nothing for me to do apparently. If anyone had had a camera I must have looked like a creature from a monster movie. The nurse left the room and left me alone, sitting there feeling like an idiot, watching a screen with flashing lights.

This must have lasted for about ten minutes. Then the nurse came back into the room and removed the pads from my now very gooey head. That apparently was that. It didn't hurt in any way and I had felt nothing. Well, my tests were all over. Now all I had to do was wait for an appointment to see the 'specialist' to get my results.

Just before Christmas I managed to have the lounge carpet cleaned and put back down and that helped to make the room cosy for all of us. But I still hadn't managed to organise getting the curtains cleaned. They would have to wait until the New Year. We did have a hedge in the garden that ran along the front of the house, but anyone walking past in the evening when the lights were on inside could see straight into our lounge. I needed to get the curtains back up at the window as soon as I could.

We had a great Christmas in our new home, plenty of

room for everyone as family and friends came to call. The only slight dampener on the festive spirit was the dark grey walls. The new plaster was still drying out. So lots of fairy lights were put up all over the house and the twelve foot Christmas tree in the front lounge helped no end. My mother came to stay with us for a few days over the holiday period, so that she was not alone. Her favourite spot was in front of the open fire, toasting her toes, along with the cats and the dog.

Mum went home just after Christmas and I began to make plans in my head as to how I could begin to start my healing work in the New Year. Our new home had an extra room that I could use to work in. If I could find a healing bed for people to lie on and get the old curtains cleaned and hung back up at the windows I could start healing.

It wasn't going to be easy for me to find patients because I didn't want to advertise. I felt in my heart that if I was meant to be doing this work the right people would be directed to my door somehow. But I was having a battle in my mind as to whether I should charge money for the healing. It just didn't seem right for me to ask for money. The healing energy that I could tap into was there for everyone to use and to me that healing energy was, and is, God's love to us, and His alone. His love has no price; to me it's priceless. Price-less - no money involved, so how could I charge people when it wasn't me doing the work?

But then if it wasn't for me channelling the energy, there would be no healing session and therefore no healing work. What a muddle my mind was in. The strange thing was I had never thought it wrong that I paid Nansi for all the healing sessions I had with her, so why did I feel the way I did? This needed a bit of thought and perhaps a good chat with the one person who would understand, Nansi.

CHAPTER THIRTY

Just when we were all nicely settling into our new home at the beginning of 1992, and I thought we were sailing into calmer waters, our world was turned upside down yet again.

We were all about to learn some more very valuable lessons.

David came home from work the second week in January and told us that the company he was working for was going to have to go into liquidation. They had been indirectly involved with Euro Disney, which had gone into receivership just a few weeks earlier. The knock-on effect was resounding through the business world, causing many businesses to fail, and David was working for one of them. He was going to lose his job and of course his income.

Now what were we going to do? We still had a very small amount of money left but that wasn't going to last long. Our immediate thought was that we might have to sell our home. We had only been in it a few weeks but it might have to be sold because we would soon have no way of paying the mortgage and, of course, for the first time in many years I had no income of any sort.

Part of the condition of the sale of my business the previous year, was that I was not allowed to practice within a ten mile radius of my old office, so there was no way I could return to accountancy work in my home area and there was nothing else that I could do to earn money.

What a muddle we were all in.

If I could get those curtains cleaned and up at the window (they were twelve feet long and much too big and heavy to fit into my washing machine) I might be able to start my healing practice but there were so many ifs and buts with this. It would take years for me to be able to build up a practice of any size, if I ever could, and if I could get my head around being able to charge for the service.

We needed income now for us to be able to keep our

home.

When the business had gone into voluntary liquidation we had had no choice but to trade both David's and my brother's cars into the garage we had bought them from, and the only deal they were prepared to offer us at the time was the two cars in part exchange for one new van so that's what we had done. At the same time I sold my expensive car to help reduce our family outgoings. (I think that was why that staff member of mine had thought I'd also gone bust) The payments on the new van were less than half the cost of my car and that made good financial sense to me. David and I shared the van between us for a few months.

But last year, after my business sold, I felt I could afford to have my own car again. Nothing flash, just something small for me to use. We managed to find a little blue second-hand mini, perfect for local journeys and also for Marie to drive when she passed her driving test, which she did very quickly.

I have mentioned this for a reason.

The curtains were taken at long last to the cleaners and would be ready the following week for us to pick up. Once they were up at the windows I could perhaps use the room to work in.

You know the saying, 'When it rains, it pours.' The last bill from the architects relating to work done on our home arrived in the post. Because there had been so much going on since we moved in we had completely forgotten that we still owed this money. The total amount due was way in excess of the estimated price that we had been given at the start of the renovation work. There was no way we were going to pay the full amount, because we had parted company with them halfway through the work, as we felt they were not doing a very good job. The problem now was we didn't have the money to pay even part of the bill. The little we did have left would be needed to pay for other things. I spent the next few nights sitting with the coffee table in front of me beside the open fire, with all the invoices relating to all the work done on the house to make sure there weren't any more outstanding invoices that could raise their heads and give us more problems.

This was history repeating itself. I kept thinking, "I've been here before," and I have to be honest, I can still remember trying to work figures out through my tears. This was just one more worry that none of us needed.

Was I stressed again? Yes I was.

The week after that final bill arrived the curtains were ready to be picked up from the dry cleaners but I was suffering from the most severe pain in my left ear and left side of my head. I'd never had earache before and, if that's what it was, the pain was almost unbearable. I had never experienced anything like it in my life. I could hardly bear to move my head.

Our daughter had passed her driving test a few weeks earlier and said she would drive me to the cleaners to pick the curtains up. I needed to go with her as I had no cash in my purse. As the cost was £65 I would pay for the cleaning with my bankcard. I know what you're thinking. I've only used the hole in the wall twice in my life and that was two years ago. In 1992 I didn't have a pin number because I didn't want one.

By the time I had gone into the cleaners and paid the bill, the pain was so bad I was fighting back tears. Marie carried the curtains to the car for me and as I got back into my seat I was crying. She was so concerned about me that she insisted she take me to the doctors to try and get me some help before we took the curtains home.

We had no appointment but she knew if we sat and waited until the end of the surgery a doctor would see me. It just so happened that the doctor on duty that day was the lady doctor who had informed me that I didn't have MS. I had not been to the surgery to see a doctor since that day over a year ago.

Marie went into the surgery with me as I could hardly see where I was walking for the pain. The doctor asked me what was wrong so I explained to her through my tears about the pain in my ear and head and then I said, "Please can you give me something to ease the pain?"

"No," was her answer. "I'm not going to give you

anything."

I was dumbfounded.

"But why?"

"Because the pain you're in probably relates to your problem."

To be perfectly honest with you, those words went right over my head at the time, probably because I was in too much distress. Marie was oblivious to the words the doctor said to me, but very worried about her mum, bless her. She had never stopped helping me all that day.

Then the doctor said to me, "What are you going to do?"

"I'm going to go home, take two painkillers and have a large glass of whiskey."

"Not a very good idea," was her response.

"Well you're not going to help me and I need to do something."

"Goodbye," she said.

My doctor's visit was apparently over. What the heck did she expect me to say? I needed help and she had refused me.

When we walked out of the doctor's surgery I said to Marie, "I can't believe this. I just don't understand why the doctor didn't help me. This just keeps happening to me every time I ask for help."

"I could take you to the hospital, Mum. I'm sure they will help."

I said, "No, let's just go home sweetheart and I can take some painkillers straight away."

Within minutes of getting through our front door I had taken two painkillers and I got myself a glass of whiskey, then I sat down and left the family to organise getting us all a takeout meal, as I was incapable of cooking or doing anything else for that matter.

As I was going over in my mind what had happened at the doctor's an hour earlier, questioning myself as to why the doctor had refused to help me, my thoughts kept saying to me, "Surely if someone, anyone, is in so much obvious pain and distress it's a doctor's job to help?"

Because I was miles away, lost in my own thoughts, I hadn't realised what I was doing. I had placed my left hand over my left ear and I was becoming aware of the heat coming from my hand. It was as if I had placed a hot-water bottle on the side of my head and actually it was very comforting. Once I was consciously aware of what I was doing, my mind was trying to comprehend the fact that perhaps I actually might be able to help myself. Could I 'heal' myself without Nansi being at my side? I'd never really given that question much thought over the past few years. What I hadn't appreciated or thought about was the fact that Nansi had taught me to heal myself from day one. There was no way I could have done it on my own but with her wonderful help, without me realising it at the time, she had given me all the tools I would need for the rest of my life. Could I 'heal' myself without her at my side? Apparently I could.

When I woke up the following morning the pain was completely gone.

It happened once more a few months later, only that time I immediately put my hand to the problem and within an hour the pain was gone and all these years on it's never come back.

Thank you, Lord.

As I've said before I'm a bit slow sometimes. My thoughts had been so full of the possibility of trying to set up a healing practice to help other people that I'd completely lost sight of the fact that Nansi had taught me how to use the healing energy to heal anyone, be it a stranger, a friend or even me!

It didn't take too long before the penny dropped and I realised that if the doctor had helped me it would have been a lost opportunity for me to learn that I could help myself. Now I understood why the doctor had said no. If she had helped me, I wouldn't have helped myself, by myself, and I obviously needed to learn that lesson. As painful and upsetting as this experience had been for me I was very grateful that it had happened. There's a right time for everything and this had been the right time for me.

CHAPTER THIRTY-ONE

By the time I had sorted through all the renovation paperwork and our current outgoings David and I both realised that we were going to need some financial help, both to clear the final bill we owed (well part of it) and also to give us the breathing space we needed for David to try and find another job, and me to find a way of earning some money. We needed a loan.

The only thing that we could both think of doing was to ask his parents for help. No bank would have lent us the money when we had no way to pay it back. We were both feeling very apprehensive about asking them but we really had no choice.

Many years earlier my father had lent us some money to buy a new carpet. At the time he said to me that he was happy to lend us the money, providing we paid him it back which, of course, we did. After all, he said, "If you pay the loan back then it's always there for you in the future should you ever need to borrow some again."

But my father was gone now, so I couldn't go to him to ask for his help and, unfortunately for me, after he had passed over my mother had said to me and other family members that she would not be lending anyone any money. As my father had only recently passed over when she told me this I never questioned her as to why. It would be a while before I was given the reason. That's why I knew not to go to her for help.

I felt sure David's parents would be angry with us for buying such a large house that needed so much money spending on it, that they would say we had 'bitten off more than we could chew'. I couldn't have been more wrong.

David decided to speak to his parents on his own to ask them and, to my surprise and delight, he came home with a cheque. God bless you Ma and Pa, wherever you are now. I was so grateful to them at the time for helping us that I asked my father to help me find the right words to use to express my thanks in writing and that night he did. When I gave David's parents the poem I had scribed for them (with Dad's help) the next time we went to visit, I knew by the tears in my mother in-law's eyes that she was pleased with the words that were written for them both.

There was a very important lesson for both David and I to learn from this. Because we had been given help without any words of reproach I made myself a promise. If in the years to come either of our children ever needed to borrow money from us, for whatever reason, if it was within our means to help then we would. We would always remember how we had been helped and, in turn, we would do the same for our children, without any words of reproach or conditions.

And thank God over the years we have been able to help them.

This lesson was learned and will never be forgotten.

A week later at the end of February, the letter arrived from the hospital. It was my appointment to see the specialist to get my results. Now I would find out once and for all who was right, me or the 'specialist.'

It's strange how our memories work. There are certain days (and nights) in my life that I can picture now as if they were yesterday. The picture of a room I was in, or the place I was visiting. I can see them and recall them in the finest detail and this day is one of them.

As I walked into his consulting room he was reading some papers on his desk and he didn't lift his head to greet me in any way. He gestured for me to sit down with a sweep of his hand. Without looking up from his desk he said, "Well, Professor Branson appears to have been right in your case." He continued by saying, "I can't find your scan to show you the scarring on your brain, but I will draw you a picture." He still had not looked at me and again gestured for me to come over to his desk. He picked up a large blank piece of paper and proceeded to draw what looked to me like the shape of a heart. Then he explained that it was a picture to represent both the left and right hand side of my brain. He then drew three separate shapes. These were to represent the three areas of scar tissue that were showing on my MRI scan. One scar was on the left hand side of my brain and was oblong in shape. It stretched up from the bottom of the drawing. Then another scar that was smaller and thinner ran along the bottom of the page, so this scar looked as if it was in both the left and right side and then he drew another scar on the right hand side, but not quite as big as the one on the left. By the drawing there seemed to be quite an area of scar tissue. (That answered a lot of questions!)

It would appear this man couldn't look me in the face because again he gestured with his hand for me to sit down. It would have been so much easier if he had just looked at me when he was talking, instead of all his hand gestures directing me around his room. Then he did look up at me and he said, "Does that answer your questions?"

"No actually, it doesn't. From my late teens when I wanted to wear eye makeup, every time I tried to apply it to my face around my eyes it hurt me, so I stopped trying. Why did that happen?"

"You didn't go for the eye test that I sent you for?"

"Yes I did."

He swivelled his chair around and picked up a telephone. "I'll ring the eye department and try and find your test results then." Obviously, I was only hearing one side of the conversation but it went something like this.

"Do you have a record of Isabella Clarence's test results? Oh good. Do you have her results to hand?" There was a pause for a few moments then, "Good. Oh very good. Ah that's good. Ah that's interesting."

He put the phone down and swivelled back around and said, "You have scar tissue behind both your eyes. Does that answer your question?"

"Yes thank you. I think it does."

Then he looked directly at me and said, "I don't know how you walked in here and I don't know how you are talking so well because the speech part of your brain has some scarring. You should not be walking," and with that, he

231

shrugged his shoulders.

I said to him, "Does this mean that I have MS?"

"Yes you have."

As I stood up to leave his consulting room he looked at me again and said, "I don't know what you are doing but, whatever it is, keep doing it." Then with a wry smile on his face, he said, "I hope I never see you again but I mean that in the nicest way." (That was the nicest thing that he ever said to me).

"You won't," said I as I walked out of his door and, all these years on, I haven't.

It's so sad that he was the way he was. I would have loved to have explained to him about the healing energy and how perhaps it could help other people like me. Well, I had proved the expert wrong, I would like to think he may have learned a lesson from this, not to always judge a book by its cover, but I think that's wishful thinking on my part.

As I walked away from the hospital gates the penny was beginning to drop big time for me. My brain was scarred. It would be fair to say my brain is damaged in quite a few places: the three scars the MRI scan picked up and also the scar, or scars, behind each of my eyes and the 'specialist had the scans to prove it.'

This is going to sound a bit odd but I was feeling very relieved and I wasn't in the least bit bothered by the picture he had drawn for me showing where the scar tissue was. I was just pleased that all the tests were now over and I now knew why I had experienced all of the symptoms or side effects that the scar tissue had caused me for many years.

But I've got to be honest and say I was feeling vindicated. I could still remember quite clearly the first time I had been in his office over a year ago and I could still hear his voice as he had gone along the scans on his wall as he explained some of them to me and, from the picture he had just drawn of my brain, mine was just as bad as any that I'd seen. But this was good. I could now understand why, when I am very tired, my speech sometimes slurs ever so slightly, or when I'm stressed.

On rare occasions when I don't get enough sleep and I'm very tired my mind tells my body that I don't need to think, but I do need to keep breathing, walking and talking if necessary. My brain keeps all my vitals operational and closes my thinking processes down.

Anyway, that's my excuse and I'm sticking to it.

This would be a good time for me to try and explain something to you. Nansi had not only healed me, she had shown me how to heal myself with her wonderful help. She had helped me to remember that how to heal was in my memory banks but I will always have the scars on my brain for the rest of my life. They are not going to go away and that doesn't matter. The important thing is that they have very little effect on me. Medically, I have Multiple Sclerosis and I always will. The medical profession would say to you that I'm in remission and that's fine by me. But they would have to admit that they have no idea how I'm walking, remission or not.

The healing energy was able to find other routes to pass the messages from my brain to my body, managing to bypass all the scar tissue. Our minds are far more powerful than we will ever realise.

Do you remember, when I started writing, I used the words, 'We are what you think'? Well, simply put, if I was to start feeling sorry for myself and if my thoughts were to keep telling me that I was ill, that I have MS and there's no cure, then that's exactly what would happen. All my MS symptoms would come back and I would be in trouble. I honestly believe that we are products of our thoughts and my thoughts are full of wellness (most of the time). Of course I have down days (I'm human) but fortunately not very often.

When I got home from my appointment and told David what had been said to me he said, "Well, you knew you had MS, so what difference does being told make?"

"An awful lot to me."

I guess he will never understand how I felt. But then no one can, unless you have walked in my shoes.

233

CHAPTER THIRTY-TWO

My birthday was fast approaching and, of course, there was no money to spare for David to be able to buy me a present but I was not bothered by that. I was more worried about the fact I hardly had any money to buy the food to put on the table.

The only thing I could think of doing was to take all my jewellery to a second-hand jewellery shop to try and raise some money for me to use. I took my engagement ring, my gold watch that my parents had bought me for my 21st birthday and a special ring that I had bought myself when I sold my business. I also took a second-hand eternity ring that I had bought years earlier. I just prayed that something would sell, so that I could have some spending money for food.

On the day of my birthday the family did manage some little things for me.

My mother, sister and her children arrived late in the afternoon (with their own food for their teas which I was pleased about for once, and again nothing for us). As they were leaving my mother handed me a five-pound note and said I could use it for food money.

I was speechless.

I do remember saying thank you, but that's not what I was feeling. The only thought that I had at the time was that my father would have turned in his grave (if he had been in it). Please don't misunderstand me. I wasn't looking for a handout. My mother knew how worried I was about our short-term finances. If she had just offered to help in some small way I would have been so grateful, but five pounds did seem like an insult.

She could have loaned me hundreds if not thousands of pounds and not missed it.

She could have gone out and bought some food and filled a box for us all, but no.

She hurt me; it's no use my trying to say anything different.

Every word spoken and unspoken, every thought and deed be it large or small, good or bad, all weave together to make the beautiful pattern of the tapestry of our lives. From the everyday run-of-the-mill tasks to the major events that change us forever, these are the things that make us who we are. We can never forget; the tapestry is our memory bank but we can let go.

It would only be a few weeks after my birthday that I did get an explanation from my mother as to why she didn't want to lend any of her family any money, ever again, and I've got to be very honest and say the reason was because of me.

Let me explain.

When I was thinking of expanding my business about eight years earlier I had gone to my father for a loan to help with my expansion plans. I had driven to my parents' home one summer evening to ask my father if he could possibly lend me some money to enable me to move to larger premises and take on some more staff. It would also enable me to buy some more office furniture and the extra equipment that I would need. He didn't hesitate, bless him, and I did pay him back.

But on the night I had gone to ask him for his help he had been sitting out in his beautiful garden, smoking his pipe. When I had come to leave to go home after saying goodbye to my mother, for some reason (and to this day I couldn't say why) I asked Mum to say goodbye to him for me. I had never done this before and I never did it again but, for whatever reason, on that night I left without going out into the garden to give him a hug, say thank you again and goodbye.

As I was driving home I had such a very strong feeling that I should turn my car around and go back to my parents' home and apologise to him for not saying goodbye and giving him his hug. My instincts had been so strong, but I reasoned with myself that I was already half way home and it would be alright to ring him tomorrow and say sorry.

If I had known then what was going on in my parents' home that night after I'd left I would have raced back to them but I was oblivious to the hurt I had caused. How I wish now

235

that I had followed my instincts that night and turned the car around, regardless of how far home I had driven. My mother explained to me that when my father found out I'd left without saying goodbye to him he had been visibly upset and had gone on and on at her to the point she was in tears, asking her over and over again why I had not said goodbye to him. I had obviously upset him beyond anything I could have realised and, in turn, he had upset my mother. From that night on she rightly associated my father being cross with her, when it was not her fault, with the night that he had lent me the money for my business. When she had explained to me what had transpired I realised it was no wonder that her hurt from that night had lain at my door.

I did apologise to my father some days later for not saying goodbye to him and he did forgive me, but I had not known at the time of his behaviour towards her. My mother had been hurt and, of course, I didn't know he had upset her or that she had been involved in any way. She had good reason never to forget the hurt she felt I had caused, all because I had not said goodbye to my father on the night he lent me money. This had been a seemingly 'non event' to me (because it hadn't hurt me) that had passed and gone.

My actions on that night caused waves for years to come in my mother's life and then, in turn, mine. Yet more thread in the tapestry.

If I was to go back over all the stories that I have been relating to you I think you would be able to see the pattern that has formed. Each and every time, without doubt, that I have found myself with a problem, the reason for the problem will always be because I haven't followed my instincts.

This has to be a huge lesson for all of us (including me). We must always, without exception, follow our instincts because they will keep us and our loved ones safe in every way, every time.

When my mother had finished explaining to me what had happened on that night, I was sorry beyond words and I told her so. This is a message to Heaven to ask their forgiveness yet again. Please, please forgive me, both of you. I love you both and always will. I would not knowingly have upset either of you for the life of me.

Well, at least now I understood. Even giving me the five-pound note must have been an effort on her part.

It's very easy for me to say now, after the event, that there was obviously a lesson for me to learn from what had transpired, but lessons are there for everyone and perhaps my parents should have told me at the time how hurt they had both been by my inaction on that night and then my mother would not have held on to that hurt for so long.

CHAPTER THIRTY-THREE

Now would we have to sell our home?

It was time for me to seek some help and the only person that I trusted to help me was Nansi so I made an appointment to go and see her as soon as possible. We had spent time together over the previous months, as she had been getting me to help some more of her patients, but it had been many months since I had had a treatment from her. I was in desperate need to clear my aura of all the negativity I was feeling. I wanted my thoughts to be positive, not negative, and I knew a treatment with her would do the trick.

A few days later my whole outlook on life had changed, my whole aura had changed. My treatment had been amazing. The only way I can describe how I felt when I arose from Nansi's healing bed is by using words that I often heard my father use: 'The peace that passes all understanding.' That's how I felt; all negativity had left me. I felt as light as air, without a care. No matter what happened, it didn't matter. All was well in my life and with the world.

My prayer for the whole of mankind would be that each and every soul on our beautiful planet, just once in each person's lifetime, could experience what I had just experienced. The actual quote is: 'And the peace of God, which passeth all understanding'. (Philippians 4:7)

Amazing, uplifting, walking on air, beyond belief, fantastic, no fear, no negative thoughts whatsoever, just bliss. All these words come nowhere near trying to convey to you how I felt and how I would like each and every one of you to feel, if only once.

When I got back home from my treatment with Nansi I knew exactly what I needed to do. I would ask God for help, knowing that somehow he would. There was nothing for me to worry about any more. The Universal energy would do the work for me. I sat down and wrote out a list. It was headed up with the word 'Help' in big letters. It was my shopping list to

God for all the things we needed help with urgently. I asked to be given the kindest words possible to say to my cleaning lady, because I was going to have to ask her to leave us as I didn't have the money anymore to pay her wages. I could no longer afford to pay the children's school fees. David and I both needed to find jobs as quickly as we could and I knew in my heart that this would be impossible for me to find, but not for God. A job I could do to earn good money. We needed the money for the mortgage payments and so much more.

Most of these things would be impossible for David and I to achieve in a short time, if at all, but I knew they were not impossible for God. That night when I went to bed after finishing the list, I was smiling to myself. Now God could start to help us. When I suddenly remembered that I had forgotten to put the van on the list, I jumped out of bed, ran down the stairs and added it to the bottom. We needed to sell it as we couldn't afford the payments anymore and when David had called at the garage two days earlier to see if they would buy it back they said they didn't want it. The salesman did say to David that he would keep it in mind should anyone come into the garage asking for a second-hand van such as ours, but he felt the chances of that happening were next to nil as they only sold new vehicles.

My shopping list was complete. I would just patiently wait now for God, the Universal energy that I trusted beyond words, to do His work and not worry anymore about being short of money. It can't have been an easy time for David with his wife telling him everything was going to get sorted and the mortgage would somehow get paid because God would help us.

I know some of you are going to say, "Ah, I've read or heard about doing this sort of thing," because there are now books written and DVDs, 'The Secret' and 'Cosmic Ordering' being just two of them. But please remember this was 1992, not 2006, long before any of the above books or DVDs had been published, written or even thought of.

This healer has been ordering her car parking spaces for

donkey's years now. I can't remember when I started to do it because it's so long ago. This healer has believed all her life that all I have ever needed to do was 'Just ask' because I have trusted all my life that God, the Universal energy, would always be there for me, no matter what. (I have said these words because in the first edition of 'The Secret' that I watched, it was said that 'healers' did not understand any of these things, silly them). They should have asked me.

But because I'm human, I kept forgetting to ask.

At the end of that week I sadly told my cleaning lady that I was so sorry but I would have to let her go because we were having financial problems. She looked so relieved when I told her and said, "I don't believe this. I was so worried because I was going to tell you today that I wanted to retire and I didn't know how to."

That was Friday, less than a week from doing my 'help' list.

On the following Monday morning our telephone rang. It was the garage asking if we still had the van, as someone had just called in asking to buy a second-hand van the exact same as ours. Amazing! That was the van sold and gone. When David took the van to the garage the salesman told him that he had been gobsmacked when this man had walked into the garage looking for a second-hand van, not just because they only sold new ones but because it had only been a few days since David had asked him for help in finding a buyer.

The next wonderful thing that happened was when my husband went to sign on the dole (he was entitled to some help because it hadn't been his fault that he lost his job). Imagine his surprise when someone at the dole office told him that we were entitled to get the interest paid on our mortgage for a few months, if he arranged to go to the office that dealt with this. As we had an interest only mortgage, that was that huge problem sorted, giving us the breathing space we so needed.

I think you will see now how the Universal energy was stepping in to help us.

Next, a friend told me that if I went to our children's

school at the beginning of the next term they had a special fund to help parents with the school fees, for exactly the situation we had found ourselves in. The fees would be paid for the last year of our children's schooling, and they were.

Then, out of the blue, I received a phone call from an old work colleague offering me a job. As it didn't contravene my contract from the sale of my business I was able to accept.

Unbelievable yet again!

We hardly had time to draw breath with all the events happening around us so quickly. Because we now had some money coming in I decided to go to the jewellery shop to collect my pieces, only to find that one had sold - the ring I had bought second-hand for myself years earlier. It was a lovely eternity ring that I paid two hundred pounds for, but I had never been able to wear it because it was too big for me and unfortunately, because it was completely surrounded by diamonds, it couldn't be made smaller. It had sold for four hundred pounds. I had doubled my money. But all my own jewellery was still there. Perfect.

Within a few weeks David also found work. We would not be losing the home we now all loved. God had answered my 'help' list better than I could have ever imagined.

Please take a lesson from all of this. If you need help, don't hesitate to ask. The Universe will help you if you ask with an open, trusting heart.

And please, always remember to say, "Thank you."

CHAPTER THIRTY-FOUR

How many times do each of us think that we have cleared all the hurts and fears that life has given us when, out of the blue, yet another old problem raises its unwelcome head again? Our thoughts then take us back to an event that left a mark on our heart and memory that we were sure we had cleared and let go of years earlier, but because it was woven into the fabric of our being we can never forget but we can forgive, let go and move forward.

Many times I'm sure.

I've lost count of the number of times both friends and patients have said to me, "Darn it, I was so sure that I had cleared that particular hurt years ago, but it's risen from the ashes yet again."

My intentions, when I started to write my story of how I have come to be working as a Spiritual Healer, were in the hope that, by sharing my experiences, it would help someone and I've still got a few more experiences to share.

As the years have gone by I have come to realise more and more that our lives are not so very different. Whether we are rich or poor, male or female, young or old, single or married it doesn't matter. Our lives are all just variations on a very similar theme. The human race is all in one big gigantic book. It's just that we are all on different pages or perhaps on a different line or in a different chapter. My hurts and fears will be another person's hurts and fears. They will not be exactly the same but they will be similar. Life has given me so many different experiences that, in turn, have enabled me to empathise with people on so many levels, and I'm very thankful for that.

Lessons and yet more lessons, clearing and yet more clearing and I'm absolutely no different in this respect from anyone else.

Because I had recently been to the hospital to see the specialist to get my results, I had been sitting thinking about how my life could have gone in a completely different direction if I had not been directed to my healer. In all probability I would not be here now on Earth if I had gone into the hospital ten years earlier, when the doctor had wanted me to. Do you remember? He wanted me to go into hospital for a few days to have some tests done. If I had gone in for those tests I would have been given drugs and I would have taken them. Where would I have been now? It didn't bear thinking about and I was quite sure that that visit had not only sparked my mind to realise how blessed I was but, in turn, it was leading me back down my time tunnel to many years earlier.

Have you ever noticed how once our mind has taken us back to one hurtful event there is a snowball effect that seems to happen? One event leads to another and the next thing we know we are recounting in our mind's eye a whole host of connected hurts. As if one wasn't enough! Those darn threads again.

These next particular events in my life all had their starting point years earlier.

Do you remember me telling you about the day I was attacked as I walked home from the bus-stop in 1968 when I was eighteen years old and how when I got home my mother left me alone in the house? A few weeks after that event, I had my interview with the psychiatrist my father had arranged for me to talk to, to see if he could get to the bottom of why I was being so quiet. Well, not long after that I developed a pain in my side and it wasn't appendicitis.

For every action there is a reaction.

For every cause there is an effect.

It was no wonder my body was beginning to respond to the hurts and fears I was keeping locked deep inside me because I had no one to talk to. If I had just been able to speak to the psychiatrist by myself that day and explain to him how hurt I was by my mother's actions I might have been able to talk my hurt out and then it wouldn't have had any long-term effect on me.

But I couldn't and I didn't.

243

If I had been able to tell someone when I was twelve years old about being so frightened when I was chased, but I had no one to talk to then either.

Can you see now how hurts and fears left unsaid begin to cause a wobble in our aura and then, in turn, in our bodies?

Because I was experiencing a severe pain in my left side my mother said I ought to go and see our family doctor who, in turn, sent me to the local hospital for it to be investigated. It was found that I had an ovarian cyst.

Memories:

Just before they wheeled me into the theatre for the operation, a nurse came to move the trolley that I was lying on and she was very angry and cross with me. As I had been given a pre-med injection I was feeling very woozy, but it did make me feel more confident than I usually was so I asked her why she was being so nasty to me.

She replied by saying, "I don't like girls who have abortions."

"I don't think I do either."

"But you're in for an abortion."

"You'll have a hard job giving me an abortion. I'm a virgin. I'm here to have a cyst removed."

"Oh!" she said. Then she picked up my arm and looked at the name tag on my hospital wrist band.

"Oh, I've got the wrong trolley! I thought you were someone else!" With that, she walked away and left me lying there.

Trust me, even in my sleepy state I was now feeling very apprehensive. I had heard stories of people having the wrong limb amputated because the surgeons had operated on the wrong person. To say I was now very frightened would be an understatement. I can even remember trying to get up off the trolley I was lying on. I don't know where I thought I was going but I knew I wanted to leave before something terrible happened to me. But I was far too woozy and drugged. I was stuck.

I went into prayer mode big time, shouting out to God in

my head, to keep me safe. There was no one else for me to ask. Even at eighteen years of age 'He' was my help when no one else was around.

So for the next 'I don't know how long' I talked to God, asking him to keep me safe and be with me through my operation and, of course, he did. I don't know how long I was on that trolley in the corridor but when I was eventually wheeled into the theatre I can remember saying to the staff that I wasn't pregnant but I did want to have a baby in the future. (They must have thought I was crackers)

It was sorted out relatively easily. I was only in hospital for twenty-four hours. The cyst was cauterised and, in all honesty, I was in no discomfort after the procedure but I was a bit shaken by what had happened. I did have a few days off work as I felt a bit weak, but that was just the after-effects of the anaesthetic. But I knew I never wanted to have to go into hospital ever again; it was a scary place.

And the ball kept rolling.

For every cause there is an effect or, better still, for every action there is a reaction. Any hurtful or frightening event will produce its effect somewhere in our futures if we don't let go of the hurt.

And here was another one.

When I was engaged to be married in 1969, my fiancé and I went for our first summer holiday together. We drove to the north-west coast of Scotland, to a beautiful little fishing village. There was a small, pure white, curved sandy beach at the top of an inlet which meant the seawater was shallow and lovely and warm.

All was going well until we went out for our evening meal on the third night. We each ordered a starter and a main course. As I started to eat my prawn cocktail I picked up a forkful of food and there on top of my fork, amongst the lettuce and prawns, was a large slimy slug, just before I was about to put the whole lot into my mouth. I dropped my fork with the contents onto my plate with a shudder. My fiancé asked me what on earth I was doing as I was sitting squirming in my seat, shaking both my hands in the air as if I was trying to dry nail varnish.

"There's a slug on my plate!"

He looked at me blankly. I asked him to please ask the waitress to take my plate away and get me a replacement.

"No," was his reply. "Just keep quiet and eat."

"I can't eat it. There may be more slugs amongst the lettuce. Please ask them to take this away for me and get me a fresh one."

"No. I've told you to keep quiet and eat."

I must have asked him three or four times but he was adamant I was to eat my starter and say nothing. While he was eating his I was sitting thinking to myself, "If he's not going to be the gentleman and say something, then I will."

I would find out in the months to come, that he didn't like me having my own mind and certainly didn't like it when I disagreed with him in a public place, yet for the first eighteen months that he had been my boyfriend I had not noticed this side of him. But on that evening all those years ago I didn't realise what I was in for.

When the waitress came to clear our plates away to then bring us our main course, my plate of food was untouched. She asked if everything was alright and I said, "No actually, it's not. I'm sorry I couldn't eat my starter because there is a large slug amongst the lettuce." And actually, when she took my fork and looked for herself she found two more.

She apologised profusely and said she would bring me another one. With another shudder I said, "No thank you. I would just rather have my main course."

By the time we had finished eating, paid the bill and left, my fiancé was not speaking to me. It was very obvious that he was furious with me because I had told the waitress about the slug. What the heck he thought I was going to do with it was beyond me. We got into our car to drive to our guest house but before he drove off he turned towards me and started shouting at me, telling me I should have done what he said. I tried to reason with him but he became enraged, and that's when he slapped me across my face and, before I had time to react in any way, he slapped me again.

I was shocked, hurting and crying. No one had ever hit me. I was shaking and very upset. We arrived back at our guest house without another word spoken. All I wanted to do now was go home, somewhere safe away from him.

I'm sure you can guess what he said next. He promised he would never do it again. I was all for abandoning our holiday and going straight back home but he insisted that we should stay because he promised on his life he would never hit me again. I had no experience of physical abuse. I was nineteen years old and very naive because I guess on the whole I had led a very sheltered life. I didn't know what abuse was. In all the years I lived at home with my parents I only ever heard my father swear once, and if I'd heard my mother swear I think I would have fainted, let alone a hand raised in anger. Being hit was something that happened to people who lived on another planet.

He was kind to me for the rest of our holiday but it didn't stop me from feeling very uneasy.

Everything was going reasonably well but four months before the wedding I went to my doctor because I wasn't sleeping. Every part of me was telling me not to go through with the wedding but I honestly felt that I could not have told my parents what my reason was for wanting to cancel it.

How I was worrying every time my fiancé and I had cross words in case he hit me again. I honestly didn't think they would have believed me if I'd told them that he had already hit me. It seemed so impossible. My fiancé was a very plausible, handsome young man. The wheels on the wagon were rolling along at a very fast pace and I was too frightened to call a halt to the wedding, too frightened to tell anyone what had happened the previous year and what my fears were. I just didn't know what to do. I told myself if my father were to ask me if I was sure I was doing the right thing in getting married I would tell him.

Even on the day of my wedding in June 1970, three

months after my twentieth birthday, I was praying that my father would ask me if I was sure I was doing the right thing, and then I could have said to him, "No Daddy, I'm not sure at all."

As I walked down the beautiful staircase in our family home, in my wedding dress and veil, to my father who was waiting at the bottom of the staircase to take my hand, he smiled at me, took my arm and helped me into the waiting car that was to drive us both to the little chapel where I was to be married. But he didn't say a word to me.

Sleeping tablets before my 20th birthday! It's very easy to see clearly in hindsight.

At the reception I burst into tears. Everyone thought it was because I was being emotional after the ceremony (if only they had known). I was in tears because every fibre of my being was telling me that I'd done the wrong thing.

My new husband and I were driving to Scotland for our honeymoon directly after the wedding reception, after we had changed from our wedding clothes. As we were leaving my parents' home, my father asked me to make sure that I rang him when we arrived at our hotel, to let him know that we had got there safely.

I didn't. I didn't ring home for three days.

I can still see myself in the hotel foyer all those years ago, standing in the phone booth as I rang my parents' telephone number. My father answered the phone. "Thank goodness you're alright. I have been worried sick about you. Why haven't you rung me before now?"

Without hesitating, I said, "Daddy, if I'd rung you when we arrived I would have said I wanted to come home. I've done the wrong thing, Daddy. I shouldn't have married him but it's my fault. I've made my bed and now I'll have to lie on it. I'll try my best to make this work. I'm so sorry, Daddy."

My father tried to reassure me that everything would probably be alright but, of course, he didn't know what I was really worried about. We said goodbye to each other and hung up.

CHAPTER THIRTY-FIVE

Within about two months of our wedding my worst fears were realised; my husband hit me again.

I'm not going to go into the number of times that I had to hide in our bathroom with the door locked, with my husband on the other side banging on it so hard I used to think the door would fall in. It was a very frightening time for me, but at the same time there was a part of me that thought that it must be my fault and that, of course, is a classic response. Like all abusers, he would make me feel that it was because of something that I'd said or done that had made him get so angry with me. After every outburst he would always say he was sorry and promise me he would never do it again.

Within a very short space of time after our wedding I wasn't feeling very well. When I think back now to all those years ago, I do remember being very tired and weary although at the time I reasoned with myself it was because I wasn't sleeping very well because of all the stress I was having to cope with. But I did have a slight niggling pain in the same place as a few years earlier.

Because it was only a few weeks after we had married (August 1970 to be precise) I hadn't had time to register with a new doctor, so I went back to see the doctor I had had since I was sixteen years old when I lived at home with my parents. She had all my records, knew me and knew I had already had one cyst removed a few years earlier.

As I sat with her in her surgery, she made me an appointment at the walk-in clinic to have my pain investigated. It was another cyst again on my left ovary. Back I went to the hospital to have it removed and, as before, I was only in hospital for a couple of days and then I went back home to my husband.

Within months of my operation, I had to hide in the bathroom yet again. I knew this situation couldn't go on and I needed help, before my husband did me some real harm.

Just after my 21st birthday I plucked up the courage to tell my father what was happening to me. He was obviously very concerned and insisted that I went to see our family solicitor as soon as possible. While I was still with my father he picked up his telephone and made an appointment for me to see the solicitor for the following morning. I'd never spoken to a solicitor before in my life so I had no idea what to expect and I was feeling very nervous when I went for my appointment with him, but he couldn't have been kinder. After I told him why I had come to see him he insisted that I was to go back to my parents and not to return to my marital home. The solicitor's instructions to me were never to go back into my own home, on my own, ever again.

That very same day, my father followed me home in his car, while my husband was at work, to help me collect as many of my clothes that I could get into my car and any other small items that my father could get into his.

The problem was that my parents, or I should say my mother, didn't want me to go back to live with them. When my father and I arrived back at my parents' home that afternoon, with our two cars full of my possessions, my mother actually said to me, "You can't stay here." She allowed me to leave all of the things that Dad and I had in our cars but she told me that she didn't want me moving in with them. She didn't want me staying in their home.

So on the very same day that I left my husband and my own home, at the age of twenty- one, I found myself having to try and find a hotel room to sleep in for that first night and, as it turned out, for the next two weeks until I was able to find myself somewhere to live. A tiny one- person flat in an area I didn't know and I didn't like, but it was the only flat I could find at the time. I was on tranquillisers and sleeping tablets, feeling lost, hurt, very lonely and desperately unhappy. What a mess my life was in. It would be fair to say I was very close to a complete breakdown.

Thank goodness I had a very good, well paid job and I could easily support myself.

My memory during this time of my life is a jumble of pictures. Some are very clear and others are dreamlike, as if the things I can see in my dream happened to someone else and not me. I'm sure that must be partly because of all the medication the doctor had put me on and partly because I was feeling so unwanted, that my young mind just couldn't cope.

My dear friend, Aunty Eileen, was a fantastic support to me during this time. She has told me recently that she remembers the night I rang her at midnight and, fortunately for me, she was up and awake because she was feeding her new baby. (He had his fortieth birthday last week) She told me that she talked to me for about an hour and a half and got me to promise her I would go and see her the next day, because I had told her I didn't want to be here anymore because nobody wanted me, no one loved me, except of course my father.

What a state I must have been in.

The one very clear memory that I do have, and it must have been within days of my ringing and seeing Eileen, is a visit that I made to my parents' home one evening to collect some more of my clothes that they were storing for me. Before I left my parents' home that night to go back to my lonely flat I took myself off upstairs and went out onto what was a lovely big balcony. It was outside and between both my mother's and my sister's bedrooms. Both their rooms had glass doors opening out onto the balcony. It was a large paved area above the lounge, where you could look out over my father's beautiful garden. Surrounding it was a wall about four feet high. I can still picture myself standing there all those years ago, leaning on the wall, thinking. And I can remember exactly what I was thinking. It's just as if it was yesterday.

My thoughts: "I can't take my own life because it's not mine to take. It's God's life, not mine."

Hand on heart, those were my exact thoughts on that night forty years ago. I would change the wording slightly now, if I was asked, because my understanding has moved on over the past forty years. That was a very 'heavy' thought for a twenty-one year old. Somehow I knew then that I was here for

251

a purpose and somehow I knew that I needed to get through this terrible time and not give up on myself.

Within minutes of this thought going through my mind, I heard my father's voice calling to me from somewhere in the house. He was frantically calling my name and, even to this day, I can still hear the fear that he had in his voice that night.

I shouted back to him, "I'm here, Daddy."

Within minutes he came running out onto the balcony as he was saying, "Isabella, I've been looking for you. Are you alright?"

"Yes Daddy, I'm alright now." I never told him what I had been thinking that night and he never told me what his thoughts had been either because I think we both knew.

Writing this has made me realise just how abandoned by my mother I was at the time. Whether I was upset or needed help in any way she was never there for me. I had just accepted that that's the way it was. Perhaps it was something to do with the conversation I had with my grandmother many years earlier or perhaps it was something completely different. I don't know and I'm never going to know in this lifetime, but that's alright because I know and understand that one day I will.

I have no sense of anger towards her because of her behaviour towards me when I was young. To be honest, I wasn't even angry at the time this all happened. Yes, I was lost and hurting and I didn't understand why but I wasn't angry. My mother didn't know me and I didn't know her and that's sad.

However, after my father passed over we became quite close because we began to talk to each other. Please don't think that I didn't love her. I did. On the day she left this world it was me holding her hand, and that's a tale I must tell in my next book, because her passing was one of the most amazing experiences of my life.

There were such a lot of lessons for me to take away from what happened during this time in my life and perhaps one or two for you. Do you remember me saying near the beginning of my story that sometimes we never find out in this lifetime why something hurtful has happened? Well, this is one of those times for me.

I would always make sure in the years to come that I would never allow any of my own loved ones to feel abandoned by me in any way. I would always be there for my children whenever they needed me.

This experience had given me the understanding to be able to empathise with anyone that comes to me feeling lonely and hurt by their own family or anyone else for that matter. If a friend should ever ask for my help I will always do my best to be there for them, as my friend had been for me. And if a patient or friend was to approach me for help because of any physical or mental abuse I would be able to empathise with them because of my own experiences.

If we can all take the negative events that happen to us in our lives and turn them around and make something positive and good come from them, then we will move forward in a positive way. Somehow I would manage to get through this horrible time. I didn't know how I was going to at the time, but I knew I would never again think about taking my life because I honestly believed that it wasn't mine to take. This didn't stop me from feeling hurt because I couldn't live with my parents, but it did help me to try my best to get on with my life.

Moving into that flat on my own was probably the worst thing I could have done, as it made me so very vulnerable. I wish I could say that that was the end of my first marriage but, over the following months, my parents convinced me to go back to my husband and try and make my marriage work. I'm not going to try and second guess why my parents did this, because they both knew they were sending me back to a man who had abused me, both physically and mentally. But because I was so lonely and unhappy with the situation I was in I found myself agreeing with them and I went back. We found a house to buy together towards the end of 1971.

But the problems had not gone away.

CHAPTER THIRTY-SIX

Within a matter of weeks I was becoming frightened again by his behaviour towards me and I wasn't feeling very well. Looking back now to what seems like another lifetime, it's almost impossible for me to comprehend how so many things could have happened to me in such a short space of time.

Not long after my twenty-second birthday, in March 1972, I decided to go and seek some help. Ever since I was married in June 1970 I had not changed my doctor. I was still registered with the family doctor where my parents lived so I went back to see her again. After I explained to her how I was feeling, she said she wanted me the following week to go back to our local walk-in clinic, the one I'd been to before. I didn't need an appointment. I was just to go along and wait my turn. She said she would ring the clinic the following day and tell them I would be coming.

I think perhaps it's important to mention and remember that this all happened nearly forty years ago now and things were very different then to how they are now.

The following week I went to the clinic on my own because I had no one to go with me. I didn't have to wait very long to be seen, because it wasn't very busy, and at the end of my examination I was told they would be in touch with me by letter to let me know the results of the tests taken and what, if anything, would need to be done.

It was about two weeks later when my father rang me at my home and told me the hospital was trying to get in touch with me. They had rung my parents' phone number, thinking I was still living there because that's the address they had for me. My father told me to ring the hospital the next day but I didn't because my mind was in such a muddle and I didn't want to go to the hospital. I guess I was hoping that whatever the problem was it would just go away.

I was due to visit my parents on the Friday afternoon after my father's phone call to me a few days earlier, and when

I arrived my mother was very cross with me and I didn't have a clue why. Apparently, the consultant from the hospital, who lived about a hundred yards from my parents' home (and knew my parents), had knocked at their door that afternoon because he thought I lived there. He spoke to my father and told him that it was very important that I was in the hospital on Monday morning as he had scheduled me in for an operation and, because I had not contacted the hospital, he wanted my parents to make sure that I was there and on time. What operation? I didn't know there was anything wrong with me that needed an operation but, of course, if I had rung the hospital like I was supposed to do, I would have known.

My heart sank.

All I knew was that I was to be at the local hospital at nine o'clock on the Monday morning and that I would be in hospital for at least four days, so I was to go prepared. That was the message given to my father. (I never did get a letter)

My husband dropped me off at the hospital before he went to work but I can remember wishing someone was staying with me. I was feeling very alone and very frightened. I desperately wanted someone to hold my hand and be there with me. I was only twenty-two years old and in so many ways still a child.

After I was settled into my bed on the ward a very nice doctor came to talk to me to explain what I was in hospital for and to fill in all the relevant forms, including a consent form that I was asked to sign. This was all very frightening and confusing for me. He told me that the tests from my clinical appointment had revealed some very suspicious cells in the entrance to my womb. I was to have a cone biopsy in the hope that they could remove them. But if they felt this would not be enough they wanted the consent form signed so they could perform a hysterectomy.

A hysterectomy not long after my twenty-second birthday? Please no.

I desperately wanted to talk to my family, but this was 1972, before the invention of the mobile phone. I would just

255

have to wait until visiting time to be able to talk to someone and tell them how frightened I was. I wanted to be able to have children sometime in the future. Let's face it, I'd wanted to have children since I was a child myself. I loved little ones so much.

After my husband left me when visiting ended that night I had never felt so alone in my life. As I lay in my hospital bed, before my operation the following morning, I prayed like I'd never prayed before. Over and over again I asked God to be with me and help me not to be so frightened. "Keep me safe Lord, please keep me safe. Help the surgeon to perform the operation so that I will be alright and they won't have to give me a hysterectomy. "

I made promises to God. I would try and make my marriage work and I would work hard and all sorts of other things if 'He' would keep me safe. (I wonder how many thousands of other people have done exactly the same thing)

When I woke up in the ward after my operation the evening meal was being served. Apparently I had been out of the ward all day and some of the ladies that were on the ward with me had thought I was a 'goner'. (That's what they told me)

I found out later that the surgeon had removed some cells and sent them to the lab and, while they were waiting for the results coming back, I had been put into a side room still fast asleep and I'm not sure if this was done more than once. Once the surgeon knew he had all the suspicious cells, I was taken back into the operating theatre and stitched up inside.

But I felt quite good when I woke up. I had no pain or discomfort. As I was getting out of bed to go to the toilet the following morning (I had slept like a log all night) I was shouted at by the sister on the ward, yelled at in fact to get back into bed. "You have a lot of stitches inside of you and you're not to get out of bed for another twenty-four hours."

I felt a bit of a fraud as I watched the ladies who had had their hysterectomy operations on the same day as me being told to get up and walk around the following morning and I was to stay in bed until the next day. We all had our operations on the

Tuesday and I wasn't allowed out of bed until Thursday.

Thank you Lord. I was going to be alright and no hysterectomy.

It may have been nearly forty years ago but I can still remember how frightened I was. I can still remember how grateful I was when it was all over. I was in hospital a total of eight days and I can still remember how kind everyone was to me.

The surgeon who performed my operation came to see me to explain what he had done. He was so nice. He told me that because I was so young he had spent quite a while making sure he removed all the cells he felt were pre-cancerous and because of that I had a lot of stitches inside me; my inside looked like a patch-work quilt. I really felt he had taken great care of me, and I was sure all my prayers skyward had helped. He then explained to me that if, in the future, I did become pregnant I may not be able to carry the baby to term, as my cervix might not be able to hold, because of all the work that had been done inside me. Or, if I did manage to carry a baby to full term, my cervix might not open when I went into labour and I would need a caesarean section but, of course, we would just have to wait and see. At least now I knew why I hadn't been allowed out of bed for forty-eight hours and why they wouldn't let me home after four days. He said I was to have a follow- up examination in a year's time so that he could keep an eye on me.

Thank goodness that was all over.

But so was my marriage.

CHAPTER THIRTY-SEVEN

I did try and make it work, but my husband was determined to make my life as difficult for me as he could. He wanted to pay me back for leaving him and I'm not going to go into all the horrible things that he resorted to in a very short space of time.

Within about six weeks of me coming out of hospital in July 1972, I visited a new doctor in the area where we were now living because I was frightened again. He said to me, "Are you stupid? You should never have gone back to him. He doesn't deserve you." Coming from a stranger, it really made me sit up and think and yes, I left my husband for the last and final time.

But this time I was more organised. I managed to find a room in a house with three other girls, close to my parents' home. Having the company of other girls would make the world of difference to me, and it did. They were all a little bit older, single and full of fun. Just what I needed. It was as if I'd taken in a huge breath of fresh air.

Had I been brave for the first time in my life, or was I just beginning to grow up and realise if I didn't do something for myself no one else would? I think I was beginning to learn to take responsibility for myself and I realised that, at long last, I was free from the cause of all my unhappiness.

The girls in the house were a bit concerned when I first moved in, in case my husband came to their door, but I assured them that he wouldn't. He was a coward and a bully and would not have wanted to show himself in a bad light.

The second half of 1972 was to be the beginning of the rest of my life and, I can't quite believe this, my story has almost come full circle without my even trying.

For the first few months after I moved in with the girls all I wanted to do was enjoy my own company at the weekends when I wasn't working, just being able to do whatever I wanted to without having to think or worry about somebody else. My housemates were very kind to me and often asked if I would like to go out with them but I always declined. The last thing I wanted to do was to go out and meet new guys.

One Friday night, just after the Christmas holidays were over and 1973 had begun, one of the girls in the house had been let down by a friend and found herself with no one to go out with on that particular night. After twisting my arm for about an hour I agreed to go out to a local pub with her to keep her company. To my surprise, the pub she took me to was the old-fashioned pub that my wedding reception had been held in two years earlier, when I had burst into tears. I said nothing but I did feel a bit peculiar for the first half an hour or so, as I hadn't set foot in the place since my wedding day.

But this was a happy fun night. She introduced me to a number of her friends, most of them young men in their early twenties, my age and older, and they were all very welcoming and chatty. Amongst them was a tall, dark-haired handsome stranger. He looked a bit like Buddy Holly to me (I'm showing my age now). The conversation was incessant, from boy talk to girl talk and everything in between, and the night was over before I knew what had happened. I hadn't enjoyed myself so much in years.

When we least expect it and we are not looking for anything, the most wonderful things can, and often do, happen. That Friday night turned out to be the first meeting with my future husband, the father of our beautiful children, my best friend and the love of my life for over forty years now.

Within a very short space of time I found myself falling in love with him and, all of these years on, I still am. I would have married him without hesitation within weeks of that first meeting. But I was still married. I needed to get divorced to free myself from the mistake I had made (huge lesson) and, unfortunately, all those years ago, getting a divorce was a long-drawn- out procedure. It took much longer than we would have liked.

My divorce finally came through on Valentine's Day 1974. That put a smile on my face and, within a matter of weeks, David and I were married. We had a happy, fun day and on our wedding night we went home to our new little house.

I can honestly say, while writing this, this is the very first time I have given a thought to the irony of that first meeting in that old-fashioned pub all those years ago, the very place the realisation hit me on my wedding day that I wasn't in love with my husband and never had been. And the exact place where I met the love of my life for the very first time.

How ironic is that?

As I would like to make sure I've left nothing of any note out of my story, there is a little bit more to tell relating to the fear I must have been carrying from my first marriage. Anyone who has been abused in any way will know that the memory of the events never go away, but they do fade with time.

The fear I had been carrying appeared just after our daughter was born towards the end of 1974. I started having terrible nightmares. I would dream that my first husband took our daughter away. The fear I had lived with must have gone very deep to make my subconscious mind think that he still had a hold over me. I would wake up crying. During the day I would be fine because obviously our baby girl had nothing to do with my first husband. But during sleep he would come and take her away, telling me she was his, not mine.

The things our minds do to us. David would keep telling me not to be so silly but he didn't understand or realise what I'd gone through just two and a half years earlier. The abuse that I had experienced, both physically and mentally, had left its mark on me big time. Fortunately the nightmares did begin to fade when she was about six months old and eventually they stopped.

I would learn to forgive and let go of all the hurts in my life from 1970-1972 but, of course, I will never forget.

When I started writing my story some three and a half years ago I started by saying I would skip forward to 1974 when I married for the second time. I have now come full circle and filled in all the missing years without even trying.

CHAPTER THIRTY-EIGHT

Right at the beginning of my story I explained to you that I wanted to answer the question that I have been asked most over the years, "How did you get into healing Isabella? " Well, with a lot of help from unseen hands, I think I almost have.

I'm sure you will be able to understand now that there was so much I needed to learn. There were so many things that I needed to remember but, more importantly for me, there were so many hurtful events that I needed to clear, forgive and let go of before I could be healed myself. Once I was healed, or perhaps I could also say released from all the major upsets in my life, I was then in a position to be able to move forward and begin the work I came into this life to do. Heal.

I'm sure you have heard the words, "Healer, heal thyself." I think it would be fair to say now that this healer has. Three very simple words, but the effort and heartache that went into my own healing can never be understated. Was it easy to move my life forward so that I could start healing? No it wasn't. But I wouldn't change a thing. I have been able to say for many years now that getting Multiple Sclerosis was the best thing that could have happened to me, and I mean it.

You may find this hard to believe but if this had not happened to me my life might have gone in a completely different direction and I might never have been so strongly directed to find the help that God had placed here on Earth, Nansi. (I'm sure she was placed on Earth for lots of other people; I'm just very grateful that I was one of them) It was she who helped me to slowly turn my life around. It was Nansi who helped me rediscover and understand my own soul's journey and, looking back, if she hadn't, that to me now would have been unthinkable.

Everything happens for a reason. Sometimes it takes us years to find out why, and we all know (now) that sometimes we never do find the reason why, in this lifetime, but one day we will. I was very fortunate. It didn't take me too long before I was able to see the reason why I had to have been so unwell, the reason why I had to experience so many different problems (lessons). I am very grateful for everything that happened.

My gratitude list would be endless if I were to go through my life, but a simple list for this 'tale' - that's easy.

I'm grateful that I followed my instincts and my 'voice' when I was only fourteen years old when I experienced my first MS attack and told no one. I'm grateful that I followed my instincts again when I walked out of the hospital with the doctor shouting after me, "You'll be back!" And yet again, I'm grateful that my own doctor ignored my pleas for help, yes very grateful. If she had investigated my symptoms I would not have met Dr Branson, experienced her kindness towards me and then I would never have met her husband, Professor Branson. And I'm also very grateful that the new lady doctor I met many years later refused to help me when I had such bad earache. Because if she had helped me I would not have helped myself, by myself, and another lesson would not have been learnt.

I have been able to see for a long time now how, over many years, I was protected from any interference from drugs of any kind, time after time. God kept me safe.

I wouldn't wish the problems I have had, and the heartache I've been through over the years, on anyone. But the insights and knowledge I have gained through all my troubles have been priceless. And for me, all the knowledge I have accumulated would mean very little in the great scheme of things unless I am able to pass it all on.

A great man once said, "If you have knowledge, let others light their candles with it." (Sir Winston Churchill) I can only hope and pray that the 'light' of my experiences will allow you to 'light' your own candle. I've been left (thank goodness) without a shred of anger or ill feelings towards anyone; grateful beyond words for all the wonders I have seen and experienced so far in my life. What a very fortunate soul am I?

This was now 1992 and I was self-employed again, charging an hourly rate to the business I was working for. I was able to choose my own working hours. This enabled me to be able to have time for my family and some spare time for myself.

My thoughts were soon back on track. It was time for me to try and start building a healing practice and, perhaps even I can say now, not before time.

We had the space and room in our new home. Now all I needed to do was find a healing bed for my patients to lie down on. I realised that I couldn't afford to buy a new one as it would cost too much but a friend suggested to me that I get in touch with the porter at our local hospital. I don't know how she knew but she said that if I got in touch with him he may be able to find me a second-hand therapy bed that I could use as a healing bed. But, thinking back, that should not have surprised me because she knew so many different people from all walks of life.

Just a few weeks earlier she had phoned to ask if I would please come to talk with someone. The young lady she would like me to meet needed some advice and words of wisdom, and Rona thought that I was the right person to do that. Rona had more faith in me than I had in myself at the time. She had been telling me for years that she loved the fact that I had a way of knowing things. It was because of this she felt I might be able to offer her daughter's friend some words of advice. Imagine my surprise when she told me the young lady I was going to meet was Kylie Minogue.

When I arrived at Rona's home that afternoon it was full of people, from her own daughters to friends of her daughters and of course Kylie, her mother and her younger sister. They were travelling with Kylie, accompanying her on her 'Let's get to it' tour of the U.K.

Over cups of tea and coffee, and a lot of laughter and giggles, I was able to spend some quiet time with Kylie. I also had a lovely talk with Kylie's mother who told me all about her family back home in Australia and how she was missing her home and all her other family members. They were obviously a very close-knit family and very supportive of each other.

Kylie, at the time of our meeting, was trying to make a very big decision that would affect the rest of her life. And, just like any young lady, she was looking for some words of reassurance to help her organise her own thoughts on the big career change she was thinking of making, looking for someone outside of her own family and friends to confirm (or disagree) that the changes she was thinking of making were the correct ones.

And as history has shown she made the correct choice. I can only hope that the time I spent with her all those years ago helped in some small way. This happened over twenty years ago now and I wouldn't expect Kylie and her family to remember the afternoon we all spent together but, of course, I do because it's not every day you get the chance to spend a few hours with such a lovely young lady who was, and still is, so famous.

You might be wondering how the heck Rona knew Kylie, and that's exactly what I asked at the time. Apparently one of Rona's daughters who lived in London was a very close friend of a girl called Lilly, who also worked in London, who just happened to be a very close friend of Kylie.

You just never know who you are going to meet in this life, but that's what makes life so exciting. And just as Rona had arranged for Kylie to get some help, Rona was now trying to help me.

Somehow she knew that the hospital had lots of old discarded bits of equipment and furniture and the porter was the right person to contact. I rang the local hospital and spoke to the porter briefly, explaining to him what I was looking for. He suggested I came to the hospital to meet him and he would take me to the area where all the old equipment was stored to see if we could find me what I was looking for. To be honest, I was very pleasantly surprised by his response to me over the telephone. He was so helpful and I had not expected this.

In the bowels of the hospital was a huge storage space where all sorts of old discarded bits and pieces were stored and, there amongst everything else, were two therapy beds. One was a bit torn but the other one was free from any ripped material;

it was just old and dusty. The porter said I could have it if I wanted it. He would not accept any money for it, so the bed was mine. I thanked him profusely. I was so very grateful. My husband was able to pick it up for me in his work's van. All it needed was a good wash down and I was in business.

The word soon spread. From friends and friends of friends, people started ringing me asking for help. But I still had my old problem. Should I charge people or should I heal for nothing? Everything began to happen so fast that I didn't have the time to sort this one out in my mind. I was just going to have to go with the flow and see how I felt after a while.

But no sooner had I started (the very first day in fact) than I learned my own lesson that helped me decide what to do, along with a very interesting conversation that I was to have with my teacher and now dear friend, the very first week I started healing total strangers.

My very first patient was a young man who came to me asking for help with a back problem. He told me he was a county cricketer and a month earlier, while playing in a match, he'd hurt his back and because he'd hurt himself he was unable to play at the moment. I was so embarrassed and unsure of myself that first day that I didn't ask him for any money when I had finished giving him his treatment. When he got up from my healing bed he said that he felt so much better and then he said, "If this works I'm going to send you a bucketful of roses."

I did hear from a friend a few weeks later that he'd told her his back was healed after his treatment and he was back playing county cricket again. But I never did get my bucketful of roses.

My second patient was another gentleman, in his late sixties, full of fun and a real character. He explained to me that he had hurt his knees and his back in an accident about two weeks earlier and he was hoping I might be able to help. I asked him to explain to me what had happened. He told me that he had done his first parachute jump and had landed badly. He described how, instead of landing on his feet when he hit the ground, he had landed heavily on both his knees and, as he

265

hit the ground, his false teeth had flown out of his mouth. So he spent the next fifteen minutes on his hands and knees in the long grass looking for them (he did find them). Well, as you can imagine, as he was explaining all this to me, we were both in fits of laughter. When I had finished giving him his treatment he asked me if I wanted some money, so I asked if five pounds would be alright, and he said, "Yes."

By the time they had both left I wasn't feeling very good about myself. Both my 'patients' were feeling much better, but not me. Having spent an hour with each of the gentlemen, I was feeling quite worthless. Of course, this was my own fault. I should have decided before I started to work what I was going to do, work for free or charge. I needed to talk to Nansi. Two hours work, or two hours of my time, for five pounds. This all needed a lot of thought.

So why did I feel I shouldn't be asking for any money, let alone a fair price for my time?

As I had been helping Nansi with some of her patients and, of course, I had had my wonderful treatment from her not that long ago, she was more than happy for me to call around and see her for a chat. I explained to her what had happened and how I was feeling and asked her to please help me understand why I was thinking the way I was. Normally she would have told me to think it through for myself but, on this occasion, she did help me straightaway and I was very grateful. And this was her answer, as best as I can remember.

"Because you have always felt, and rightly so, that it is God sending you the healing energy and, without it, you can do nothing. Because of your upbringing you find it very hard to be able to ask for money for something you feel should be free because God's healing energy is free to you."

"Yes."

"Think about this, Isabella. Have you worked hard over many years to free your own energy to enable you to be the wonderful channel that you are, allowing the healing energy to flow through you? Have you worked hard over many lifetimes to bring you to this life, born with an inbuilt trust in God

266

because of all the work you did in your past lives? Do you want people in this life to owe you something because you have given them something wonderful for nothing? The laws of Karma will come into play if they cannot pay you for the healing. They will be in your debt whether they realise it or not. If you were to spend the rest of your life healing and didn't charge a penny, think of the number of lifetimes you will have to come back and live through to allow that debt to be repaid to you, allowing the scales to be rebalanced."

I just sat there shaking my head, thinking I didn't want to have to do that.

"Does a teacher get paid? Does a priest get paid? Does a doctor get paid?"

"Well yes, but I'm not a teacher Nansi, or a doctor or anything else for that matter."

"Oh yes you are," was her reply.

"You are going to spend the rest of your life healing, teaching and much more, and the last thing I want for you is for you to have to come back into many more lives just to allow the karmic debt owed to you to be cleared. But you know all of this. You just haven't had the time to sit and think about everything quietly by yourself. Your upbringing has left its mark on you and it's time for you to move away from your old ways of thinking."

"Oh boy!"

She then told me a little story about a healer that she knew who was registered with a healing organisation. This lady apparently never charged but asked people to please put a donation into her envelopes, which she then sent to the organisation she was registered with. At the end of a particularly busy week she decided to open the envelopes to see how much she would be sending to her organisation, instead of sending them sealed and unopened as she normally did. She had seen about fifteen people that particular week and when she opened and counted all the money it totalled about five pounds thirty-six pence. People had been putting in anything from a new penny piece to a few ten pence coins or fifty pence pieces. She sat and cried and, from that day on, she started to charge each person a fair price instead of asking for a donation. The word here is fair. A fair price for her time and also to cover the cost of heating the room she was working in.

"Now do you understand why you must charge? That lady had felt worthless when she counted up the money in those envelopes, worthless and used. We all need to feel we are of worth, no matter what task we are performing. Your time is worth money, Isabella, your knowledge is worth money, you are worth money. Just be fair in the amount you charge. You could earn a fortune if you wanted to. You could charge a lot of money for your treatments because you can, and do, genuinely help and heal people and, over the coming years, you are going to be amazed at the people who will seek you out."

I've never forgotten what she said to me all those years ago and, over the years, I have been fair with my charges.

CHAPTER THIRTY-NINE

I spent the summer and early autumn of 1992 healing in the evenings, my days being filled with either work or family, but the rest of the family were not very happy with me. They didn't like having strangers coming into our home in the evenings. It was important to me that peace reigned in our house. The only thing I could think of doing was to set aside a day a week to work, while the family were out of the house at either school or work. That way they wouldn't see the people who were coming into our home for healing. But I found out very quickly that I still needed to work at least one evening, because most of the people that were coming to me for help worked during the day. It would take quite a while before I could stop the evening sessions. Not quite the support I would have liked from my family at the time, but never mind.

Nansi had been asking me for a few months to get myself registered with a healing organisation, as she felt it would be the way forward for me in the years to come. I wasn't so sure but because I respected and trusted her opinion, I agreed. To become registered I would need to work with six patients under the guidance of two registered healers who would act as my sponsors. Nansi said she would act as one of my sponsors but I needed to find a second one.

Just before I met my second sponsor for the first time, my friend Rona sadly died. She had had a brain tumour quite a few years earlier and, unfortunately, the cancer had come back. She was a fantastic lady, a real character, a loving mother and a friend. Always amazingly dressed, always beautifully turned out, right down to her long painted fingernails.

I was to go to her funeral with another of our friends. They had both been partners in a high-end clothing wholesale business and were clients of mine when I had my business and, of course, Rona and I had kept in touch with each other.

Obviously it was going to be a sad time at the crematorium. The place was packed with family and friends. So imagine my horror as the coffin was brought down the centre isle while we were all standing. There on the top of the coffin sat my friend. She was sitting on the end of her own coffin, with her legs crossed, dangling both of them over the end as if she was posing for a model shoot, while waving her hands in the air with her brightly polished red nails and shouting at me, "You can see me."

I didn't know which way to turn. Was I seeing things?

She kept shouting at me, "I know you can see me," as she waved her hands in the air. I had to bite the inside of my mouth to stop myself from laughing. I felt as if I was in a Carry On film, the whole scene was so bizarre.

Then she said to me "I'm going to stop this lot in their tracks." I just sat there wondering what on earth was going to happen next.

When the time came to close the curtains around the coffin they wouldn't budge. I lost count of the number of times the button was pressed trying to close them, but to no avail. All I could hear from the direction of the coffin was laughter. With a look of embarrassment, one of the undertakers closed them by hand.

I couldn't wait to get outside, say my goodbyes as quickly as I could and get in my car and leave! As I was driving away from the crematorium I was crying with laughter. The only regret I felt was that I had not been given the chance to tell her daughters what I'd seen, but I mustn't have been meant to.

I've related this tale because, when I was introduced to my second sponsor about two weeks later, she blew me away with what she said to me.

I can't remember who gave me Betty's name and phone number or who told me she was a registered healer with the organisation I was going to try and register with, but whoever it was thought that she would probably be able to help me. I had phoned her and she agreed to meet me to see if she thought I would be suitable.

That first meeting with Betty is one of those days in my life that I can still remember very clearly. As soon as I entered her house she said, "I can't help you to become a healer because you are a healer, you always have been and actually, I would like you to heal me of a problem that I have had for a long time. Perhaps we could organise for you to do this next week. But I can help you with your clairvoyant gift." I just looked at her blankly, not knowing what was coming next.

"You have just recently been to a funeral haven't you?"

"Yes."

"And you saw your friend sitting on her coffin, didn't you?"

Dear Lord, I'd told no one because I wasn't sure whether I had imagined the whole thing.

"No, you didn't imagine it. It really happened. That's what I think I can help you with, help you develop your clairvoyant gift."

Good grief. Not only did she know what had happened to me, but she had been reading my mind as well. I was used to reading other people's minds but no one had ever read mine before. Betty was not only to be my second sponsor but she would also be one of my six patients. It was now 'all systems go' to get me registered.

Within days, I had the other five people that I needed. They were all happy to allow me to work with them, with one of my sponsors looking on. Most of them had been to me before for a treatment which made it easy for me to be able to ask for their help in getting my certificate of registration. My sponsors would only be with me to observe and then they were both going to write reports on my performance. The other five people I was to work on were also asked to write their own reports on their treatments from me. Oh gosh, this was going to be very interesting for everyone, including me.

The first person I was to work on was my second sponsor. I was feeling a little bit apprehensive as I walked to her front door and rang the bell. Betty hadn't told me what her problem was or what she expected from me. But she had given me the impression that she had been very pleased to meet me, as if she had been waiting for someone to 'magically appear' that could help her with her problem.

It was eleven o'clock in the morning when she welcomed me into her home with open arms and a cup of tea. Then she began to explain to me that she had been 'sitting' on a letter from the hospital. They had been trying to get her to go into hospital for an operation for about a year but she didn't want to. Now this I could understand. She had been diagnosed with a prolapsed womb nearly two years earlier and it was getting worse. I sat there and said to her, "I really don't know how to start to help you with this."

"You don't have to do anything. My guide will work through you and perform the operation I need, and I will tell you exactly what to do before I fall asleep because I will fall asleep."

If I'd felt apprehensive before, my stomach was doing somersaults now. I had no idea what she meant but I was about to find out. Betty led me like a lamb to the slaughter into her healing room. It was a little room all set up with her healing bed and, as my eyes swept around the room, the object that caught my eye was a picture on the wall. I felt drawn to it. She smiled when she saw me looking at it. It was a drawing of a Chinese gentleman. He was dressed in clothes from hundreds of years ago, with a thin face and a very long thin beard that went to a point on the end. I kept thinking he could be 'Mandarin' but I didn't really know what that meant.

"That's my guide. He will work on my problem through you and put me right."

"But how will he work through me?"

Without answering my question she climbed up onto her healing bed, lay down and said to me, "Just relax and let the healing energy flow for a few minutes and then you will feel as if you are stuck to the spot. When that happens just keep your hands over me and stand as still as you can as he works through you. He is going to use your body as an instrument for him to be able to perform a psychic operation on me. Don't be frightened."

I wasn't sure what I was thinking at that precise moment,

but my instincts were not telling me to run.

"Once he starts to work on me I will fall asleep. You can just leave me when he's finished and I will sleep for a while. You can go home; I'll be fine. I'll speak to you tomorrow."

With that she closed her eyes and I started, just as I had for a few years now, only this time within minutes I felt a bit odd to say the least. I did feel as if I couldn't move, just as she had said I would. I kept my hands over her lower body and watched in amazement as unseen hands (but I could see the shape of hands in the energy) worked on the inside of her.

It really did feel as if I was in the twilight zone. Let's face it, I was in the twilight zone.

After a while, and I had no idea how long, I felt her 'spirit guide' leaving me as my body relaxed, and I knew whatever had been done was finished. So I did what she told me. I quietly left her room and her house and drove home in a daze.

That day is carved into my memory bank and, quite frankly, what she did to me that day was a bit naughty of her to say the least. I could have freaked out and run from her house, but I didn't. Talk about being thrown in at the deep end. This was something that I had never experienced before and I didn't expect it to ever happen again. But I have to be honest and say the whole experience had been amazing.

Betty didn't ring me until the end of that week, by which time I was getting a little bit worried about what had happened to her, although I knew I'd done nothing. I had just stood beside her on that day, feeling a bit peculiar with my arms outstretched over her. When she did eventually ring she asked if she could see me again, as whatever had been done hadn't worked and she wanted me to 'do it again'. I was confused by what she was saying and I wasn't sure how I felt about being asked to go back and 'do it again'. But because she was one of my sponsors I felt that I ought to do as she asked. She asked me to go back to her home the following Monday morning.

As soon as I arrived, Betty said she was sorry. I was even more confused now. Then she explained to me what had happened when I left her. She told me that she had slept for about half an hour and, when she got up from her healing bed, she said she knew she had been healed because she felt wonderful. Her prolapsed womb had given her many other related problems and she said she knew immediately that they had all gone.

I said; "That's wonderful for you, so why do you need me to do it again?"

"Because after I got up and had my lunch, I then had six patients booked in to see me. It was early evening before I finished seeing everyone and I had been on my feet for hours." I just looked at her in disbelief. Until I saw her I had honestly thought that somehow I must have done something wrong but I had reasoned with myself that, actually, I hadn't done anything.

If Betty was reading my mind she would have known that I was cross with her. What she should have done was to take it very easy for the rest of that day and a few days after, but she knew that. After all she had been worked on by those unseen hands inside of her. I had actually seen the 'hands' stitching her up after the internal work had been done (twilight zone), and she knew it. Betty was the person who had instigated her own healing. She was the experienced person between the two of us and she knew she should have rested. I was to do it again.

Betty didn't say very much after that because I'm sure she realised that I was cross with her. She had used me and then she had abused the wonderful work that had been done. Off we went again and exactly the same thing happened. But this time, when I knew her guide had left me, I asked God to make sure she slept for a few hours.

"Please Lord, make sure she stays asleep until her body has fully healed so she doesn't undo the amazing work that I have just witnessed."

Three days later Betty rang me and told me that she had got up from her healing bed after about an hour and she had sat down with a cup of tea. The next thing she knew, she woke to find it had turned dark outside. She had slept for eight hours.

She said she made herself something to eat and then went straight to bed and she had not woken up until after lunch the following day.

Unknown to me she had made appointments for more of her patients to see her on that Monday afternoon, after I had left. Betty was going to work again for the rest of the day after she had had her own healing. Her patients had been knocking on her door but she never heard them, all six of them.

Then the following day more of her patients had arrived in the morning for their appointments but no one answered the door. No one was at home, or so they thought. I told her I had asked that she be kept asleep until her body had had time to heal. Betty sounded a bit cross with me when I told her but not as cross as I was with her. I just said, "Thank you Lord," under my breath. I don't think she thought that I had it in me to ask the Universe to help me, let alone the fact that my request would be answered so wonderfully.

"Are you healed Betty?"

"Yes I am," was her reply.

Betty told me a few weeks later that she kept her next appointment at the hospital because she knew they would discharge her, as she no longer had a prolapsed womb. And that's exactly what they did, after scratching their heads in disbelief.

The next time I spoke to her on the telephone was to arrange for her to come to my home to act as my sponsor while I was to work with a lady I had seen once before. Because Betty arrived about half an hour before my patient was due I was able to question her as to what on earth had happened to me during the twice I had 'been present' at her healing. I don't know what other words to use because it wasn't me doing any healing work. It was the spirit of her guide working through me.

Betty tried to shrug me off with, "You don't need to know," but I wasn't going to let this one go. I needed to know what I had done, or not done. She explained that she worked, not only as a healer, but also as a transfiguration medium. This meant that spirit people could, and did, use her body. They

275

could transform her features to make her look like the spirit person had looked while they were here on Earth. They could not only change her face, but they could also change the appearance of her clothing. I was to witness this in the weeks to come and all I can say is that it is an amazing event to see and an even more amazing thing to be able to do, as I would experience for myself in the years to come.

Betty then explained that the spirit world also used her body to be able to perform spirit surgery and that's what had happened to me. I had been used by the spirit world to heal her.

Apparently the spirit surgeon enters the channel (that was me with Betty) through our energy centres, and then the spirit surgeon can utilise our hands to perform whatever needs doing. The spirit person didn't actually use my hands. He used my hands to be able to use his. Don't ask because I can't explain this any better.

Betty then explained that there are no barriers or boundaries with psychic surgery, as the spirit surgeon can get to bits that a surgeon here on Earth would not be able to reach. She continued by saying that the minute she met me she knew I was the person she had been waiting for for nearly two years. I was the answer to her prayers. She knew her guide would be able to use me to heal her because I was such a good channel and she also said that she knew I would be able to handle the experience, even though I had no idea what was going to happen at the time.

Betty finished our conversation by saying that this would never happen to me again because obviously it was her guide (not mine) that had worked through me, and he would not be doing 'that' again with me.

Okay, at least now I had an explanation, I think.

CHAPTER FORTY

The next person I was to work on was the wife of an ex-client of mine. We were still in touch by telephone because David was now working for her husband on a self-employed basis so we occasionally had a chat on the telephone.

I explained to her that I was starting to try and build up my healing practice and, as I knew she was having problems with her back, I asked if she would like to come for a treatment but she declined my offer.

Then, not very long after my first approach, she rang me and said she had changed her mind. She would like to 'give it a go' in the hope it would help the severe pain she was having.

I had seen her for one treatment before that day and she said she would be happy to have another one with my sponsor present. Cath arrived with her daughter who would have been about fourteen years old at the time. She wanted to sit in the room and be with her mum while I worked, and that was fine by me. Firstly I worked around Cath's aura as she sat on a stool, and then I asked Cath to climb up onto my healing bed. I asked her to lie on her stomach so that I could work down her spine with the healing energy.

She told me that she was feeling a little bit dizzy, so I tried to reassure her that she would be fine and if she were to gently breathe deeply and slowly it might help. It was just after this that I heard a voice say to me. "We are going to give her an injection to numb the area where she has pain and she will fall asleep."

Cath started telling me that her bottom was turning numb and the numbness was travelling down her legs, and then she stopped talking mid-sentence; she was asleep.

I had no sooner realised she was asleep when I heard the same voice again say, "Now we can work on her spine." As I was now standing at the bottom of her spine with my hands about six inches above her, thinking I was going to direct the wonderful healing energy into where she said her pain was, I realised I 'felt' stuck to the spot and I knew what that feeling meant. All I can remember thinking was, "Dear Lord, it's happening to me again," and at the same time I said to my sponsor, "Something's starting to happen."

"Just keep still," was all she said to me.

I could see hands working inside of Cath, as I was standing over her in complete awe and amazement. Golden light surrounded the area the spirit person was working in. First it looked as if some sort of padding was being placed between two discs in her spine and then a golden fluid was poured over the padding.

Next I could see a file (that's the only word I can think of to describe the tool I could see) as it was being used on a bit of bone that seemed to stick out where it shouldn't be. The hands were busy filing the bone down and then they smoothed it off. Then more golden fluid was painted on the bone that had been filed.

I saw the hands coming out of her and a voice said to me, "It's all done now. You can relax." I felt the spirit person leaving me. My legs felt a bit wobbly. In fact, the whole of me was feeling a little bit strange, but that was no surprise. I turned to my sponsor, who was sitting on my settee with her mouth open. She had witnessed the whole thing but not only my sponsor, Cath's daughter, who was clairvoyant herself, had also witnessed the whole operation and she was in tears.

"Mum's healed, isn't she?"

I said, "I think she is, sweetheart. I think your mum is going to be fine now."

Cath was still fast asleep, oblivious to the events of the past twenty minutes.

My sponsor was almost speechless. When she did speak, a few moments later, she seemed to be speaking to me as if she didn't believe her own eyes when she said, "I'm the only healer for hundreds of miles that performs spirit operations. The only reason this has happened to you today is because I'm here with you."

I said, "That's fine. I'm just very pleased you are here

with me because Cath obviously needed this help and if this never happens to me again it doesn't matter."

"It won't," was her response.

Cath started to wake up and she immediately needed the loo. When she came back from the toilet I tried to explain to her what had happened. She was smiling and that's all I needed to see. She would go home and let me know in a few days time how she felt.

It would be a few months before Cath wrote her report to send to the organisation I was trying to register with. This was a good thing, as a few months had gone by and she was still well. As Cath and I are still in touch with each other, after all these years, I have asked her permission to include her report so that you can read her story from her own perspective.

The following is Catherine's report word for word. The only thing I have left out is her surname and address:

Catherine D.

Re: Isabella Clarence

This may help you to understand the amount of help I have received from Isabella. My name is Catherine. I am married with two children. My doctor informed me about six years ago that if I did not follow his instructions I would be in a wheelchair.

I had had a niggly pain in my back for a number of years, but this time I had terrible back pain. I would collapse on my knees with tears running down my face, it was so bad. When the doctor came to examine me he said, "It's just a slipped disc." Just. I didn't think I could stand any more pain. This went on for four weeks with me taking more and more painkillers.

After a further consultation with the doctor he agreed to send me immediately for an x-ray. When the x-ray was checked, they showed a badly slipped disc and, more unusual, an extra piece of bone growing in-between the vertebra of my spine. This was causing pressure on the nerves, so causing me continual pain.

I was then sent for physiotherapy, traction, manipulation and given gentle exercise routines to do. This was over a period of two and a half years. The slipped disc seemed better but I was informed that the bone was still growing and that there was nothing more that could be done for me.

The bone growth was situated where it was impossible to operate on. I would have to learn to live with it, take the painkillers and adjust my life accordingly to accommodate my back or the alternative, to be in a wheelchair. This meant no stretching, carrying or any exertion of any kind as this could begin weeks of continual pain. I was even shown how to lift a kettle properly, how to load a washing machine properly and the correct way to get in and out of bed.

Can you imagine what it is like for a mother of two lively children to be virtually housebound, not even to be able to pick them up for a cuddle, or a woman who had to rely on other people to clean windows, hang washing out and bring it back in, or even something as simple as carry a shopping bag?

It was very hard to believe that this was going to be 'it' for the rest of my life.

My husband knew Isabella for about fifteen years, through business, the last five of which she was his accountant. I came to know her through this. I occasionally spoke to her on the telephone and I had met her once or twice. On one of these occasions the pain was very bad and Isabella asked if she could help. I refused.

I couldn't believe in 'that sort of thing' then I began to wonder and I thought if it helps, give it a try, so I arranged it with Isabella.

I had my first healing on Wednesday, 11ᵗʰ November 1992. It took approx. forty minutes. I was very nervous to begin with. Isabella sat me down and began talking to me. She explained what she would be doing and told me if I wanted her to stop or I felt unsure about anything I just had to ask and she would try to explain. After I took some deep breaths, Isabella began. I was sitting on a stool and Isabella was behind me; her hands were above and around my neck. After a few moments I began to feel very light-headed and relaxed. Isabella asked if I was alright. I said, "Yes," and she asked if I could lie down on her bed.

Once I was in a comfortable position Isabella began to follow the length of my body, from head to toe. She told me to breathe deeply and slowly and explained what she was doing.

It's hard to believe that anyone can be doing anything, when they are not even touching you. By now I was totally relaxed. I began having tingling sensations on my neck and down my back and I felt really warm. I was asked to turn over onto my back. Isabella continued. A warm tingling sensation passed down from my head to my stomach, my back and hips, to my legs and finally my toes. My legs felt very warm and my back felt as though I had pins and needles in it. I felt totally relaxed and sleepy. Isabella advised me to rest for a while and covered me with a blanket. About ten minutes later I got down from the bed. My back still felt warm and tingly. The numbness lasted for about two hours. Isabella advised me to take things easy. She asked me how I felt and asked if I would care to come again. I said, "Yes." I had very little pain. That night I had my first full night's sleep for approx. six years. I couldn't believe it.

I had my second healing on Wednesday, 18th November 1992. Again I was nervous, though not as much as the first time. I asked Isabella if my daughter could be present while I was being given healing. She said, "Of course she can."

Isabella enquired how I had been feeling since the week before. I said, "Fine, but I am still in some pain."

I got onto the bed and, once I was comfortable, Isabella began. Almost immediately I began to feel light-headed and dizzy. I was face down on the bed, so I couldn't really see what was happening. Later, I'll tell you what my daughter told me. Isabella explained that her hands had stopped moving, so something was happening. I felt really warm and relaxed. I can remember saying that my bottom was really cold on the left hand side and the coldness was travelling down my left leg. I said I felt really strange and that the coldness was beginning in my left leg.

I can remember Isabella saying, "Don't worry. Just relax and breathe deeply," and then I'm afraid I don't remember anything more as I was unconscious. The next thing I knew I woke up with an overwhelming urge of needing the toilet. Isabella helped me down from the bed. She told me to be very careful.

When I came back from the loo I was very surprised when my daughter informed me that I had been asleep and that I had stayed asleep for about twenty-five minutes. I felt very strange.

Isabella sat me down and explained what had happened. I had been put to sleep while 'they' went to work on me. Isabella said that she had had a sensation of a sanding process going on, on my spine. I couldn't feel anything. My back was totally numb.

This was strange. How could you have an operation inside you without being cut? How could an operation be done when I was told by a specialist that this condition was inoperable? This was very hard to believe.

Isabella advised me to take things very gently and quietly as I had had major surgery. From the way I was feeling I believed her. How could I doubt this, feeling as I did? As you can see by the date of my visit to Isabella it was nearing Christmas. I took things very easy for the next two to three weeks.

Can you imagine what it feels like not to be doped by painkillers, not to be in constant pain?

It is a totally new way of life.

For Christmas I washed and polished the tiles in my kitchen myself. I cleaned windows. Me. I never thought I would enjoy ordinary household chores. Isabella did tell me off for doing so much and I know a slipped disc can happen in any part of the spine, so I still do my special exercises, but I have a totally different way of life now. I would never have believed it possible.

I thank God the day I was introduced to Isabella Clarence because it must surely have been meant for me to have this miracle worked on me.

Thank you, Isabella.

Your friend forever,

Catherine D

Reading this as I have being typing the words that Catherine wrote down about an event that happened at the end of 1992, so many years ago now, has brought a smile to my face.

Catherine and I still talk to each other by phone at least once a fortnight and I can tell you that her back has never given her any problems since that night (nineteen years ago now).

Yes, I told her off because she told me she had climbed up onto her kitchen bench to clean the tiles about three weeks after her treatment and please don't worry, she was not unconscious during that treatment; she was just in a very deep sleep, quite safe.

That was the second and the last treatment that Catherine ever had. She didn't need another one. She had been healed.

It was definitely a miracle for Catherine.

CHAPTER FORTY-ONE

My next guinea pig was to be a dear friend of mine. Do you remember me telling you about the reading I had with a clairvoyant at a friend's house a little while after my father died and how the clairvoyant was able to relay my father's words to me? My next patient was to be that very same friend. We had known each other for years, as we both used to live on the same road and we had spent many hours chatting over cups of tea and coffee.

Betty said there was no need for her to be with me anymore, even though she had only been with me the once, with one of my patients. She said she would be wasting her time being with me as I was a healer and there was nothing she could teach me. After all, she said, "You healed me."

Nansi, who was my main sponsor, said there was no need for her to be present as she had been watching me heal for at least three years now. I was to be on my own for the rest of my 'tests', if that's what they were.

When Jean arrived she was a little bit nervous, as she had no idea what was going to happen. She had been listening to me for years, telling her my stories of my travels outside of myself. She had most of my father's poems in a drawer beside her bed. She had been the friend who was there for me to talk to when I needed to unload the unloadable. Most people would have run a mile from me if they had heard just a few of the stories I used to tell her. So I think I understood just a little bit of her apprehension. I just said to her, "It's only me." She looked at me and said, "Yes, and who else?"

Once she was up on my healing bed I started to work as I always do, by going around her with my hands about a foot away from her body and, just as I got to her lower stomach, I felt myself becoming 'stuck' yet again. I was on my own this time, but that was alright. I knew now what was happening and I was fine with it. If the spirit world could work through me and help someone, I was very privileged.

Trying to explain to someone who is awake and wanting to know what's going on, when all the while all I wanted to do was watch in amazement, was hard but I did try and give her a running commentary. After all it was her body we were working on.

"A baggy loose bladder," was what I was told. It needed everything lifting and tightening up and that's exactly what 'he' did. I was even able to tell her when it was almost finished and he was stitching her up internally.

She was going to have to be very careful for a few days. I can also remember when 'he' first started working on Jean she kept saying to me that she needed the toilet. He told me to tell her that the sensation she was feeling would pass in a few moments and she wasn't to worry, and it did. I think I would have preferred it if she had been asleep, but knowing my friend the way I did, I knew she wanted to be in on the act, and she was. It was most definitely a man who performed the work but to this day I can't give you his name, because he never gave me one. All I can do again is say a heartfelt thank you, as I did on the day this amazing work was done.

Jean has given me her permission to use her testimonial.

This is her report, word for word:

Where can I start to tell of the wondrous things I have heard and seen and experienced through my lovely friend Isabella? I spent a most unpleasant summer in 1992 constantly troubled with a very weak bladder. Every morning, padded up and clutching spares, I set off for the office. I used to dread, more than most, catching a cold or a cough; sneezing and coughing were my worst enemies. Each was followed by a deluge. Hot days were a nightmare.

Having coffee with Isabella, I would listen with interest to her relating to me people she was helping and with great success. I feel I have followed her steps along the road to the spirit world, since her father died and spoke to her for the first time, beautiful words of poetry, many poems kept in a book by my bed, which I often read for the sheer pleasure and sweetness of them.

I have listened and discussed all aspects of the subject with my friend and seen with interest as she has progressed into what, to me, was the unknown. The experiences she has had have brought her great joy and I have been more than delighted to share in the knowledge of them.

The answer to my problem was so obvious to me. It was staring me in the face. Why not let Isabella help me? I didn't need a doctor; I needed Isabella.

I was nervous as I climbed onto her bed. Would I feel invisible hands and would I feel pain? I felt nothing, just relaxation. I was told my bladder was baggy. A tuck here, a tuck there and stitches everywhere as invisible fingers gently solved my embarrassing problem. "Just lie there and relax," said my friend when it was all over. I did. It was all over.

But had it, I wonder, worked? Two days later I was still wearing my pads but they were now dry. Then came the first day I went to the office unpadded. All was well. I felt I had been liberated. I even felt I had lost weight. Well in a way I had; no more bulky pads.

I have been worked on again and taught to really relax. I now have no problem with my bladder. I feel more feminine. To me it is my miracle.

I am spreading the word about Isabella, who coyly says it is not her, but I know better. Yes, spirit is working, but it is she, the person, loving and caring for people, who makes this possible.

They of the great beyond didn't just choose anyone to work through. She is special and I am more than privileged to have her as a very dear and loving friend.

Jean C

When I read through this report it always brings a tear to my eye. Bless you, Jean.

The next person I was to see was actually a work colleague and friend of Jean's. Jean asked me if she could have a treatment in the evening, to allow her friend Pat, who worked all day, to come along with her. Pat wanted to see with her own eyes what it was all about before she herself had her first treatment. Because Jean was such a good family friend I didn't think my family would complain about this evening appointment, because she wasn't a stranger in our home. Jean had a short treatment first (not that there was anything wrong with her). She just loved to feel relaxed and it did give her lots more energy for her busy life.

Once I had finished Jean's treatment I asked Pat if she felt comfortable enough to be able to have one herself. She said after seeing Jean survive her treatment (jokingly) she was happy to give it a go, as she had nothing to lose and yes, she was quite happy to write a report when we had finished, to go to the healing organisation.

Once Pat was settled on my healing bed I began working in her aura, first around her head for a few minutes and then moving slowly down her body and, just as I was passing my hands over her lower stomach area, I instinctively knew I had to stop and stand still. It was happening again.

Pat was so relaxed she wasn't quite with it. All she said to us was that she felt wonderful, so peaceful and so relaxed, in a very sleepy voice. I stopped and stood still to allow my new 'help' to start his work. His hands were inside of her within seconds of me stilling myself, working away at great speed.

Over the years I've tried to explain to people what I see. It's like watching a movie in fast forward. It's not a long-drawn-out affair. Depending on what work needs doing, the whole event can be over in a matter of minutes.

My first three 'twilight zone' events had gone relatively slowly and, thinking back, it was probably the spirit world getting me used to the way 'they' worked. But, working on Pat, everything seemed to be going at full speed. It was a bit difficult for me to know what 'he' was doing because everything was being done in fast forward.

The only thing I can clearly remember was as if a blast of energy was directed through her intestines and then the work began. First on her right side and then on her left, it seemed as if something was being held open, as if a little tunnel on both sides was collapsing in on itself and what was being done was to hold each one open with what looked like two small springs. That unfortunately is the best explanation I can give.

More golden liquid was used when 'he' had completed whatever he had done and then he left me. Pat was still in a very relaxed, sleepy state and that's how I left her for a little while.

Over the following years Pat has occasionally come to see me for a treatment and I can honestly say she relaxes quicker and deeper than anyone else I have ever worked on. Pat has also given her permission for me to use her testimonial from 1992.

These are her words:

Wonderful Feelings

When Jean first told me about the woman who used to live along the road from me, who was doing wonderful things to people but could not describe quite how, I thought what a load of rubbish. But the more she told me I became very curious, but still could not believe what she was saying was really true, and I never thought I would ever be going as a patient, if that is the right word.

I had a problem which had been with me for about fifteen to twenty years. Everyone close to me was aware exactly what it was; it became a joke but, unfortunately, was no joke to me.

I never ever got a feeling that I wanted to go to the toilet, unless I used a suppository. So when Jean suggested that I accompanied her to Isabella's on her next visit I thought, okay it's a night out, a chat and a coffee. So when it came to lying on the table I was under the impression nothing could ever happen to me. Well, I was wrong. I went into a relaxed, most wonderful feeling I had ever experienced. I was not asleep, yet I was. I was there, but I wasn't there. I felt nothing. It took me about half an hour to pull myself together. I thought I had been on the table about ten minutes. I was later told I was there about forty-five minutes.

I was so tired all I wanted was to go to bed and sleep. As I explained to Isabella what had happened, this feeling, I could not really put into words. My feelings were nothing will happen to me, or my bowels. WRONG. Isabella said I would go to the toilet in the next few days. Oh yes, I thought. After fifteen years she'll be lucky, or I would.

I went to see Isabella on the Wednesday. The Monday previous I had gone to the loo with usual help. By Friday I thought to myself, "Idiot. Nothing. Told you so."

Never mind. Sat, Sun, Monday came. By afternoon I had this wonderful feeling. Yes, you're right, I went to the toilet, and yes I did again

287

Monday evening. Tuesday, Wednesday twice. Thursday once, Friday twice.
Friday, I visited Isabella again. The same experience as Wednesday
the week previous. It is now Tuesday, thirteen days later. I have had the
most marvellous two weeks. If I never go again I believe it's been a miracle.
So I must thank this wonderful lady called Isabella who used to live
along the road. I did not think it was possible.
I thank you from the bottom of my, not my heart but yes, you've
guessed.
Thanks,
Pat.

CHAPTER FORTY-TWO

There were two more people that came to me to be helped during this time but, unfortunately, I have lost touch with them both over the years and it would be unfair of me to include their stories in my book without their permission. Never mind.

Betty was to write two reports for me, one as my sponsor and the other one as a patient, but unfortunately she never provided me with a copy of either of her written reports. I have a 'feeling' that she would not have told the whole story, because what she did to me was a bit unprofessional to say the least, but obviously meant to be. But I do understand why she did it. That was probably why she never gave me a copy, even though I asked her several times. She wanted to be healed and the only way for that to happen was to have a spirit operation.

Well, God bless her, she got it.

Nansi on the other hand did give me her written report and I would like to almost finish my story with her own words. This is part of Nansi's report, as it would be unfair of me to include her personal information:

I was first introduced to Isabella Clarence when she attended me as a patient after being medically diagnosed as an advanced Multiple Sclerosis case and being told she would soon be wheelchair-bound. For months she had treatments and asked many questions, and the treatment sessions also became teaching sessions. After termination of treatments, contact was maintained and, whilst Isabella pursued her own individual path of learning, she frequently came to me for more explanations, demonstrations and instructions. Teaching was mostly by questions and answers, loans of relevant books, plus practical demonstrations on patients, demonstrating healing hands, flow of energies through the body centres etc. She then pursued her own path, learning from many aspects. Lately she has been working on some of my patients and I have been impressed with the results. They are all long-standing chronic cases rejected by orthodox medical practitioners. She has had success where I have failed.

Miss Nansi Morgan

I did become registered as a Spiritual Healer after all the reports were sent to the healing organisation at the beginning of 1993, and I have remained so to this day.

When I began writing this I honestly thought that it wouldn't take me very long to be able to answer the question, "How did you get into healing, Isabella?" If I'd known then how soul-searching writing my story was going to be I may not have even started. But I'm glad I did. I just hope and pray that by being so open and honest I may have helped someone. I may have helped someone to 'light' their own 'light' of understanding.

Do you remember what my daughter said to me at the beginning of my writing nearly four years ago, that whatever I thought I was going to write would not be what I ended up with? She was absolutely right. I honestly thought I would write a chapter on answering that question and then I would be able to write healing stories from the many years that I have been helping people, but that's not what has happened.

You were right my precious girl. The book took on a life of its own and now it's done.

I have dedicated my first book to the two precious souls who helped me so much through my troubles (lessons) and, as I have just written down Nansi's words, I would like to finish with some words from my father.

On the day I passed my driving test my father handed me a set of keys to the car he was going to allow me to drive and said to me, "Now go and learn to drive." This is a perfect analogy for now. The time had come for me to learn to be the healer God always wanted me to be. Time to learn how to deal with strangers, and the only way I could do that was by 'jumping into the deep end' and 'doing it.'

Thanks Dad. You always had the right words and you still do.

When I first started to heal outside of my own circle of family and friends in 1989, I asked my father to please send me some words that I could use every day to help keep me in my right space and thank you Dad, you did.

I would like to finish my book with those words.

If you ever feel you need a little bit of help, please use them with our love.

A Prayer to Hold

O wondrous source of peace and love
O wondrous source of life,
I pray your Grace will fill the years
With love, for this soul's life.

Be near me, Lord
And guide my path,
That every step I take
Be filled with goodness from the source
Of peace and love and Grace.

All I can hope for now is two things. The first is that I have accomplished my mission and that you have been able to take something away from my story that has helped you. And, last but not least, that my second book will be as well guided as this one has been.

Thank you, Lord.

This is now the end of the beginning.

INFORMATION

Just in case anyone is wondering what symptoms I have experienced over the past forty odd years of my life I thought it might be a good idea to list them all for you and tell you the effect they had on me. So here is my list:

MY LEGS: the words that come to my mind - buzzing, tingling, pins and needles and sometimes numbness, but numbness I could feel. That sounds daft, but it's the best way I can describe it. Not necessarily all at once; one at a time, or one or two together. Also sometimes I would have a feeling as if lead weights had been attached to both my legs. They would feel so heavy that it was hard for me to move them. And the worst of all, the day they just would not move forward and I ended up having to sit on the pavement for I don't know how long. This happened more than once but, fortunately, I was in my own home the other times it happened.

MY HANDS: the same tingling, sometimes numb and lots of dropping things because I would misjudge my hold on a cup, glass or plate, or anything else that I was trying to pick up and hold onto, which left me with lots of broken crockery in the kitchen!

TINGLING: along with a feeling of pins and needles across my shoulders, sometimes on one side or the other and sometimes both at the same time. This could also be very painful. It would come and go over the years for no particular reason.

TIREDNESS: as I have said, it was like a wave coming over me out of the blue and there was no fighting it. One minute I would be fine and the next I would be feeling so exhausted that I had no choice but to sit down or lie down, before I fell down.

FEELING LIKE A FLY ON THE WALL: as if I was not there, not connected. A feeling as if I was not part of myself, as if I was not part of anything at all. (Very odd)

CHOKING SENSATION: when I was lying in bed at

night, just as I was beginning to fall asleep, I would sometimes suddenly find myself not being able to breathe, as if my throat had somehow closed. I would gulp and swallow in air and then realise I was still breathing. This was a very strange and a horrible sensation and quite frightening while it lasted, but it did pass quickly. And it definitely had nothing to do with acid reflux.

MY EYES: I have described the net curtain that sometimes appeared from nowhere and when it did appear I had to strain my eyes to be able to see through it which, in turn, gave me a bad headache. This could last for a few weeks then, for no reason, the net curtain would disappear along with the headache. Also in any brightly lit shop or shopping mall, within minutes of entering I would begin to feel panicky. This was due to the lighting systems. They would (and still do on occasions) flicker slightly, but enough to cause me a problem. Sunglasses put a stop to this symptom. Also, on more than one occasion I suffered from pupil dilation in one eye. The episodes didn't last very long, but when it happened it was very uncomfortable.

KNOCKING MYSELF: against the side of a wall or door frame as I turned to go into a room, or when a corridor had a left or right hand turn I would bang my shoulder against it because I was forever misjudging the distance which, in turn, left me with a lot of bruises!

MY SPEECH: when I was very tired my speech would become very slurry and I would sometimes say my words backwards. This was quite funny for everyone listening to me but not very funny for me. It sometimes sounded as if I'd had too much to drink. I would also find some words impossible to say. I could 'see' them in my mind but, for the life of me, I couldn't pronounce them.

FACIAL TENDERNESS: from about fifteen years of age, when I started to try and apply make-up to my face, especially around my eyes, I couldn't. Because my face was very sore to the touch, it really hurt me when I applied even the slightest pressure. During my late teenage years and early twenties I periodically tried again but, by my mid-twenties, I gave up trying. So no makeup for me. Lipstick didn't hurt to apply but I never did learn how to apply anything else. Consequently I still don't wear very much make-up, as I never learned how. Thankfully my face has not hurt to the touch since my late thirties.

MY WATERWORKS: this next symptom has been with me since I was about sixteen years of age and this is one of the symptoms that I still have. But for me it's never been a problem, so I've never given it much thought. When anyone has asked me over the past thirty odd years if I have a problem with my waterworks, I have always answered no. Because I always thought they meant did I occasionally have lack of control and the need to wear incontinence pads. What I have (apparently) is urinary retention, due to lack of muscle tone in the bladder, but how the MS has caused this I still have to find out. When I go to the loo to pass water, I could pee for England sometimes. I have often thought (but I know I haven't) I have got two or even three bladders because as one flow finishes, a second or two later, another flow starts. I just have to be patient and make sure my bladder is completely empty before I get up off the loo seat.

Okay, that was a bit embarrassing for me but I promised myself that I was going to be one hundred percent honest with everything I write down. So if you ever go out with me for the night and I'm in the 'Ladies' for a while, it's not that I've fallen down the toilet bowl (although I have done that before when David left the toilet seat up one night and I wasn't looking). It's just that my bladder will be very full and it takes a few minutes to empty.

FEELING LOPSIDED AND FALLING SIDEWAYS: Feeling as if I was going to fall down because I felt lopsided and obviously, when I felt like this, I just wanted to lie down before I fell down. And I did fall sideways, quite a few times.

BRAIN FUZZ: not being able to think straight, not being able to remember things that I had just said. Again tiredness and stress would bring this on. The more stressed I got, the worse this and my speech would become. Even now, if

I'm very tired or upset or stressed, my speech will be affected.

FUNNY FEET: this one has to be experienced to see the funny side. Try and imagine what it would feel like to walk on bubble wrap for weeks on end; that's exactly what it feels like, the souls of your feet full of bubbles. It feels so real when it happens that I would keep touching the bottom of my feet just to reassure myself that I didn't have bubbles in them. This would last about four to six weeks and then disappear. It has happened to me about once in every seven years over the past forty odd years, so it's not very often it happens but it does.

VOICE TIREDNESS: I can feel my voice starting to trail away to a mere whisper. On the rare occasions this still happens, I know it's time to be quiet or I could spark off the worst symptom of all, problems with my throat.

THROAT: I have already mentioned what happens to me sometimes as I'm falling asleep, but this next problem is different. It can happen at any time during the day. My throat appears to almost close and I can't breathe. Only once has my throat closed completely. One night when I was all alone in our home, I stupidly had my head tilted back, as I was trying to get the juice out of a pomegranate. A drop of juice hit the back of my throat and I was in serious trouble. I tried to breathe (stupidly) through my mouth and I couldn't. The harder I tried to breathe the more frantic I became. Fight and flight response must have taken over because I ran to our front door, opened it and knelt down on the door step trying desperately to get air into my lungs through my mouth. I can still remember the horrible noise I could hear myself making, as if a wild animal was being skinned alive. All the while this was happening, I was screaming out to God in my head to help me. I've never been so frightened in my life. At this point I heard my father's voice shouting at me, "Calm down Isabella, calm down. I'm here beside you. Calm down." He kept repeating this to me. Obviously I did, because I'm still here to tell the tale. Thank the Lord my throat has never completely closed again. But it's got very close on a few occasions. I think because of that one terrifying experience I must be honest and say, when it does

295

start to happen I do panic....and not without cause.

There are a number of things that can trigger my 'almost throat closure' : a tickle at the back of my throat, forcing me to breathe through my mouth, when I have a cold; a very bad coughing fit can spark it; a drop of fluid can catch the back of my throat and start an episode. I once breathed in when I had a crumb in my mouth. The crumb caught the back of my throat and that sparked it. And as stupid as this sounds, an intake of breath can catch my throat and start me gasping for breath. I can assure you it's not food or drink coming back up or going down. I feel as if I can't get any air. It's very frightening while it is happening.

Just to be on the safe side, I have learned to eat my food slowly (although as I have said, food has never been a problem) and I try to remember not to talk when I'm drinking or eating because I once spoke while eating and a tiny piece of ground peppercorn caught the back of my throat and sparked an episode.

When it does happen I have to try and stay calm (while I'm panicking inside and shouting out to God in my head, to help me) Rescue Remedy helps, so I keep a bottle in the fridge and a bottle in my handbag, just in case. It helps to calm me down. I need to remember to 'breathe' in though my nose, not my mouth, and that's not easy when you are panicking (and almost impossible if you have a tickle in your throat, or your nose is blocked because of a cold). This is horrible when it happens and yes, it does still happen to me on rare occasions when I'm very tired or stressed, or when my vocal cords seem to want to give up, all because of tiredness.

What I have just described is called a 'Laryngospasm' or also known as 'dry drowning' and the terrifying noise I heard myself making as I tried to get air into my lungs, as I knelt on our front doorstep, is called a 'stridor'. This is all very scary when it happens but it does pass. I will explain how I found this all out in my next book.

But I understand now why this happens. It's a warning for me to rest and be kind to myself.

I like those words, "Be kind to myself." If we were all a little bit kinder to ourselves, we would all feel so much better. So let's all be kind to ourselves.

Printed in Great Britain
by Amazon